Better Homes and Gardens®

simple secrets

TO BETTER EVERYDAY COOKING

Better Homes and Gardens® Books

Des Moines, Iowa

Better Homes and Gardens® Books
An imprint of Meredith® Books

Simple Secrets to Better Everyday Cooking

Editors: Kristi Fuller, Chuck Smothermon
Associate Art Director: Lynda Haupert
Graphic Designer: Craig Hanken
Contributing Writers: Cynthia Adams, Ellen Boeke,
    Lisa Kingsley, Winifred Moranville
Recipe Developers: Ellen Boeke, Brett Champion,
    Linda Henry, David Kennedy, Susan Lamb Parenti,
    Marcia Stanley
Copy Chief: Catherine Hamrick
Copy and Production Editor: Terri Fredrickson
Managers, Book Production: Pam Kvitne,
    Marjorie J. Schenkelberg
Contributing Copy Editor: Angela K. Renkoski
Contributing Proofreaders: Jessica Kearney Heidgerken,
    Gretchen Kauffman, Garland Walton
Contributing Indexer: Elizabeth Parson
Wine Consultant: John Teeling
Photographers: Jim Krantz, Pete Krumhardt,
    Kritsada Panichgul
Food Stylists: Susan Draudt, Dianna Nolin, Susie Skoog,
    Judy Vance, Charles Worthington
Prop Stylist: Karen Johnson
Electronic Production Coordinator: Paula Forest
Editorial and Design Assistants: Judy Bailey,
    Mary Lee Gavin, Karen Schirm
Test Kitchen Director: Lynn Blanchard
Test Kitchen Product Supervisor:
    Marilyn Cornelius

Our seal assures you that every recipe in *Simple Secrets to Better Everyday Cooking* has been tested in the Better Homes and Gardens® Test Kitchen. This means that each recipe is practical and reliable and meets our high standards of taste appeal. We guarantee your satisfaction with this book for as long as you own it.

Pictured on front cover: Turkey Tender Steaks & Sweet Pepper-Citrus Salsa (page 131)

Meredith® Books

Editor in Chief: James D. Blume
Design Director: Matt Strelecki
Managing Editor: Gregory H. Kayko
Executive Food Editor: Jennifer Dorland Darling

Director, Retail Sales and Marketing: Terry Unsworth
Director, Sales, Special Markets: Rita McMullen
Director, Sales, Premiums: Michael A. Peterson
Director, Sales, Retail: Tom Wierzbicki
Director, Book Marketing: Brad Elmitt
Director, Operations: George A. Susral
Director, Production: Douglas M. Johnston

Vice President, General Manager: Jamie L. Martin

Better Homes and Gardens® Magazine

Editor in Chief: Jean LemMon
Executive Food Editor: Nancy Byal

Meredith Publishing Group

President, Publishing Group: Stephen M. Lacy
Vice President, Finance & Administration: Max Runciman

Meredith Corporation

Chairman and Chief Executive Officer: William T. Kerr

Chairman of the Executive Committee: E. T. Meredith III

All of us at Better Homes and Gardens® Books are dedicated to providing you with the information and ideas you need to create delicious foods. We welcome your comments and suggestions. Write to us at: Better Homes and Gardens Books, Cookbook Editorial Department, 1716 Locust St., Des Moines, IA 50309-3023.

If you would like to purchase any of our books, check wherever quality books are sold. Visit our website at bhg.com.

Frozen Caramel Custard,
page 186

Fresh Greens Salad with Herbed Croutons, page 17

Irish Coffee Meringues, page 192

Potato & Leek Soup, page 35

Chile Pork Ribs with Chipotle Barbecue Sauce, page 155

table of contents

Unlock the secrets to great cooking!

Were you one of those inquisitive kids who often asked "Why?" and "How?" Are you still curious about how things work, particularly the ingredients in a recipe? *Better Homes and Gardens® Simple Secrets to Better Everyday Cooking* doesn't just say "because." It answers your questions in detail.

Each recipe in this book reveals its own secret, such as how to caramelize sugar for desserts, how to cook pasta to perfection, and how to select the best potato for mashing.

Tips throughout the book will help you make your everyday cooking better. For example, do you know how to get the most punch out of herbs and spices? Learn how to crush dried herbs and toast spice seeds for maximum flavor. Many ingredients are identified, too, to help you select, store, and use them.

To make meal planning easier, read pages 209 to 212 for the secrets to a well-stocked pantry. Uncertain about what foods make a great meal? Turn to pages 213 to 219 for complete menus—featuring recipes from this book. The glossary on pages 220 to 225 can help when you're not sure about a certain cooking term. And, in a pinch, the Emergency Substitutions chart on page 238 will come to your rescue when you've run out of an ingredient.

One cookbook is all you need to begin making great meals!

Pork au Poivre with Mustard & Sage, page 162

Identifying Foods

Salads

SIMPLE SECRET INDEX

USING FENNEL

With its wispy fronds and bulbous base, fennel looks like a feather-topped, potbellied cousin to celery, but its flavor is deliciously different. The white bulb and bright green fronds have a gentle, slightly sweet anise flavor (the stalks aren't usually eaten).

A great way to incorporate fennel into cooking is to use the bulbs as you would celery: chopped or sliced for soups, stir-fries, vegetable medleys, and salads (see recipe, right). Or, substitute wedges of it for another vegetable in pot roast.

Don't throw away all of the fronds. A sprig makes a nice garnish, and a few snipped leaves add flavor to just about any dish.

fennel & orange salad

prep: 15 minutes   *makes:* 4 servings

2 medium fennel bulbs	1 tablespoon snipped fresh chervil
2 medium blood oranges	or ¹/₂ teaspoon dried chervil, crushed
¹/₄ cup olive oil	Bibb lettuce leaves
2 tablespoons balsamic vinegar	1 green onion, sliced

1 Cut off and discard upper stalks of fennel bulbs, reserving some of the feathery leaves. Cut off a thin slice from base of fennel bulbs. Remove and discard any wilted outer layers. Wash fennel and cut each bulb into ¹/₄-inch slices, discarding core. Set aside.

2 Working over a bowl, section oranges, catching juice in bowl (see tip, page 24). For dressing, in the same bowl, whisk together orange juice, olive oil, vinegar, and chervil.

3 Line 4 salad plates with lettuce leaves. Arrange the fennel slices and orange sections on lettuce; sprinkle with green onion. Drizzle dressing over salads. If desired, garnish salads with reserved fennel leaves.

Nutrition Facts per serving: 159 cal., 14 g total fat (2 g sat. fat), 0 mg chol., 31 mg sodium, 10 g carbo., 15 g fiber, 1 g pro. **Daily Values:** 1% vit. A, 41% vit. C, 3% calcium, 2% iron.

singapore beef slaw

prep: 15 minutes   *broil:* 13 minutes   *marinate:* 6 hours   *makes:* 4 servings

12 ounces boneless beef sirloin steak,
    cut 1 inch thick
¼ cup snipped fresh cilantro
3 tablespoons salad oil
2 tablespoons cider vinegar
1 teaspoon sugar
⅛ to ¼ teaspoon crushed red pepper
    (optional)
1 clove garlic, minced

4 cups shredded cabbage
1 cup thin, bite-size jicama strips
1 medium red sweet pepper, cut
    into thin, bite-size strips
½ to 1 teaspoon cumin seeds, toasted
    (see tip, right)
   Coarsely shredded carrot (optional)
   Lime wedges (optional)
   Fresh cilantro leaves (optional)

1 Place meat on the unheated rack of a broiler pan. Broil 3 inches from heat for 13 to 17 minutes or to desired doneness, turning once. When meat is cool enough to handle, cut into bite-size strips.

2 For marinade, in a non-metal bowl combine cilantro, oil, vinegar, sugar, crushed red pepper (if desired), and garlic. Add steak strips; stir to moisten. Cover and marinate in the refrigerator for 6 to 24 hours.

3 To serve, in a large salad bowl combine undrained meat strips, cabbage, jicama, and sweet pepper; toss lightly to coat. Sprinkle toasted cumin seeds over salad. If desired, garnish with shredded carrot and serve with lime wedges and cilantro leaves.

Nutrition Facts per serving: 292 cal., 18 g total fat (5 g sat. fat), 57 mg chol., 59 mg sodium, 12 g carbo., 2 g fiber, 21 g pro. **Daily Values:** 22% vit. A, 143% vit. C, 4% calcium, 21% iron.

TOASTING SEEDS

To bring an irresistible smokiness to their already nutty aroma, toast the cumin seeds before adding them to Singapore Beef Slaw (see recipe, left).

To toast, place the seeds in a small skillet over low heat. Don't add any oil to the pan. Cook, stirring, for 2 to 3 minutes. Or, spread the seeds in a shallow baking pan and toast, stirring occasionally, in a 350° oven about 10 minutes or until brown and aromatic.

Other spice seeds such as sesame and fennel seeds—as well as flaked coconut and many nuts—often benefit from a little toasting, too. As a general rule, to toast these ingredients, spread them in a single layer in a shallow baking pan. Bake in a 350° oven for 5 to 10 minutes or until light golden brown, watching carefully and stirring once or twice so they don't burn.

CHOOSING EDIBLE FLOWERS

Edible flowers add unexpected color and flavor to salads and other foods. Here are a few favorites to choose from:

Pansies are slightly spicy.

Calendulas are bland, but with their yellow and gold colors, they make a pretty garnish.

Nasturtiums are peppery.

Chive blossoms have an oniony flavor.

Squash blossoms taste a little like the squash they come from.

Roses offer a slight sweetness.

Violas or **violets** bring a sweet—but sometimes tangy or spicy—flavor.

Geranium flavors vary, so taste before using.

Borage has a cucumber-like flavor.

Note: Use only flowers that have been grown without pesticides or other chemicals.

mesclun salad
with walnut vinaigrette

start to finish: 20 minutes   *makes:* 4 servings

3 tablespoons walnut oil
3 tablespoons orange juice
1 teaspoon Dijon-style mustard
1 tablespoon honey butter
$^1/_3$ cup coarsely chopped walnuts

6 cups mesclun
2 apples, cored and thinly sliced
1 ounce Parmesan cheese shavings
  Edible flowers (such as zucchini, chive, or calendula blossoms)

1 For vinaigrette, in a screw-top jar combine walnut oil, orange juice, and mustard. Cover and shake well.

2 In a small skillet melt honey butter; add walnuts. Cook and stir over medium heat about 3 minutes or until nuts are golden brown.

3 Place mesclun in a large salad bowl. Drizzle with vinaigrette; toss lightly to coat. Divide mesclun among 4 salad plates. Top each serving with apple slices. Sprinkle with toasted walnuts and Parmesan cheese. Garnish each serving with edible flowers.

Nutrition Facts per serving: 252 cal., 20 g total fat (2 g sat. fat), 9 mg chol., 134 mg sodium, 15 g carbo., 3 g fiber, 6 g pro. **Daily Values:** 5% vit. A, 20% vit. C, 7% calcium, 5% iron.

Mesclun

For cooks looking to bring spicy, herblike flavors and more varied textures to their salads, mesclun is a delicious option. Mesclun includes a variety of young, tiny salad greens, such as arugula, radicchio, oak leaf lettuce, chervil, chickweed, dandelion, and other greens with a variety of contrasting bitter, mild, and peppery flavors. While mesclun once was found only in specialty markets of cosmopolitan areas, the mix is now widely available at larger supermarkets across the country. If you're lucky, during your region's growing season, local farmers might bring their own organically grown mixes to your community's farmers' market. Try it for a picked-that-day freshness only locally grown produce has.

Cutting up a pineapple isn't tricky—but it can be prickly. To make cutting easier, use a large, sharp knife to slice off the bottom stem end and the green top.

Stand the pineapple on one cut end and slice off the skin in wide strips, from top to bottom.

To remove the eyes—those rough brown dots that spiral up the pineapple—cut diagonally around the fruit, following the pattern of the eyes and making narrow wedge-shaped grooves into the pineapple as you cut away the eyes (see photo, above). When trimming, cut away as little of the fruit as possible.

Slice the fruit away from the core and discard the core.

romaine & fruit
with balsamic vinaigrette

start to finish: 20 minutes   ***makes:*** 4 servings

1	small pineapple
¼	cup sifted powdered sugar
4	teaspoons white balsamic vinegar
½	teaspoon dry mustard
¼	teaspoon salt
⅛	teaspoon ground red pepper

⅓	cup salad oil
6	cups torn romaine
2	medium peaches or nectarines, peeled, pitted, and thinly sliced
½	cup quartered strawberries

1 Peel and core pineapple (see tip, left). Cut pineapple into bite-size chunks. Set pineapple aside.

2 For vinaigrette, in a blender container or food processor bowl combine powdered sugar, vinegar, mustard, salt, and red pepper. Cover and blend or process until combined. With blender or processor running, slowly add oil in a thin, steady stream through hole or opening in top, blending or processing until mixture is thickened.

3 In a large salad bowl combine pineapple chunks, romaine, peach or nectarine slices, and strawberries. Drizzle vinaigrette over salad mixture; toss lightly to coat.

Nutrition Facts per serving: 289 cal., 19 g total fat (3 g sat. fat), 0 mg chol., 154 mg sodium, 31 g carbo., 4 g fiber, 2 g pro. **Daily Values:** 25% vit. A, 86% vit. C, 4% calcium, 8% iron.

White balsamic vinegar

When you want balsamic vinegar's flavor but not its color, use white balsamic vinegar. Technically this vinegar is not classified by the Italians as a true balsamic vinegar (only the dark balsamic vinegar gets the *Aceto Balsamico Tradizionale di Modena* label). However, white balsamic vinegar offers much of the same concentrated sweet-tart flavor so loved in the traditional variety.

couscous-artichoke salad

start to finish: 20 minutes   **makes:** 8 servings

1½ cups chicken broth
1 cup quick-cooking couscous
⅓ cup finely chopped onion
1 to 2 tablespoons finely chopped
    fresh jalapeño pepper*
¼ teaspoon ground cinnamon
¼ teaspoon pepper

1 9-ounce package frozen artichoke hearts,
    thawed and cut up
1⅓ cups coarsely chopped tomatoes
¾ cup chopped green sweet pepper
¼ cup raisins
¼ cup olive oil
¼ cup balsamic vinegar

1 In a medium saucepan bring chicken broth to boiling; stir in couscous and onion. Remove from heat; cover and let stand for 5 minutes. Stir in the jalapeño pepper, cinnamon, and pepper; cool.

2 In a bowl combine couscous mixture, artichoke hearts, tomatoes, sweet pepper, and raisins. Whisk together the olive oil and balsamic vinegar; pour over couscous mixture, tossing lightly to coat. Serve immediately.

*Note: Because hot peppers contain pungent oils, protect your hands when preparing them. Wear gloves or sandwich bags so your skin doesn't come in contact with the peppers. Always wash your hands and nails thoroughly in hot, soapy water after handling chile peppers (see tip, page 48).

Nutrition Facts per serving: 209 cal., 7 g total fat (1 g sat. fat), 0 mg chol., 189 mg sodium, 31 g carbo., 7 g fiber, 6 g pro. **Daily Values:** 4% vit. A, 56% vit. C, 2% calcium, 10% iron.

EASY-COOK COUSCOUS

Ready in minutes, the quick-cooking couscous used in Couscous-Artichoke Salad (see recipe, left) is possibly the speediest side dish on earth. Could that be why it has gained so much popularity lately as cooks have become more crunched for time? Perhaps, but cooks also enjoy the way this North African staple's bead-shaped grains, made from ground semolina, provide a mild yet texturally interesting side dish that goes with just about anything.

Though regular couscous can take up to 60 minutes to cook, the quick-cooking form is ready in a fraction of that. Boil water, pour the couscous into the pan, and let it stand about 5 minutes (follow specific package directions). You will find quick-cooking couscous in the rice or pasta section of the supermarket.

fresh greens salad
with herbed croutons

prep: 30 minutes   *bake:* 45 minutes   *makes:* 6 servings

1 8½-ounce package corn muffin mix
2 tablespoons snipped fresh parsley
1 tablespoon snipped fresh rosemary
1 tablespoon snipped fresh cilantro
¼ cup butter or margarine, melted
¼ cup grated Parmesan cheese

6 cups torn romaine
1½ cups torn arugula or spinach
⅓ cup snipped fresh cilantro
¼ cup sliced green onions
½ cup bottled Italian salad dressing

1 Prepare corn muffin mix in an 8×8×2-inch baking pan according to package directions, adding the parsley, rosemary, and the 1 tablespoon cilantro with liquid ingredients. Bake according to package directions. Cool in pan on wire rack for 10 minutes. Remove from the pan; cool completely.

2 Cut corn bread into 1-inch cubes. Toss cubes with melted butter or margarine and Parmesan cheese; spread in a 15×10×1-inch baking pan.

3 Bake in a 300° oven about 25 minutes or until crisp, stirring twice. Transfer croutons to a piece of foil; cool completely. Place half of the croutons in a freezer container or bag and freeze for up to 3 months.

4 In a salad bowl combine romaine, arugula or spinach, the ⅓ cup cilantro, green onions, and remaining croutons. Drizzle with bottled salad dressing; toss lightly to coat. Serve immediately.

Nutrition Facts per serving: 220 cal., 16 g total fat (5 g sat. fat), 12 mg chol., 357 mg sodium, 17 g carbo., 1 g fiber, 4 g pro. **Daily Values:** 22% vit. A, 25% vit. C, 6% calcium, 7% iron.

STORING LETTUCES

Having plenty of lettuce ready for salad at a moment's notice is convenient. But washing and storing lettuces properly makes a big difference in how long they will stay at the peak of freshness.

Remove any brown-edged, bruised, wilted, or old leaves. Wash greens under cold running water, then separate the leaves and rinse them in a colander under cold water. If the leaves are very sandy or gritty, repeat the rinsing step.

Use a salad spinner to dry washed lettuce greens or shake them dry. Layer the leaves between paper towels and store in a sealable container or plastic bag in the refrigerator. Cleaned lettuce will keep this way for a week.

Next time you accidentally
leave salad greens in the
refrigerator a couple days past
their prime, turn them into
a wilted greens salad. Often,
spinach, lettuce, and other
greens that have become too
droopy to use raw in a salad
will taste great when cooked
until wilted.

Use our recipe, right, as a
guide for proportions of greens
to oil. Then experiment with
other greens (such as mustard
greens, chard, or sorrel) to
perfect your own version of the
wilted greens salad.

wilted greens salad
with port dressing

prep: 30 minutes   **makes:** 4 servings

$\frac{1}{3}$ cup dried tart red cherries

$\frac{1}{4}$ cup port wine

4 ounces pancetta or 3 slices
       bacon, cut into small pieces

1 tablespoon walnut oil or almond oil

$\frac{1}{3}$ cup sliced green onions

1 clove garlic, minced

3 tablespoons red raspberry vinegar
       or balsamic vinegar

1 teaspoon sugar

1 10-ounce package prewashed fresh spinach,
       torn (about 10 to 12 cups)

$\frac{1}{4}$ cup broken walnuts, toasted (see tip,
       page 11)

1 In a small saucepan combine cherries
and port. Bring to boiling; remove
from heat. Let stand for 10 minutes.

2 Meanwhile, in a 12-inch skillet cook
pancetta or bacon over medium heat
until crisp. Remove pancetta or bacon with
a slotted spoon, reserving 1 tablespoon
drippings in skillet. Add walnut or almond
oil to skillet. Cook green onions and garlic
in hot oil until onion is tender. Stir in
vinegar, sugar, and cherry mixture. Bring
just to boiling; reduce heat.

3 Add spinach to skillet, half at a time,
tossing for 30 to 60 seconds or until just
wilted. Add pancetta or bacon and walnuts;
toss to combine. Serve immediately.

Nutrition Facts per serving: 207 cal., 14 g total fat
(3 g sat. fat), 7 mg chol., 163 mg sodium, 14 g carbo.,
7 g fiber, 5 g pro. **Daily Values:** 44% vit. A, 31% vit. C,
7% calcium, 30% iron.

raspberry-cranberry
spinach salad

prep: 25 minutes   *chill:* 1 hour   *makes:* 6 servings

- 1 10-ounce package frozen red raspberries in syrup, thawed
- 1/4 cup sugar
- 2 teaspoons cornstarch
- 1/2 cup cranberry-raspberry juice cocktail
- 1/4 cup red wine vinegar
- 1/4 teaspoon celery seeds
- 1/4 teaspoon ground cinnamon

- 1/8 teaspoon ground cloves
- 1 10-ounce package prewashed fresh spinach, torn (about 10 to 12 cups)
- 1/2 cup broken walnuts
- 1/3 cup dried cranberries
- 1/4 cup shelled sunflower seeds
- 3 green onions, thinly sliced

1 For dressing, place raspberries in a blender container or food processor bowl. Cover and blend or process until raspberries are smooth. Strain through a sieve to remove the seeds; discard seeds.

2 In a medium saucepan stir together the sugar and cornstarch. Stir in the cranberry-raspberry juice cocktail, vinegar, celery seeds, cinnamon, cloves, and strained raspberries. Cook and stir over medium heat until thickened and bubbly. Cook and stir for 2 minutes more. Transfer mixture to a non-metal container; cover and chill at least 1 hour before serving.

3 To serve, in a large salad bowl toss together spinach, walnuts, dried cranberries, sunflower seeds, and green onions. Drizzle with half the dressing; toss lightly to coat. (Cover and chill the remaining dressing in a non-metal container for up to 1 week.)

Nutrition Facts per serving: 178 cal., 9 g total fat (1 g sat. fat), 0 mg chol., 82 mg sodium, 23 g carbo., 3 g fiber, 4 g pro. **Daily Values:** 33% vit. A, 31% vit. C, 5% calcium, 13% iron.

FRUITY VINAIGRETTES

Traditionally vinegar is what gives vinaigrette its bite. However, another way to spark salad dressings is to use fruit juices to replace all or some of the vinegar. Doing so adds a different kind of edge—a spark that's light, fresh, and fruity. Lemon juice (a hallmark ingredient in the classic Caesar) or lime juice adds tartness. Grapefruit juice can bring a pleasantly bitter quality; orange juice lends sweetness. Any fruit juice or nectar can be used to create your own version of a house dressing.

As a rule, start with one part juice to one part oil. Season with salt and pepper, and experiment with other spices, herbs, and flavorings as desired. With tart juices, such as lemon and lime juice, you can replace all the vinegar. But if you use a less-tart juice—such as orange, apple, or cranberry-raspberry juice—team it with vinegar to bring both tartness and fruitiness to a vinaigrette, as in the recipe, left.

Preparing asparagus is a snap—literally. For slim, tender stalks, all you need to do is snap off and discard the woody base.

For thick stalks of asparagus, which can be so much tougher than thin ones, peel away the tough outer layer. The easiest way is to grasp the base of the asparagus in one hand and use a vegetable peeler in the other (see photo, above), carefully peeling toward (but stopping short of) your hand and rotating the asparagus as you peel. You'll wind up with a short piece of stalk with the peelings attached; you can easily snap it off at the point where the peeling stops.

asparagus & carrots
with asian vinaigrette

prep: 20 minutes   **cook:** 6 minutes   **makes:** 4 servings

 8 ounces baby carrots with tops, trimmed to 2 inches or ½ of a 16-ounce package peeled baby carrots
 12 asparagus spears, trimmed (see tip, left)
 4 cups torn red-tip leaf lettuce or leaf lettuce
 1 cup fresh enoki mushrooms
 1 recipe Asian Vinaigrette
 2 teaspoons sesame seeds, toasted (optional) (see tip, page 11)

1 In a medium skillet cook carrots, covered, in a small amount of boiling water for 2 minutes. Add asparagus spears. Cover and cook for 4 to 6 minutes more or until vegetables are crisp-tender. Drain; immediately plunge vegetables into ice water. Let stand for 1 minute. Drain and pat dry.

2 Line 4 salad plates with lettuce. Arrange carrots, asparagus, and mushrooms on lettuce. Drizzle with Asian Vinaigrette. If desired, sprinkle with sesame seeds.

Asian Vinaigrette: In a small bowl, combine ¼ cup bottled Italian salad dressing, 1 tablespoon soy sauce, 1 teaspoon toasted sesame oil, and ¼ teaspoon crushed red pepper.

Nutrition Facts per serving: 128 cal., 9 g total fat (1 g sat. fat), 0 mg chol., 416 mg sodium, 12 g carbo., 3 g fiber, 3 g pro. **Daily Values:** 134% vit. A, 26% vit. C, 3% calcium, 6% iron.

The quick chill
Many vegetables cook so quickly they can go from perfectly crisp-tender to limp in seconds. When serving vegetables chilled, as in the recipe above, it's essential you stop the cooking process as soon as the vegetables are crisp-tender. To do this, quickly drain the vegetables, plunge them into a bowl of ice water, and let them stand until they're completely cold (asparagus takes about 1 minute). Then drain them, pat dry, and use as directed in recipes.

TURN OLD BREAD INTO NEW CROUTONS

Homemade croutons make any salad or soup more special, and your family or guests don't need to know how easy they are to prepare.

Although Italian Salad with Garlic Polenta Croutons (see recipe, right) uses polenta to make homemade croutons, a similar method works well for leftover bread.

To make herbed croutons from leftover bread, in a large skillet melt ¼ cup butter or margarine. Remove from heat.

Stir in ½ teaspoon dried thyme, crushed, and ⅛ teaspoon garlic powder.

Add 2 cups French, sourdough, or other firm-textured bread cubes; stir until the cubes are coated with butter or margarine mixture.

Spread in a single layer in a large baking pan. Bake in a 300° oven about 15 minutes or until dry and crisp, stirring twice; cool.

The bread croutons will keep for up to 1 week at room temperature if stored tightly covered.

italian salad
with garlic polenta croutons

start to finish: 20 minutes   ***makes:*** 4 servings

½ of a 16-ounce tube refrigerated cooked polenta or 8 ounces leftover polenta
1 tablespoon olive oil
½ teaspoon garlic-pepper seasoning
6 cups torn romaine or torn mixed greens

½ of a 7-ounce jar roasted red sweet peppers, drained and cut up (½ cup)
½ cup chopped tomato
⅓ cup sliced pitted ripe olives
2 tablespoons grated Parmesan cheese
¼ cup bottled Italian salad dressing

1 Cut polenta into ¾-inch cubes; toss with oil and sprinkle with garlic-pepper seasoning. Spread cubes in a greased shallow baking pan. Bake in a 425° oven for 15 to 20 minutes or until golden, turning once halfway through.

2 Meanwhile, in a bowl toss together romaine or mixed greens, roasted sweet peppers, tomato, and olives. Divide salad mixture among 4 salad plates. Top each salad with warm polenta croutons; sprinkle with Parmesan cheese. Serve with Italian salad dressing.

Nutrition Facts per serving: 199 cal., 13 g total fat (2 g sat. fat), 3 mg chol., 515 mg sodium, 18 g carbo., 4 g fiber, 5 g pro. **Daily Values:** 36% vit. A, 130% vit. C, 7% calcium, 10% iron.

mixed salad
with lime-pistachio vinaigrette

start to finish: 20 minutes   ***makes:*** 4 servings

3 tablespoons lime juice
3 tablespoons honey
2 tablespoons snipped fresh cilantro
$\frac{1}{4}$ teaspoon crushed red pepper
$\frac{1}{4}$ teaspoon salt
$\frac{1}{3}$ cup salad oil

$\frac{1}{3}$ cup pistachio nuts
6 cups baby spinach or mesclun
1 medium mango, seeded, peeled,
    and coarsely chopped (see tip, right)
1 cup raspberries

1 For vinaigrette, in a blender container or food processor bowl combine lime juice, honey, cilantro, red pepper, and salt. Cover and blend or process until nearly smooth. With blender or processor running, slowly add salad oil in a thin, steady stream through hole or opening in top, blending or processing until mixture is thickened.

2 Coarsely chop pistachio nuts. Sift chopped nuts through a small colander. Reserve $\frac{1}{4}$ cup of the coarsely chopped pistachio nuts; set aside. Add fine shavings from colander and remaining coarsely chopped nuts to vinaigrette. Cover and blend or process until nuts are finely chopped.

3 In a large salad bowl combine spinach or mesclun, mango, and raspberries. Pour 2 to 3 tablespoons of the vinaigrette over salad; toss lightly to coat. Divide salad among 4 salad plates. Sprinkle with the reserved $\frac{1}{4}$ cup pistachio nuts. Serve salads with remaining vinaigrette.

Nutrition Facts per serving: 342 cal., 24 g total fat (3 g sat. fat), 0 mg chol., 203 mg sodium, 32 g carbo., 6 g fiber, 5 g pro. **Daily Values:** 78% vit. A, 82% vit. C, 9% calcium, 22% iron.

CUTTING A MANGO

The best way to manage a mango is to start by looking at its shape. See how it has a broad, flat side? That shows you the shape of the seed inside.

Using a sharp knife, slice all the way through the mango next to the seed. (In the top photo, the seed is just next to the knife, toward the fruit's center.) Repeat on the other side of the seed, resulting in two large pieces of fruit. Cut away all the fruit that remains around the seed. Remove the peel, and slice, chop, or puree the fruit.

23

To section oranges, use a
serrated knife and proceed
as follows:

1. Remove the peel.
2. Holding the orange over a
   bowl to catch the juice, cut
   between one orange section
   and the membrane (see
   photo, above), slicing to the
   center of the fruit.
3. Turn the knife and slide it up
   the other side of the section
   alongside the membrane.
4. Repeat with remaining
   sections.

For grapefruit, first cut off the
ends of the fruit. Then, with a
long, thin-bladed knife, cut out
the core. Resting one end of
the grapefruit on a cutting
board, cut off the peel in strips.
From there, pull the fruit apart
and lift or pull each segment
from the membrane.

citrusy chicken salad

prep: 25 minutes   *makes:* 4 servings

$\frac{1}{3}$ cup frozen orange juice
     concentrate, thawed
$\frac{1}{4}$ cup olive oil
 2 to 3 tablespoons white wine vinegar
     or white vinegar
 1 teaspoon ground cumin
$\frac{1}{8}$ teaspoon ground red pepper

 4 cups torn mixed greens
10 ounces cooked chicken, cut into
     bite-size pieces (2 cups)
 2 medium oranges, peeled and sectioned
     (see tip, left)
 1 cup thin, bite-size jicama strips
 1 medium red sweet pepper, cut into rings

1 For dressing, in a small bowl stir
together orange juice concentrate,
olive oil, vinegar, cumin, and ground
red pepper. Set aside.

2 In a bowl toss together mixed greens,
chicken, orange sections, jicama, and
sweet pepper rings. Pour dressing over
salad; toss lightly to coat. Serve immediately.

Nutrition Facts per serving: 348 cal., 20 g total fat
(3 g sat. fat), 68 mg chol., 73 mg sodium, 20 g carbo.,
2 g fiber, 24 g pro. **Daily Values:** 25% vit. A, 162% vit. C,
4% calcium, 16% iron.

know your salad greens

Red-tip leaf lettuce has a tender, sweet, delicate flavor that makes it versatile for many types of green salads.

Leaf lettuce has a mild, delicate flavor and may be used interchangeably with red-tip leaf lettuce.

Radicchio is bitter and peppery-tasting when eaten alone, but small amounts add a nice accent to other greens.

Spinach has a mildly hearty flavor and is often used raw in salads.

Swiss chard has large stems with a delicate flavor similar to celery; leaves have a hearty spinach-like flavor.

Romaine has large, crisp leaves and a slightly sharp flavor that make this the classic lettuce for Caesar salad.

Curly endive has a mildly bitter flavor and adds visual interest to salads.

Arugula has a peppery, pungent flavor that is an ideal contrast when mixed with milder greens.

fresh mozzarella salad

start to finish: 20 minutes   **makes:** 4 servings

1   15-ounce can black beans or garbanzo
      beans, rinsed and drained
1   15-ounce can butter beans or Great
      Northern beans, rinsed and drained
1   small cucumber, quartered
      lengthwise and sliced (1 cup)
2   red and/or yellow tomatoes, cut into
      thin wedges

¼   cup thinly sliced green onions
1   recipe Basil Dressing or ½ cup bottled
      oil-and-vinegar salad dressing
8   ounces round- or log-shaped fresh
      mozzarella cheese or fresh part-skim
      scamorza cheese

1 In a large bowl combine black beans or garbanzo beans, butter beans or Great Northern beans, cucumber, tomatoes, and green onions.

2 Add dressing; toss lightly to coat. Cut cheese into thin slices; gently toss with salad mixture. Serve immediately.

Basil Dressing: In a screw-top jar combine ¼ cup red wine vinegar; ¼ cup olive oil or salad oil; 1 tablespoon snipped fresh basil or 1 teaspoon dried basil, crushed;
1 teaspoon Dijon-style mustard; ¼ teaspoon crushed red pepper; and 1 clove garlic, minced. Cover and shake well. (If desired, cover and chill dressing for up to 2 days.) Makes about ½ cup.

Nutrition Facts per serving: 434 cal., 23 g total fat (8 g sat. fat), 32 mg chol., 919 mg sodium, 37 g carbo., 6 g fiber, 27 g pro. **Daily Values:** 16% vit. A, 24% vit. C, 36% calcium, 24% iron.

Storing fresh tomatoes

It's tempting to set under-ripe fresh tomatoes in the sun to ripen, but doing so can cause the tomatoes to become mushy. Instead, place them in a brown paper bag or in a fruit-ripening bowl with other fruits, and store them at room temperature. Ripe tomatoes should yield slightly to pressure when touched.

Once ripe, do not refrigerate tomatoes because they'll lose their flavor and become mushy. Instead, store them at room temperature; they'll keep for 2 to 3 days.

If tomato season finds you with more tomatoes than you can use, freeze them. Because frozen tomatoes soften when thawed, they work best in soups, stews, and casseroles.

FABULOUS FRESH MOZZARELLA

Although related to the solid mozzarella that is a staple on pizza, fresh mozzarella is much softer and moister. Salads such as Fresh Mozzarella Salad (see recipe, left) are the perfect way to show off this mild, luxuriously creamy cheese. (In Italy, fresh mozzarella is often served sliced with tomatoes as a salad or with fresh fruit for dessert.)

It's worth seeking out Italian markets, good cheese shops, and large delis to find fresh mozzarella. Usually, you'll find it packaged in whey or water. It must be eaten within a few days of purchase for the best flavor and texture.

A similar Italian cheese is scamorza (also spelled scamorze or scamorzo). It is often aged and smoked but can be eaten fresh when young, like mozzarella.

USING FRESH FAVA BEANS

When you're lucky enough to find them, fresh fava beans will add a hint of subtle sweetness to your favorite salads and soups. Because their growing season is short, favas are available only occasionally. Look for them at farmers' markets, in produce sections of the supermarket, and in specialty food markets in early spring; they're out of season by early summer. Choose fresh-looking, even-shaped pods without spots. Avoid older, bulging beans.

To prepare favas, follow the cooking and cooling directions in step 1, right. Then remove the outer skin by using your thumbnail (see photo, above) to peel the skin back and pop the bean out.

middle eastern
fresh fava bean salad

prep: 35 minutes   ***cook:*** 10 minutes   ***makes:*** 6 servings

1 pound fresh fava beans (3$\frac{1}{4}$ cups)	1 cup chopped tomato
3 tablespoons olive oil	3 tablespoons snipped fresh parsley
2 tablespoons lemon juice	Salt
$\frac{1}{4}$ teaspoon salt	Pepper
$\frac{1}{4}$ teaspoon cracked black pepper	$\frac{1}{2}$ cup crumbled feta cheese
1 clove garlic, minced	2 tablespoons capers, drained
1 cup chopped cucumber	

1 Shell fresh fava beans (remove outer pods). You should have about 2 cups. In a medium saucepan cook shelled beans, uncovered, in enough boiling water to cover for 1 minute; drain. Transfer to cold water; drain. To remove outer skin, peel it back with your thumbnail and pop out the bean.

2 In a medium saucepan cook beans, uncovered, in boiling water about 10 minutes or until tender; drain. Let cool.

3 In a large bowl whisk together oil, lemon juice, salt, pepper, and garlic. Stir in cooled beans, cucumber, tomato, and parsley. Season to taste with additional salt and pepper. Divide bean mixture among 6 salad plates. Top each serving with feta cheese and capers.

Nutrition Facts per serving: 185 cal., 9 g total fat (2 g sat. fat), 8 mg chol., 578 mg sodium, 18 g carbo., 12 g fiber, 9 g pro. **Daily Values:** 3% vit. A, 24% vit. C, 8% calcium, 2% iron.

Capers

It's amazing how much piquancy a spoonful of capers can add to a dish. These little buds, which grow on a spiny shrub found from Spain to China, have an assertive flavor that can be described best as the marriage of citrus and olive, with the tang from the salt and vinegar of the brine in which they are packaged.

At the supermarket, you'll likely find two varieties of capers: the smaller ones, which are considered by experts to be the finest; and the milder larger buds, which also work well in recipes. You'll usually find capers next to the olives.

If you want to experiment by adding capers to such dishes as spaghetti sauces and pizza, start with just a teaspoon or two. They pack plenty of flavor, and a heavy dose can bring a briny taste to a dish.

Soups & Stews

SIMPLE SECRET INDEX

basic soup stock

prep: 35 minutes   *simmer:* 5 hours   *stand:* 5 minutes   *makes:* 8 cups

6	pounds meaty beef soup bones (beef shank crosscuts or short ribs), 4 pounds bony chicken pieces (backs, necks, and wings), or 3 pounds meaty smoked pork hocks
3	carrots, cut up
1	large onion, sliced
12½	cups water
1	small head cabbage, cut up
2	stalks celery with leaves, cut up
1	large tomato
8	whole black peppercorns
4	sprigs fresh parsley
1	bay leaf
2	teaspoons dried thyme, crushed
2	teaspoons salt
1	clove garlic, halved
¼	cup cold water (optional)
1	egg (optional)

1 Preheat oven to 450°. Place soup bones or meat pieces, carrots, and onion in a large shallow roasting pan. Bake, uncovered, about 30 minutes or until well browned, turning occasionally. Drain off fat. Transfer browned bones, carrots, and onion to a 10-quart Dutch oven. Pour ½ cup of the water into roasting pan and rinse; pour this liquid into Dutch oven.

2 Add remaining water, cabbage, celery, tomato, peppercorns, parsley, bay leaf, thyme, salt (omit if using ham hocks), and garlic to Dutch oven. Bring to boiling; reduce heat. Simmer, covered, for 5 hours.

3 Strain stock by ladling it through a colander or sieve lined with 1 or 2 layers of 100-percent cotton cheesecloth; discard bones, vegetables, and seasonings.

4 If desired, clarify stock (see tip, left). If using stock while hot, skim fat using a metal spoon. Or, ladle stock into pint or quart jars; cover and chill immediately. When thoroughly chilled, lift off hardened fat with a fork. Stock may be stored in the refrigerator for up to 3 days or in the freezer for up to 6 months.

Nutrition Facts per 1-cup serving: 17 cal., 1 g total fat (0 g sat. fat), 0 mg chol., 782 mg sodium, 0 g carbo., 0 g fiber, 3 g pro. **Daily Values:** 1% calcium, 2% iron.

turkey meatball
& vegetable soup

prep: 20 minutes   ***cook:*** 43 minutes   ***makes:*** 6 servings

2 sprigs fresh thyme
3 fresh sage leaves
3 bay leaves
1 slightly beaten egg
1 cup soft bread crumbs
1 tablespoon snipped fresh sage
2 teaspoons snipped fresh thyme
1 pound raw ground turkey
2 tablespoons cooking oil

1 cup sliced celery
1 cup sliced carrots
½ cup chopped onion
5 cups chicken Basic Soup Stock (see recipe,
     page 30) or canned chicken broth
¼ teaspoon pepper
1 10-ounce package frozen Italian
     green beans, thawed

1 For the bouquet garni (see tip, right), place thyme sprigs, sage leaves, and bay leaves in the center of a double-thick, 8-inch square of 100-percent cotton cheesecloth. Bring the corners of the cheesecloth together and tie with clean string; set aside.

2 In a large bowl combine egg, bread crumbs, the 1 tablespoon sage, and the 2 teaspoons thyme. Add ground turkey; mix well. Shape into 1-inch balls.

3 In a large nonstick skillet cook meatballs in 1 tablespoon of the oil over medium heat about 10 minutes or until no pink remains, turning occasionally to brown evenly. Set meatballs aside.

4 Meanwhile, in a large saucepan cook celery, carrots, and onion in remaining 1 tablespoon hot oil about 4 minutes or until just tender. Stir in soup stock or broth, pepper, and bouquet garni. Bring to boiling; reduce heat. Simmer, covered, for 25 minutes. Add meatballs and thawed green beans. Return to boiling; reduce heat. Simmer, covered, for 4 to 5 minutes more or until green beans are tender. Discard bouquet garni.

Nutrition Facts per serving: 238 cal., 13 g total fat (3 g sat. fat), 108 mg chol., 635 mg sodium, 11 g carbo., 3 g fiber, 20 g pro. **Daily Values:** 109% vit. A, 10% vit. C, 8% calcium, 12% iron.

MAKING A BOUQUET GARNI

Tired of fishing herbs out of hot liquids? Use a bouquet garni. Bundling up herbs in a piece of 100-percent cotton cheesecloth (see photo, above) allows you to remove herbs neatly from a cooked dish in one quick motion.

A traditional French bouquet garni includes thyme, parsley, and bay leaf, but you can create one from just about any herbs you'd like. The bouquet garni is especially handy for herbs such as bay leaves, which should always be removed before serving.

31

WHAT'S IN A NAME?

A soup isn't always called "soup." It can be labeled one of the following:

- **A bisque** is a rich, thick, smooth soup that's often made with shellfish, such as lobster or shrimp.

- **A chowder** is a thick, chunky soup. Traditionally, a chowder is made with seafood or fish, but chowders made with poultry, vegetables, and cheeses have become popular.

- **Stock or broth** is a strained, thin, clear liquid in which meat, poultry, or fish has been simmered with vegetables and herbs (see recipe, page 30). While normally used as an ingredient in other soups, it can be enjoyed as a light course on its own.

- **Bouillon** is basically the same as broth, but the term often refers to commercial dehydrated products sold as granules or cubes.

- **Consommé** is a strong, flavorful meat or fish broth that has been clarified (see tip, page 30).

vegetable & smoked turkey chowder

prep: 15 minutes   *cook:* 16 minutes   *makes:* 6 servings

1 cup sliced celery	2 cups water
1 cup sliced carrots	2 cups cubed, unpeeled red potatoes
1/2 cup chopped onion	1 10-ounce smoked turkey leg
1/2 teaspoon dried thyme, crushed	2 small zucchinis, halved lengthwise and sliced
1/2 teaspoon dried sage, crushed	1 10-ounce package frozen whole kernel corn
1/2 teaspoon pepper	
2 tablespoons cooking oil	
2 cups chicken Basic Soup Stock (see recipe, page 30) or canned chicken broth	

1 In a large saucepan cook celery, carrots, onion, thyme, sage, and pepper in hot oil over medium heat for 4 minutes. Stir in soup stock or broth, water, and potatoes; add turkey leg. Bring to boiling; reduce heat. Simmer, covered, about 5 minutes.

2 Stir in zucchini and corn. Return to boiling; reduce heat. Simmer, covered, about 5 minutes or until potatoes are tender.

3 Remove from heat. Remove turkey leg from saucepan; let stand until cool enough to handle. Remove meat from turkey leg; discard turkey bone and skin. Coarsely chop meat and return to saucepan. Heat through.

Nutrition Facts per serving: 180 cal., 6 g total fat (1 g sat. fat), 20 mg chol., 515 mg sodium, 23 g carbo., 4 g fiber, 11 g pro. **Daily Values:** 109% vit. A, 25% vit. C, 4% calcium, 7% iron.

knowing a slice from a dice

Mince
Cut into tiny, irregular pieces.

Dice
Cut into small, uniform pieces, usually with 1/8- to 1/4-inch sides.

Chop
Cut into small, irregular pieces— can be coarsely or finely chopped.

Slice
Cut into flat, usually thin, pieces from a larger piece.

Matchstick
Cut into thin, bite-size strips— also known as julienne.

Cube
Cut into large, uniform pieces, usually with 1/2-inch sides.

potato & leek soup

prep: 20 minutes   **cook:** 28 minutes   **makes:** 4 servings

1 pound russet or Idaho potatoes, peeled and cubed

1¾ cups chicken Basic Soup Stock (see recipe, page 30) or one 14½-ounce can chicken broth

1 medium leek

1 cup sliced celery

2 tablespoons butter or margarine

2 cups peeled, cubed sweet potato

¼ teaspoon pepper

¼ teaspoon ground nutmeg

1½ cups milk

½ teaspoon salt

Salt

Pepper

1 In a medium saucepan combine the cubed russet or Idaho potatoes and 1 cup of the soup stock or broth. Bring to boiling; reduce heat. Simmer, covered, about 10 minutes or until potatoes are tender; do not drain. Cool slightly.

2 Transfer potato mixture to a blender container or food processor bowl. Cover and blend or process until smooth; set aside.

3 Meanwhile, wash leek well (see tip, right). Cut into thin slices.

4 In a large saucepan cook leek and celery in butter or margarine for 3 to 4 minutes or until tender. Add sweet potato, the remaining soup stock or broth, pepper, and nutmeg. Bring to boiling; reduce heat. Simmer, covered, for 10 minutes. Stir in pureed potato mixture, milk, and salt. Cook and stir about 5 minutes more or until thickened. Season to taste with salt and pepper.

Nutrition Facts per serving: 280 cal., 9 g total fat (5 g sat. fat), 30 mg chol., 696 mg sodium, 42 g carbo., 5 g fiber, 9 g pro. **Daily Values:** 283% vit. A, 50% vit. C, 16% calcium, 9% iron.

Pureed soups

Ever have a vegetable cream soup that tasted more like butter or cream than vegetables? Most likely, such a soup relied on cream, cornstarch, and/or a mixture of butter and flour to thicken the soup. Such thickening agents work fine in some recipes but can mask the delicate flavors of vegetable-based soups. The thickening agent used for the soup above is made by first cooking potatoes in chicken stock, then pureeing, or finely mashing, the mixture. The resulting puree is all the thickening this soup needs because the starch from the potatoes acts as a thickener. What's more, the puree allows the full flavors of the vegetables to come through. You also can rely on the starch in rice to thicken soups. The next time you make your favorite rice soup, try pureeing some of the cooked rice to act as a thickener.

CLEANING LEEKS

Prized by gourmets, leeks are more mellow than their cousins onion and garlic. Before they're washed, they're also more gritty because their tightly packed leaves easily collect soil. Here's how to remove the grit:

Remove any outer leaves that have wilted. Slice the leek lengthwise in half, all the way through the root end. Holding the leek under a faucet with the root end up (see photo, above), rinse the leek under cold running water, lifting and separating the leaves with your fingers to allow the grit to flow down through the top of the leek. Continue rinsing until all grit is removed. Slice off the root end before using.

35

meet the onion family

Chives have a mild onion flavor and make a nice garnish.

White onions often have a sharp flavor; smaller varieties include pearl onions, about ½ inch in diameter, and boiling onions, ⅞ to 1½ inches in diameter.

Leeks have a mellow onion flavor and can be used interchangeably with onions.

Shallots have a mild, delicate flavor that is outstanding when added to sauces.

Green onions also are known as scallions and usually have a mildly pungent flavor.

Red onions generally have a sharp flavor. They are valued for their color when served raw.

Yellow onions can be round or flattened; sweet varieties include Vidalia, Walla Walla, and Maui, which are great for caramelizing.

Garlic is strongly scented and pungent. Elephant garlic is larger, milder, and more closely related to a leek.

potato-shrimp soup
with chives

prep: 20 minutes   *cook:* 12 minutes   *makes:* 4 servings

½ cup finely chopped onion
⅓ cup chopped leek
3 cloves garlic, minced
1 tablespoon olive oil
½ cup dry white wine
3½ cups chicken Basic Soup Stock (see recipe,
    page 30) or two 14½-ounce cans
    chicken broth
2 cups cubed, unpeeled new potatoes

1 cup water
¼ teaspoon freshly ground pepper
2 bay leaves
8 ounces cooked, peeled, and deveined
    shrimp, halved lengthwise
¼ cup snipped fresh chives
1 tablespoon snipped fresh thyme
    Salt
    Pepper

1 In a large saucepan or Dutch oven cook onion, leek, and garlic in hot olive oil until tender. Stir in wine. Bring to boiling; reduce heat. Boil gently for 3 to 5 minutes or until wine is reduced by half.

2 Stir in soup stock or broth, potatoes, water, pepper, and bay leaves. Bring to boiling; reduce heat. Simmer, covered, for 12 to 15 minutes or until potatoes are tender.

3 Stir in shrimp, chives, and thyme; heat through. Remove bay leaves. Season to taste with salt and pepper.

Nutrition Facts per serving: 225 cal., 5 g total fat (1 g sat. fat), 126 mg chol., 688 mg sodium, 17 g carbo., 2 g fiber, 22 g pro. **Daily Values:** 7% vit. A, 30% vit. C, 8% calcium, 18% iron.

SUBSTITUTING DRIED HERBS FOR FRESH HERBS

All out of fresh herbs? In a pinch, you can substitute dried herbs. To do so, use one-third the amount of dried herb for the amount of fresh herb called for in a recipe. For example, substitute 1 teaspoon dried herb for 1 tablespoon fresh herb.

Before adding a dried herb to a recipe, crush it between your finger and thumb to help release the herb's flavors.

If you use a dried herb, add it to the recipe at the beginning of cooking to develop its flavor. If you use a fresh herb, add it at the end because long cooking can destroy its flavor and color. The exception to this rule is fresh rosemary, which can withstand long cooking times.

Cook up a big pot of soup and, if you're lucky, you'll have leftovers to freeze for another meal. Here's how to do it safely:

Cool the hot soup quickly by placing it in a bowl set over another bowl filled with ice water. This method allows less time for bacteria to grow.

Once cool, quickly transfer the food to moisture- and vapor-proof freezer containers. Use small containers to allow food to freeze quickly, which slows bacteria growth. Remember, soups and other liquids or semi-liquids expand when they freeze, so leave about ½ inch space below the rim.

Thaw frozen foods in the refrigerator or in the microwave, never at room temperature.

grilled chicken & vegetable soup

prep: 8 minutes   **cook:** 34 minutes   **makes:** 4 servings

2   medium carrots, sliced
1   large red, green, or yellow sweet pepper,
       cut into bite-size pieces
1   medium zucchini, cut into bite-size pieces
1   small onion, coarsely chopped
2   tablespoons olive oil
½   teaspoon pepper
¼   teaspoon salt
2   cloves garlic, minced

8   ounces skinless, boneless chicken
       breast halves or thighs
3½ cups chicken Basic Soup Stock (see recipe,
       page 30) or two 14½-ounce cans
       chicken broth
2   cups water
1   cup dried radiatore, cavatelli,
       or farfalle (bow ties)
2   tablespoons snipped fresh basil,
       cilantro, or parsley

1 In a small saucepan cook carrots in a small amount of boiling water for 2 minutes; drain.

2 In a large bowl combine cooked carrots, sweet pepper, zucchini, and onion. Combine olive oil, pepper, salt, and garlic. Drizzle over the vegetables; toss lightly to coat. Spoon vegetable mixture into a grill wok (see tip, page 51) or onto a large piece of heavy foil.

3 Grill vegetables on the rack of an uncovered grill directly over medium heat about 20 minutes or until lightly charred, stirring often. Remove vegetables from grill; set aside. Add more coals, if necessary.

4 Add chicken to grill. Grill for 12 to 15 minutes or until chicken is tender and no longer pink, turning once halfway through grilling. Cool chicken slightly; cut into bite-size pieces.

5 Meanwhile, in a 4-quart Dutch oven bring soup stock or broth and water to boiling; add pasta. Cook according to package directions. Stir in vegetables, chicken, and basil, cilantro, or parsley; heat through.

Nutrition Facts per serving: 268 cal., 10 g total fat (2 g sat. fat), 58 mg chol., 734 mg sodium, 24 g carbo., 3 g fiber, 19 g pro. **Daily Values:** 198% vit. A, 114% vit. C, 5% calcium, 11% iron.

minestrone

prep: 25 minutes   *cook:* 34 minutes   *makes:* 6 servings

1   cup chopped onion or
    2 medium leeks, sliced
1/2   cup chopped carrots
1/2   cup sliced celery
1   clove garlic, minced
2   tablespoons olive oil or cooking oil
3 1/2   cups chicken Basic Soup Stock (see recipe,
    page 30) or two 14 1/2-ounce cans
    chicken broth
1   14 1/2-ounce can tomatoes, cut up
    and undrained
1   cup shredded cabbage

3/4   cup tomato juice
1   teaspoon dried basil, crushed
1   15-ounce can cannellini or Great Northern
    beans, rinsed and drained
1   medium zucchini, sliced 1/4 inch thick
1/2   of a 9-ounce package frozen Italian
    green beans
2   ounces dried spaghetti or linguine,
    broken (about 1/2 cup)
2   ounces prosciutto or cooked ham, diced
1/4   cup finely shredded Parmesan cheese

1 In a 4-quart Dutch oven cook onion or leeks, carrots, celery, and garlic in hot oil about 4 minutes or until onion is tender.

2 Stir in the soup stock or broth, undrained tomatoes, cabbage, tomato juice, and basil. Bring to boiling; reduce heat. Simmer, covered, for 20 minutes.

3 Stir in the drained cannellini or Great Northern beans, zucchini, green beans, spaghetti or linguine, and prosciutto or ham. Return to boiling; reduce heat. Simmer, covered, for 10 to 15 minutes more or until vegetables and pasta are tender. Top each serving with Parmesan cheese.

Nutrition Facts per serving: 323 cal., 10 g total fat (2 g sat. fat), 13 mg chol., 1,665 mg sodium, 50 g carbo., 11 g fiber, 19 g pro. **Daily Values:** 129% vit. A, 164% vit. C, 27% calcium, 28% iron.

THE FASTEST WAY TO CHOP AN ONION

It's easy to make quick work of chopping an onion:

Slice off the stem and the root ends of the onion; remove peel. Halve the onion from top to root end. Place each onion half flat side down and make vertical slices across the half (see photo, top). Holding the vertical slices together, cut across the slices (see photo, above).

QUICK SWEET PEPPER STEMMING & SEEDING

Here's how to make stemming and seeding sweet peppers quick and easy:

Holding the pepper upright on a cutting surface, slice each of the sides from the pepper, using a sharp knife (see photo, above). You should have 4 large, flat pieces of pepper—free of seeds and ribs—that are easy to slice or chop. The stem, seeds, and ribs should all be in one unit and can be easily discarded. Or, if there is enough pepper left, trim it from the seeds and ribs to use in your recipe.

italian country
bread soup

prep: 20 minutes   *cook:* 10 minutes   *makes:* 6 servings

  8 ounces Italian flat bread (focaccia), cut into ³/₄-inch cubes (4 cups)
2¹/₂ cups chopped zucchini and/or yellow summer squash
  ³/₄ cup chopped green sweet pepper
  ¹/₂ cup chopped onion
  1 tablespoon olive oil

3¹/₂ cups chicken Basic Soup Stock (see recipe, page 30) or two 14¹/₂-ounce cans chicken broth
  1 14¹/₂-ounce can diced tomatoes with basil, oregano, and garlic, undrained
     Finely shredded Parmesan cheese (optional)

1 Spread bread cubes in a single layer on an ungreased baking sheet. Bake in a 375° oven for 10 to 15 minutes or until lightly toasted.

2 Meanwhile, in a large saucepan cook zucchini or yellow squash, sweet pepper, and onion in hot oil for 5 minutes. Stir in soup stock or broth and undrained tomatoes. Bring to boiling; reduce heat. Simmer, uncovered, about 5 minutes or until vegetables are just tender.

3 Ladle soup into bowls. Top each serving with toasted bread cubes and, if desired, Parmesan cheese.

Nutrition Facts per serving: 172 cal., 4 g total fat (1 g sat. fat), 9 mg chol., 526 mg sodium, 27 g carbo., 3 g fiber, 8 g pro. **Daily Values:** 5% vit. A, 45% vit. C, 8% calcium, 6% iron.

THICKENING SOUPS

Soups can be thickened several ways, including adding a roux (see tip, page 43); pureeing all or some of the ingredients (see tip, page 35); using a beurre manie (see tip, page 170); or adding cream, cornstarch, or flour. Thai Lime Custard Soup (see recipe, right), however, is thickened with eggs, similar to stirred custard.

The secret to successfully making the soup is combining the eggs with the hot liquid without causing them to curdle. This is accomplished by gradually stirring a small amount of hot liquid into the eggs before adding the eggs to the rest of the soup (see step 2, right). This step, called tempering, assures the gradual heating and mixing needed to avoid curdling the eggs.

thai lime custard soup

prep: 15 minutes   **cook:** 9 minutes   **makes:** 5 servings

2 baby eggplants or Japanese eggplants (1 pound), halved and sliced (about 5 cups)
1 tablespoon grated fresh ginger
¼ teaspoon crushed red pepper
2 to 3 cloves garlic, minced (optional)
1 tablespoon cooking oil

3½ cups chicken Basic Soup Stock (see recipe, page 30) or two 14½-ounce cans chicken broth
3 slightly beaten eggs
2 cups chopped fresh spinach
¼ cup lime juice
¼ cup fresh basil leaves, cut into thin strips

1 In a large saucepan cook eggplants, ginger, red pepper, and, if desired, garlic in hot oil over medium-high heat for 2 minutes. Stir in soup stock or broth. Bring to boiling; reduce heat. Simmer, covered, for 5 minutes.

2 Place eggs in a small bowl. Gradually stir about ½ cup of the hot broth into eggs. Return all to saucepan. Add spinach. Cook and stir over medium-low heat about 2 minutes or until soup is slightly thickened and spinach is wilted. Stir in lime juice and basil; heat through.

Nutrition Facts per serving: 114 cal., 6 g total fat (1 g sat. fat), 138 mg chol., 482 mg sodium, 7 g carbo., 3 g fiber, 8 g pro. **Daily Values:** 21% vit. A, 14% vit. C, 4% calcium, 10% iron.

Thai Lime Custard-Chicken Soup: Prepare as directed at left, except add 1½ cups chopped cooked chicken with the spinach.

Thai Lime Custard-Shrimp Soup: Prepare as directed at left, except add 8 ounces cooked shrimp with the spinach.

chicken & sausage gumbo

prep: 45 minutes   **cook:** 1 hour 2 minutes   **makes:** 10 servings

1 cup all-purpose flour
²/₃ cup cooking oil
³/₄ cup sliced celery
¹/₂ cup chopped onion
¹/₂ cup chopped green sweet pepper
2 cloves garlic, minced
2 pounds meaty chicken pieces
   (breasts, thighs, and drumsticks)
6 cups water

8 ounces cooked smoked sausage,
   cut into 1-inch pieces
8 ounces andouille sausage, cut into
   ¹/₂-inch pieces
1 teaspoon salt
1 teaspoon ground red pepper
¹/₄ teaspoon black pepper
   Hot cooked rice

1 For roux, in a large heavy saucepan combine flour and oil until smooth. Cook over medium-low heat about 20 minutes or until roux is caramel-colored, stirring constantly. Stir in celery, onion, sweet pepper, and garlic; cook for 5 minutes more, stirring occasionally.

2 Meanwhile, if desired, skin chicken. Add the chicken pieces, water, smoked sausage, andouille sausage, salt, red pepper, and black pepper to the saucepan. Bring to boiling; reduce heat to medium-low. Simmer, covered, about 1 hour or until chicken is tender and no longer pink. Skim off excess fat. Remove chicken pieces from gumbo.

3 When chicken pieces are cool enough to handle, remove meat from bones; discard bones. Return chicken to saucepan. Cook for 2 to 3 minutes more or until heated through. Serve in bowls with rice.

Nutrition Facts per serving: 462 cal., 36 g total fat (9 g sat. fat), 57 mg chol., 487 mg sodium, 33 g carbo., 1 g fiber, 26 g pro. **Daily Values:** 2% vit. A, 16% vit. C, 2% calcium, 16% iron.

WHAT IS A ROUX?

Roux [ROO] is a French term for a mixture of flour and fat, such as cooking oil or butter, that is cooked, then used for thickening soups, sauces, gravies, and gumbos. A roux can be cooked to several stages, depending on the color and flavor you want to achieve.

- If cooked for only a couple minutes, the roux mixture won't change color, making it perfect for thickening white, delicately-flavored sauces.
- Heating a roux for a few minutes more gives it a golden color and a little more flavor. This is sometimes referred to as a *blond roux*.
- A *brown or caramel-color roux*, such as in the recipe at left, takes 20 to 30 minutes of cooking and stirring to achieve its deep brown color (similar to the color of a penny). This type of roux, with its rich, nutty flavor and aroma, is a perfect match for the strong flavors of gumbo. Roux will keep, tightly covered, in the refrigerator for 2 weeks or in the freezer for 6 months.

43

ROASTING GARLIC

Roasted garlic adds a sweet, mellow caramel flavor to soups (see recipe, right) and salad dressings. It also can be served as an appetizer spread for crackers and focaccia. Here's how to roast a whole head of garlic:

With a sharp knife, cut off the pointed top portion from 1 medium head of garlic, leaving the bulb intact but exposing the individual cloves. Place in a small baking dish or custard cup; drizzle with 2 teaspoons olive oil (see photo, above). Bake, covered, in a 325° oven for 45 to 60 minutes or until the cloves are very soft. Set aside until cool enough to handle. Squeeze garlic paste from individual cloves and use as directed in recipes, or serve garlic bulbs whole on an appetizer platter.

portobello mushroom
& roasted garlic soup

prep: 25 minutes   *cook:* 51 minutes   *makes:* 6 servings

1 pound fresh portobello mushrooms
1 cup sliced celery
1 cup chopped red or yellow sweet pepper
2 tablespoons olive oil
1 tablespoon snipped fresh thyme
 or ½ teaspoon dried thyme, crushed
¼ teaspoon pepper

3½ cups beef Basic Soup Stock (see recipe, page 30) or two 14½-ounce cans beef or vegetable broth
10 to 12 cloves garlic (1 entire head), roasted (see tip, left) and mashed (about 2 tablespoons)
½ cup brown rice or pearl barley

1 Cut off mushroom stems even with caps; discard stems. Clean mushrooms as directed in tip on page 45. Thinly slice mushroom caps; cut slices into 2-inch pieces. Set aside.

2 In a large saucepan cook celery and sweet pepper in hot oil over medium-high heat for 3 minutes. Add mushrooms, dried thyme (if using), and pepper. Cook for 3 to 4 minutes more or until vegetables are just tender, gently stirring occasionally.

3 Stir in soup stock or broth; bring to boiling. Stir in mashed roasted garlic and brown rice or pearl barley. Return to boiling; reduce heat. Simmer, covered, about 45 minutes or until rice or barley is tender. Just before serving, stir in fresh thyme (if using).

Nutrition Facts per serving: 152 cal., 6 g total fat (1 g sat. fat), 3 mg chol., 375 mg sodium, 20 g carbo., 4 g fiber, 5 g pro. **Daily Values:** 28% vit. A, 73% vit. C, 6% calcium, 6% iron.

creamy mushroom
and wild rice soup

prep: 25 minutes   *cook:* 46 minutes   *makes:* 6 servings

1¼ cups sliced fresh shiitake mushrooms
 1   cup sliced fresh white mushrooms
 ¼   cup thinly sliced carrot
 ¼   cup sliced celery
 ¼   cup sliced green onions
 3   tablespoons margarine or butter
1¾ cups chicken Basic Soup Stock (see recipe, page 30) or one 14½-ounce can chicken broth

 ½   cup water
 ¼   cup wild rice, uncooked
 ⅛   teaspoon dried marjoram
 1   cup half-and-half or light cream
 2   tablespoons all-purpose flour
 1   cup milk
     Thin carrot strips (optional)
     Fresh marjoram sprigs (optional)

1 In a large saucepan cook shiitake and white mushrooms, carrot, celery, and onions in hot margarine or butter for 5 minutes, stirring occasionally. Remove several shiitake mushroom slices for garnish; set aside. Place remaining mushroom mixture in a blender container. Add about half of the soup stock or broth. Cover and blend until smooth. Return mixture to saucepan.

2 Add remaining stock or broth, water, uncooked wild rice, and dried marjoram to the mixture in the saucepan. Bring to boiling; reduce heat. Simmer, covered, 45 to 50 minutes or until rice is tender.

3 In a small bowl gradually stir half-and-half or light cream into flour until smooth. Add to mixture in saucepan. Add milk. Cook and stir over medium heat until slightly thickened and bubbly. Cook and stir for 1 minute more.

4 Top each serving with reserved mushrooms. If desired, garnish with carrot strips and marjoram sprigs.

Nutrition Facts per serving: 188 cal., 12 g total fat (4 g sat. fat), 22 mg chol., 289 mg sodium, 16 g carbo., 2 g fiber, 6 g pro. **Daily Values:** 39% vit. A, 4% vit. C, 11% calcium, 4% iron.

CLEANING & STORING MUSHROOMS

When it comes to cleaning and storing mushrooms, follow these helpful hints:

The best way to clean fresh mushrooms is to wipe them with a clean, damp cloth. If you must rinse them, do it lightly, then dry them immediately—and gently—with paper towels. Never soak fresh mushrooms in water because it ruins their texture.

As for storage, prepackaged mushrooms should stay in the package, but loose mushrooms or those in an open package should be stored in a paper bag or in a damp cloth bag in the refrigerator. This allows them to breathe so they stay firm longer. Storing mushrooms in a plastic bag causes them to deteriorate quickly. (See also mushroom tips, pages 56 and 57.)

country french beef stew

prep: 30 minutes   *stand:* 1 hour   *simmer:* 1 hour 55 minutes   *makes:* 6 servings

½ cup dry navy beans or one 15-ounce can
     white beans,* rinsed and drained
4 cups water
¼ cup all-purpose flour
½ teaspoon pepper
2 pounds boneless beef chuck pot roast,
     cut into 1-inch pieces
3 tablespoons olive oil
1 medium onion, cut into thin wedges
3 cloves garlic, minced

⅔ cup dry red wine
1¾ cups beef Basic Soup Stock (see recipe,
     page 30) or one 14½-ounce can
     beef broth
1 cup chopped tomato
2 teaspoons dried thyme, crushed, or
     2 tablespoons snipped fresh thyme
4 medium carrots, cut into ½-inch slices
2 medium parsnips, cut into ½-inch slices
     Snipped fresh parsley (optional)

1 If using dry beans, rinse beans. In a large saucepan combine drained beans and the 4 cups water. Bring to boiling; reduce heat. Simmer, uncovered, for 2 minutes. Remove from heat. Cover and let stand for 1 hour. (Or, place beans in water in pan. Cover and let soak in a cool place for 6 to 8 hours or overnight.) Drain and rinse beans.

2 Place flour and pepper in a plastic bag. Add beef pieces, a few at a time, shaking to coat. In a 4- to 6-quart Dutch oven brown half of the beef in 1 tablespoon of the hot oil; remove beef. Add remaining oil, remaining beef, onion, and garlic to Dutch oven. Cook until beef is brown and onion is tender. Drain fat, if necessary.

Stir in wine, scraping until the brown bits are dissolved. Return all beef to Dutch oven. Stir in beans, soup stock or broth, tomato, and dried thyme (if using). Bring to boiling; reduce heat.

3 Simmer, covered, for 1½ hours. Add carrots and parsnips. Return to boiling; reduce heat. Simmer, covered, for 25 to 30 minutes more or until beef and vegetables are tender. Stir in fresh thyme (if using). If desired, garnish with parsley.

Nutrition Facts per serving: 554 cal., 31 g total fat (10 g sat. fat), 99 mg chol., 295 mg sodium, 29 g carbo., 8 g fiber, 34 g pro. **Daily Values:** 211% vit. A, 26% vit. C, 8% calcium, 30% iron.

*Note: If using canned beans, decrease soup stock or broth to 1 cup.

STEWING FOR TENDERNESS

Stewing is a cooking technique perfectly suited for when you want to make the most of less expensive, tougher cuts of meat, such as beef chuck or round.

Stewing simply means to cook food in liquid in a covered pot for a long time (see recipe, left). You can stew meats either on the range-top or in the oven. The long, slow, moist cooking softens the tough fibers of the meat, making it tender, juicy, and delicious.

Naturally tender cuts, such as most steaks, however, don't require this sort of cooking. That's why they often are grilled, broiled, or pan-fried for a short period of time.

47

Chiles, such as jalapeños, habañeros, and serranos, contain volatile oils that can burn your skin and eyes. Avoid direct contact with them as much as possible.

When working with fresh chiles, wear rubber gloves or disposable plastic gloves, or cover your hands with small plastic bags.

If your bare hands do touch the peppers, wash your hands and nails well with soap and hot water. If you get some of the oils in your eyes, flush them with cool water.

Oils from chiles can transfer to knives and cutting surfaces, so wash tools and surfaces with hot, soapy water after using to prevent the oils from transferring to other foods.

green chile pork stew

prep: 30 minutes ***simmer:*** 50 minutes ***makes:*** 6 servings

$\frac{1}{4}$ cup all-purpose flour
1 teaspoon ground cumin
$\frac{1}{2}$ teaspoon salt
$\frac{1}{4}$ teaspoon pepper
2 pounds boneless pork shoulder roast, cut into $\frac{3}{4}$-inch pieces
2 tablespoons cooking oil
3 fresh Anaheim peppers, finely chopped (about 1 cup)
$\frac{1}{2}$ cup chopped onion

2 cloves garlic, minced
$1\frac{3}{4}$ cups chicken Basic Soup Stock (see recipe, page 30) or one $14\frac{1}{2}$-ounce can chicken broth
1 $14\frac{1}{2}$-ounce can diced tomatoes with basil, oregano, and garlic, undrained
2 small zucchinis, thinly sliced
1 $14\frac{1}{2}$- to 15-ounce can hominy
Snipped fresh cilantro (optional)

1 Place flour, cumin, salt, and pepper in a plastic bag. Add pork pieces, a few at a time, shaking to coat.

2 In a large saucepan or Dutch oven brown half of the pork in 1 tablespoon of the hot oil; remove pork from pan. Add remaining oil, remaining pork, peppers, onion, and garlic to saucepan. Cook until pork is brown and onion is tender. Drain fat, if necessary. Return all pork to saucepan.

3 Stir in soup stock or broth and undrained tomatoes. Bring to boiling; reduce heat. Simmer, covered, for 45 minutes. Stir in zucchini and hominy. Return to boiling; reduce heat. Simmer, covered, about 5 minutes more or until pork and zucchini are tender. If desired, garnish with cilantro.

Nutrition Facts per serving: 368 cal., 16 g total fat (4 g sat. fat), 105 mg chol., 760 mg sodium, 21 g carbo., 3 g fiber, 34 g pro. **Daily Values:** 6% vit. A, 123% vit. C, 7% calcium, 18% iron.

Vegetables

SIMPLE SECRET INDEX

THE PERFECT EAR

Biting into fresh sweet corn is a summer pastime to savor. But how do you ensure the corn you choose is at its best? If possible, find out when the corn was picked—if it was picked no more than 24 hours earlier, it should be fine. If you don't know when the corn was picked, opt for a supersweet variety—some of the sweetest varieties will retain their sweet flavor for several days.

Sort through the corn to find the best ears. Pull down the husk and listen as you pull—a fresh ear will squeak. Look at the kernels. Whether yellow or white (or both), kernels should be in even, tightly-spaced rows and look plump and milky. Look for well-filled-out ears without lots of underdeveloped kernels. Husks should be bright green and healthy-looking, and they should fit tightly together and be snug on the ear.

grilled corn relish

prep: 10 minutes   *grill:* 10 minutes   *makes:* 4 to 6 servings

2   tablespoons fresh lime juice
1   tablespoon vegetable oil
2   cloves garlic, minced
2   ears corn on the cob, husked
1   teaspoon chili powder or hot chili powder

1   small ripe avocado, peeled, seeded, and diced
½   cup diced red sweet pepper
¼   cup chopped cilantro
¼   teaspoon salt

1 In a medium bowl combine lime juice, oil, and garlic. Brush corn lightly with mixture, leaving remaining mixture in bowl. Sprinkle corn with chili powder. Grill on the rack of an uncovered grill over medium coals about 10 minutes or until tender, turning occasionally.

2 Meanwhile, add avocado, sweet pepper, cilantro, and salt to bowl with lime juice mixture; toss well. Cut corn kernels from cob; stir into avocado mixture. Serve immediately.

Nutrition Facts per serving: 159 cal., 12 g total fat (2 g sat. fat), 0 mg chol., 152 mg sodium, 15 g carbo., 3 g fiber, 3 g pro. **Daily Values:** 15% vit. A, 51% vit. C, 1% calcium, 6% iron.

How to keep vegetables fresh

Ideally, you would buy your vegetables one day and eat them that night or the next. As a practical matter, however, you'll probably want to store your vegetables for several days. How do you keep vegetables fresh after you buy them? The keys are keeping them chilled (with some exceptions, such as onions, garlic, potatoes, and tomatoes), maintaining an appropriate moisture level (too much and they'll rot, too little and they'll dry out), and limiting oxygen—that is, keeping them wrapped or sealed in plastic bags or other containers. Fresh greens require special handling (see tip, page 17).

grilled vegetable fajitas
with chipotle cream

prep: 25 minutes **grill:** 12 minutes **makes:** 4 servings (2 fajitas per serving)

¹⁄₃ cup dairy sour cream
1 tablespoon snipped fresh cilantro
1 to 2 teaspoons minced chipotle peppers
    in adobo sauce
1 medium green sweet pepper
1 medium red sweet pepper
1 medium yellow sweet pepper
2 tablespoons olive oil

¹⁄₂ to 1 teaspoon Mexican seasoning
1 medium sweet onion, cut into
    ¹⁄₂-inch slices
1 Japanese eggplant, halved lengthwise
8 10-inch flour tortillas
¹⁄₄ teaspoon salt
¹⁄₂ cup chunky salsa

1 For chipotle cream, in a small bowl combine sour cream, cilantro, and chipotle peppers; set aside.

2 Halve sweet peppers lengthwise; discard stems, membranes, and seeds (see tip, page 40). Combine olive oil and Mexican seasoning; lightly brush cut sides of sweet peppers, onion, and eggplant with oil mixture. (Or, place vegetables in a heavy-duty, large plastic bag; add oil mixture. Close bag; shake bag to coat vegetables.)

3 Grill vegetables, cut sides up, on the rack of an uncovered grill directly over medium coals until tender, turning occasionally. (Or, use a grill wok. See tip, right.) (Allow 8 to 12 minutes for eggplant and sweet peppers and 12 to 14 minutes for onion.) Remove vegetables from grill; cool until easy to handle.

4 Meanwhile, wrap tortillas in foil. Place tortillas on grill rack directly over coals. Grill about 10 minutes or until heated through.

5 Cut sweet peppers into thin strips; cut eggplant into ¹⁄₂-inch slices. Separate onion into rings. Place all vegetables in a large serving bowl; toss lightly with salt. Serve vegetables in warm tortillas with chipotle cream and salsa.

Nutrition Facts per serving: 420 cal.,19 g total fat (5 g sat. fat), 8 mg chol., 651 mg sodium, 57 g carbo., 4 g fiber, 8 g pro. **Daily Values:** 26% vit. A, 151% vit. C, 11% calcium, 24% iron.

EASY GRILLING WITH A GRILL WOK

Grilling works wonders on your favorite fresh vegetables. They get smoky, crisp, and slightly caramelized.

An easy way to keep cut-up vegetables from falling into the fire as you grill them is to use a grill wok. Start by coating the wok with nonstick cooking spray to prevent sticking. Coat the vegetables you plan to grill lightly with cooking oil and season them with salt and pepper, seasoned salt, or the seasoning called for in your recipe. Add vegetables to the grill wok. Grill as the recipe directs, turning the vegetables occasionally with tongs (see photo, above) or a large metal spatula to avoid burning and to cook all of the vegetables evenly.

51

cheesy garlic potato gratin

prep: 15 minutes   **cook:** 1 hour 15 minutes   **makes:** 6 to 8 servings

1½ pounds Yukon gold or other yellow-fleshed
       potatoes, thinly sliced (about 5 cups)
⅓ cup sliced green onions
1½ cups shredded Swiss cheese

2 teaspoons minced garlic
1 teaspoon salt
¼ teaspoon pepper
1 cup whipping cream

1 Grease a 2-quart square baking dish. Layer half of the sliced potatoes and half of the green onions in prepared dish. Sprinkle with half of the cheese, garlic, salt, and pepper. Repeat layers. Pour whipping cream over top.

2 Bake, covered, in a 350° oven for 1 hour. Uncover and bake 15 to 20 minutes more or until potatoes are tender and top is golden brown.

Nutrition Facts per serving: 365 cal., 23 g total fat (14 g sat. fat), 80 mg chol., 454 mg sodium, 30 g carbo., 1 g fiber, 12 g pro. **Daily Values:** 25% vit. A, 31% vit. C, 26% calcium, 10% iron.

Selecting the best potato for the job

Whether you're in the mood for mashed, baked, boiled, or fried potatoes will determine which potato is the best type to use. The starch content of each variety dictates the preparation method that works best for that type of potato.

High-starch potatoes, such as russets—which have a light, mealy texture—are best for baked potatoes, potato pancakes, French fries, and mashed potatoes. The fluffy quality that makes them good for these types of foods makes them a poor choice for salads, however, because they will crumble when boiled.

Medium-starch potatoes, such as yellow Finns and Yukon golds, are all-purpose potatoes. They contain more moisture than high-starch potatoes and don't fall apart as easily. They're a good choice for roasting or making into gratins, such as the recipe above.

Low-starch potatoes, often called waxy potatoes, are dense and hold their shapes better than other types, making them the ideal choice for potato salad and roasting. Most round red and round white varieties are low-starch potatoes. All new potatoes are low-starch potatoes.

know your potatoes

Sweet potatoes have sweet orange flesh that cooks to a moist texture (they're often mislabeled "yams," a starchier vegetable).

New potatoes are young, very thin-skinned, waxy-fleshed potatoes that are low in starch. They can be of any variety.

Russets are high in starch and the ultimate baking potato, with a dry, fluffy texture.

Round white potatoes are waxy-fleshed potatoes with more moisture and less starch than russets or golden potatoes.

Round red potatoes are like round white potatoes, with waxy flesh, and are good for boiling. They are low in starch.

Golden potatoes have yellow flesh and are all-purpose potatoes; Yukon gold is a popular variety. These are medium-starch potatoes.

COOKING BRUSSELS SPROUTS

The secret to bringing out the best in Brussels sprouts is simple. Don't overcook them. Sautéed Brussels Sprouts (see recipe, right) requires only 14 to 16 minutes to cook the sprouts. Like all vegetables, crisp-tender is best.

Another way to fix Brussels sprouts is to toss them with olive oil and coarse sea salt and slightly steam or oven-roast them.

When shopping for Brussels sprouts, buy small, compact ones with good green color. Store them in the refrigerator for up to 3 days; any longer and they'll develop a strong, unpleasant flavor.

sautéed
brussels sprouts

prep: 15 minutes   *cook:* 18 minutes   *makes:* 4 servings

- 1 pound Brussels sprouts
- 3 tablespoons butter or margarine
- ¼ cup finely chopped shallots
- 2 cloves garlic, minced
- 1¼ cups chicken broth
- ½ cup broken walnuts, toasted
- ¼ teaspoon freshly ground pepper

1 Trim stems and remove any wilted outer leaves from Brussels sprouts; wash. Cut any large sprouts in half.

2 In a large skillet melt butter or margarine. Cook shallots and garlic in melted butter or margarine over medium heat for 4 to 5 minutes or until tender and golden. Add Brussels sprouts; cook for 2 minutes more. Stir in broth. Bring to boiling; reduce heat. Simmer, uncovered, for 12 to 14 minutes or until liquid is almost evaporated and sprouts are crisp-tender. Transfer to a serving dish; sprinkle with walnuts and pepper.

Nutrition Facts per serving: 248 cal., 19 g total fat (7 g sat. fat), 25 mg chol., 367 mg sodium, 15 g carbo., 5 g fiber, 8 g pro. **Daily Values:** 19% vit. A, 140% vit. C, 7% calcium, 13% iron.

roasted asparagus & red peppers

prep: 20 minutes   **stand:** 20 minutes   **bake:** 10 minutes   **makes:** 4 servings

- 1 medium red sweet pepper
- 2 tablespoons olive oil
- 1 teaspoon snipped fresh thyme
- ¼ teaspoon salt
- ¼ teaspoon freshly ground pepper

- 1 pound fresh asparagus spears, trimmed
- 2 tablespoons shredded Parmesan cheese
- 2 tablespoons snipped fresh parsley
-   Olive oil (optional)
-   Cracked black pepper (optional)

1 Halve sweet pepper lengthwise; discard stem, membranes, and seeds (see tip, page 40). Place sweet pepper, cut side down, on a foil-lined baking sheet. Broil 4 to 5 inches from heat for 8 to 10 minutes or until blackened and blistered. Carefully bring foil up and around pepper halves to enclose. Let stand about 20 minutes or until cool enough to handle. Peel skin off sweet pepper (see tip, right). Cut pepper into ½-inch-wide strips. Set strips aside.

2 Combine oil, thyme, salt, and ground pepper; pour over asparagus spears. Toss lightly to coat. Arrange spears in a single layer in a 15×10×1-inch baking pan. Bake, uncovered, in a 400° oven for 10 to 12 minutes or until lightly browned and tender, turning asparagus once.

3 Arrange asparagus spears and sweet pepper strips on warm serving platter. Combine Parmesan and parsley. Sprinkle mixture over vegetables. If desired, drizzle with olive oil and sprinkle with cracked black pepper. Serve immediately.

Nutrition Facts per serving: 102 cal., 8 g total fat (2 g sat. fat), 3 mg chol., 186 mg sodium, 6 g carbo., 2 g fiber, 3 g pro. **Daily Values:** 22% vit. A, 99% vit. C, 6% calcium, 6% iron.

Roasted peppers on call

You can use roasted sweet peppers in a variety of ways. Add them to soups or chili, puree them to use in pasta sauces, blend them with mayonnaise for a quick dip, or drizzle them with olive oil and balsamic vinegar to top toasted baguette slices. To keep some on hand, roast a supply when peppers are plentiful and stash them in your freezer.

To prepare the peppers, roast and peel them according to the directions in the recipe above and in the tip at right. To freeze the peppers, place the individual roasted pepper pieces between sheets of waxed paper. Place them in a sealable plastic freezer bag and freeze for up to 3 months. To use, thaw at room temperature about 30 minutes. (Or, after roasting, place the peppers in a little olive oil in an airtight container and refrigerate for up to 1 week.)

EASY SWEET PEPPER ROASTING & PEELING

Freshly roasted sweet peppers taste so much better than what you can buy in a jar. They're easy to prepare, too.

To roast the peppers, follow the process in step 1 at left. Steaming is the key to softening the skins, making it easier to peel the peppers. So don't be tempted to skip the 20-minute standing time. To peel the peppers, use a sharp knife to loosen the edges of the skins from the peppers. Then peel off the skins (see photo, above).

mushrooms—beyond the basics

Trumpet mushrooms have a mellow, woodsy taste.

Enoki (*eh*-NOH-*kee*) mushrooms come vacuum-packed. Show off their delicate flavor raw in salads.

Savory **morels** (*more*-EL) have an intense mushroom flavor and aroma.

Oyster mushrooms come in many colors and sizes. All have a soft texture and mild taste.

Shiitakes (*shee*-TAH-*kee*) are prized for their meaty flavor and texture.

Buttery-flavored **chanterelle** *(shant-uh-REL)* mushrooms are best in simple recipes.

Wood ear mushrooms are favored for their yielding, yet crunchy, texture.

Portobellos are velvety brown mushrooms boasting a deep mushroom flavor. You'll find them in large, medium, and small sizes.

wild mushroom toss

prep: 10 minutes   ***cook:*** 16 minutes   ***makes:*** 6 servings

12 ounces dried linguine or spaghetti
4 cups sliced fresh mushrooms (such as shiitake, morel, oyster, and/or cremini)
2 small red or green sweet peppers, cut into strips

1 medium onion, cut into thin wedges
¼ cup butter or margarine
¼ teaspoon seasoned salt
¼ teaspoon pepper
   Shaved or grated Parmesan cheese

1 Cook linguine or spaghetti according to package directions; drain. Keep warm.

2 Meanwhile, in a large skillet cook mushrooms, sweet peppers, and onion in hot butter or margarine until tender.

3 Stir in seasoned salt and pepper. Toss with hot pasta. Top with cheese.

Nutrition Facts per serving: 351 cal., 10 g total fat (5 g sat. fat), 23 mg chol., 168 mg sodium, 59 g carbo., 4 g fiber, 10 g pro. **Daily Values:** 22% vit. A, 81% vit. C, 3% calcium, 13% iron.

Tarragon Mushroom Toss: Prepare as directed above, except add 1 tablespoon snipped fresh tarragon or 1 teaspoon dried tarragon, crushed, along with vegetables.

Madeira Mushroom Toss: Prepare as directed above left, except add ¼ cup Madeira or dry sherry to vegetable mixture after cooking. Bring to boiling. Boil gently until sauce is reduced by half.

WILD MUSHROOMS

Wild mushrooms, with their hearty, earthy flavor, are worth seeking out to use in recipes.

Many wild mushrooms, such as oyster, shiitake, and trumpet, are grown on farms and are wild in name only. The commercially raised versions retain the same unfettered mushroom flavor as their counterparts that grow in the wild.

Look for the varieties shown on page 56 at your local supermarket. Some of these may be found either fresh or dried. (For advice on using dried mushrooms, see the tip on page 73.)

Many varieties in the wild— including some that appear identical to familiar edible types—are poisonous and can be harmful, even fatal, to eat. Buying wild mushrooms at a supermarket ensures you'll get only ones that are safe to eat.

Caramelized onions add a scrumptious sweetness to lots of dishes, dips, and sauces, but you may wonder just what caramelizing is.

All vegetables and fruits contain natural sugars. When heated, these sugars brown and caramelize, becoming more intense in flavor. Onions are great candidates for caramelizing because they contain plenty of natural sugars.

Onions can be caramelized by cooking them slowly in oil as in Caramelized Onion & Leek Tart (see recipe, right, and photo, above). Or, they can be caramelized using a little sugar (see tip, page 102).

caramelized onion
& leek tart

prep: 35 minutes   **bake:** 25 minutes   **makes:** 6 servings

1 recipe Pastry for Single-Crust Pie	2 tablespoons snipped fresh basil or Italian parsley
1 small onion, thinly sliced	½ teaspoon salt
1 leek, halved lengthwise and sliced	⅛ teaspoon pepper
1 shallot, coarsely chopped	6 ounces shredded Italian cheese blend (1½ cups)
1 tablespoon olive oil	
3 eggs	
1½ cups milk	

1 Prepare Pastry for Single-Crust Pie; set aside. In a medium skillet cook onion, leek, and shallot, uncovered, in hot olive oil over medium-low heat, about 20 minutes or until golden, stirring occasionally.

2 Meanwhile, on a lightly floured surface, roll pastry from center to edges into a circle about 12 inches in diameter. Line a 10-inch tart pan with pastry. Trim edges even with tart pan. Do not prick. Line pastry shell with a double thickness of foil.

3 Bake in a 450° oven for 5 minutes. Remove foil. Bake for 5 to 6 minutes more or until pastry is set and dry. Remove from oven; set aside. Reduce oven temperature to 375°.

4 In a medium bowl beat eggs slightly with a fork. Stir in milk, basil or Italian parsley, salt, and pepper; set aside.

5 Spoon caramelized onion mixture into the hot, baked pastry shell. Sprinkle with cheese. Carefully pour egg mixture over cheese in pastry shell. Bake in the 375° oven about 25 minutes or until a knife inserted near the center comes out clean. Let stand 5 minutes before serving.

Pastry for Single-Crust Pie: In a medium bowl stir together 1¼ cups all-purpose flour and ¼ teaspoon salt. Using a pastry blender, cut in ⅓ cup shortening until pieces are pea-size. Sprinkle 1 tablespoon water over part of the mixture; gently toss with a fork. Push moistened dough to side of bowl. Repeat moistening dough, using 1 tablespoon water at a time, until all dough is moistened (4 to 5 tablespoons of water total). Form dough into a ball.

Nutrition Facts per serving: 376 cal., 25 g total fat (9 g sat. fat), 131 mg chol., 535 mg sodium, 24 g carbo., 1 g fiber, 15 g pro. **Daily Values:** 12% vit. A, 4% vit. C, 26% calcium, 9% iron.

SELECTING CHILES

Chiles are so popular entire cuisines, such as Mexican, seem to be built around them. A variety of types now can be found in most grocery stores. To find some of the less common peppers, such as pasilla and pequín (see photos, page 61), check Latin and Asian markets.

Jalapeños probably are the most popular chiles with Americans. But if the heat is too much for you, substitute the milder Anaheim.

For fiery flavor, habañeros rate high; their heat is intense, but it doesn't seem to linger as long as many other chiles. Fresh habañeros also have a fruity element to their flavor that makes them good in fruit salsas, such as Caribbean Salsa (see recipe, right).

When shopping for fresh chiles, look for bright colors and avoid any that are shriveled, bruised, or broken. Store them, covered, in your refrigerator for up to 5 days. (See the tip on page 48 for hints on handling fresh chiles.) Dried chiles will keep for up to a year in airtight containers in a cool, dark place.

caribbean salsa

prep: 20 minutes   *chill:* 1 hour   *makes:* 12 servings (3 cups)

1 cup finely chopped mango
1 cup finely chopped papaya
½ cup finely chopped green sweet pepper
¼ cup finely chopped onion
¼ cup snipped fresh cilantro
2 tablespoons lime juice
1 tablespoon honey
1 teaspoon minced garlic
½ to 1 teaspoon finely chopped fresh habañero pepper or 1 medium fresh jalapeño pepper, seeded and finely chopped
Dash salt

1 In a medium bowl combine mango, papaya, sweet pepper, onion, cilantro, lime juice, honey, garlic, habañero pepper or jalapeño pepper, and salt.

2 Cover and chill in the refrigerator for 1 to 24 hours, stirring occasionally. Serve salsa with a slotted spoon as a condiment for fish, chicken, or pork.

Nutrition Facts per ¼-cup serving: 24 cal., 0 g total fat, 0 mg chol., 14 mg sodium, 6 g carbo., 1 g fiber, 0 g pro. **Daily Values:** 7% vit. A, 31% vit. C, 1% calcium, 1% iron.

know your chiles

Pasilla chiles are long, slender, sometimes twisted dried chiles with wrinkly skin. They are medium to very hot, with a rich flavor that works well in sauces.

Popular **jalapeños** are also available dried and smoked. Called **chipotles** in this dried form, they also are found canned in adobo, a spicy chile sauce.

Thai chiles are spunky for their size, with lots of intense heat. For spicing up Thai-inspired dishes, this chile is the choice.

Pequín are tiny chiles, loaded with blistering heat—use them sparingly and with caution!

Poblanos and anchos are the same variety of chile—but poblanos are fresh; anchos are dried. Both are mild to medium-hot, with deep, complex flavors.

Anaheim chiles are available in fresh and dried forms. They are versatile and offer medium heat.

Cascabel chiles have a medium heat level and are most often sold dried. Pick one up, shake it, and you'll hear how it gets its name— "cascabel" is Spanish for "rattle."

Habañeros are native to the Caribbean. They pack searing heat and are available fresh and dried. The fresh form is most popular.

SIMPLE COMPOUND BUTTER FOR FLAVOR

Compound butter is a fancy name for butter that's flavored with other ingredients. The addition of this simple fix-up can make ordinary foods extraordinary. As a pat of compound butter melts over vegetables, grilled meats, poultry, or seafood, it transforms into a delicious sauce. Compound butters also complement freshly baked and toasted breads.

If you haven't tasted a compound butter, try the vermouth, whiskey, or jalapeño-lime butters, right. Or, experiment with hot peppers, pepper jelly, edible flowers, coarsely ground black pepper, citrus peel, liqueurs, onions, garlic, shallots, spices, cheeses, toasted nuts, and snipped fresh herbs.

green beans with
vermouth butter

prep: 20 minutes   **chill:** 1 hour   **cook:** 10 minutes   **makes:** 6 servings

2 tablespoons finely chopped shallots
2 teaspoons olive oil
½ cup butter, softened

2 tablespoons dry vermouth
1 pound green beans

1 For vermouth butter, cook shallots in olive oil over medium-low heat for 10 to 12 minutes or until shallots are golden. Remove from heat; cool. Combine cooled shallot mixture with softened butter; stir in vermouth, 1 tablespoon at a time.

2 Transfer butter mixture onto a piece of plastic wrap. Shape into a 6-inch log by rolling the plastic wrap around the butter and rolling the wrapped butter back and forth between your hands. Twist ends of wrap tightly. Chill in the refrigerator at least 1 hour or freeze butter until ready to use. (For longer storage, wrap butter tightly in plastic wrap, then wrap in aluminum foil. Store in the refrigerator for up to 1 week or in the freezer for up to 1 month.)

3 Wash beans; remove ends and strings, if necessary. Leave whole or cut into 1-inch pieces. Cook, covered, in a small amount of boiling, salted water for 10 to 15 minutes or until crisp-tender; drain.

4 To serve, transfer hot beans to a serving bowl. Top with 3 tablespoons vermouth butter; toss lightly to coat.

Nutrition Facts per serving: 78 cal., 6 g total fat (3 g sat. fat), 15 mg chol., 60 mg sodium, 6 g carbo., 3 g fiber, 1 g pro. **Daily Values:** 10% vit. A, 16% vit. C, 3% calcium, 4% iron.

Whiskey Butter: In a medium bowl combine ½ cup softened butter with 1 tablespoon dark brown sugar and 1 tablespoon bourbon whiskey. Mold and store butter as directed in step 2 at left.

Jalapeño-Lime Butter: In a medium bowl combine ½ cup softened butter with 2 teaspoons seeded and finely chopped fresh jalapeño pepper, 2 teaspoons finely shredded lime peel, and 1 clove garlic, minced. Mold and store butter as directed in step 2 at left.

roasted root medley

prep: 15 minutes   **roast:** 30 minutes   **makes:** 6 servings

3 to 3½ pounds peeled root vegetables
   (such as sweet potatoes, rutabagas,
   parsnips, and/or white potatoes),
   cut into 1-inch cubes (6 cups)
¼ cup olive oil
½ teaspoon salt
¼ teaspoon pepper

¼ cup finely chopped shallots
1 tablespoon sugar
2 teaspoons all-purpose flour
½ teaspoon salt
¼ cup cider vinegar
¼ cup water

1 Place root vegetables in a large shallow roasting pan. Combine 3 tablespoons of the olive oil, ½ teaspoon salt, and pepper; drizzle over vegetables in pan. Toss lightly to coat. Roast, uncovered, in a 425° oven for 30 to 35 minutes or until vegetables are lightly brown and tender, stirring occasionally.

2 Meanwhile, for vinaigrette, in a small saucepan cook shallots in the remaining 1 tablespoon hot oil over medium heat, about 5 minutes or until tender. Stir in sugar, flour, and ½ teaspoon salt. Cook and stir for 1 minute. Gradually whisk in vinegar and water. Cook and stir until thickened and bubbly.

3 To serve, transfer vegetables to a large serving bowl; drizzle with vinaigrette. Toss lightly to coat. Serve immediately.

Nutrition Facts per serving: 247 cal., 9 g total fat (1 g sat. fat), 0 mg chol., 378 mg sodium, 40 g carbo., 6 g fiber, 3 g pro. **Daily Values:** 94% vit. A, 58% vit. C, 5% calcium, 10% iron.

DELICIOUS ROOT VEGETABLES

Roasting is an extremely easy cooking technique that is well-suited for root vegetables because it brings out their subtle sweetness (see recipe, left). It also gives the vegetables great texture—a crisp crust with a tender, creamy interior. Roasted root vegetables, such as parsnips, beets, carrots, potatoes, sweet potatoes, and rutabagas, make an ideal companion for roasted or grilled meats.

MAKING A SMOOTH WHITE OR CHEESE SAUCE

The key to silky, lump-free white or cheese sauces is low heat and frequent stirring. Follow these tips:

• When you add the flour to the melted butter, be sure to keep the heat low so the butter-flour mixture doesn't cook too fast and form lumps or burn.

• Add the cream or milk slowly, stirring constantly with a whisk or wooden spoon. If you like, heat the milk or cream slightly before adding it to the butter-flour mixture to help it mix in more easily.

• If your finished white sauce is destined to become a cheese sauce (see recipe, right), shred the cheese or cut it into small cubes. Add the cheese a little bit at a time, with the heat on low or turned off. Low-fat cheeses, in particular, require this treatment to melt into the sauce.

baby vegetable platter
with brie dipping sauce

prep: 15 minutes   ***cook:*** 12 minutes   ***makes:*** 10 to 12 servings

1 8-ounce baguette-style French bread, cut into ¼-inch slices
2 tablespoons olive oil
¼ cup finely chopped shallots
2 tablespoons butter or margarine
2 tablespoons all-purpose flour
⅛ teaspoon salt
Dash pepper
¼ cup dry white wine
¾ cup half-and-half or light cream
1 teaspoon snipped fresh thyme or ¼ teaspoon dried thyme, crushed
4½ ounces Brie cheese, rind removed and cut into ½-inch pieces
Assorted steamed baby vegetables (artichokes, carrots, summer squash, haricots verts)

1 Lightly brush both sides of bread slices with olive oil. Place slices on ungreased cookie sheet. Bake in a 400° oven for 6 to 8 minutes or until light brown; set aside.

2 Meanwhile, in a small saucepan cook shallots in hot butter or margarine until tender. Stir in flour, salt, and pepper. Stir in wine all at once. Cook and stir for 1 minute. Stir in half-and-half or cream and, if using, dried thyme. Cook and stir over medium heat until thickened and bubbly. Cook and stir for 1 minute more. Reduce heat to low. Stir in cheese until melted. If using, stir in fresh thyme. Serve warm with toasted bread slices and steamed baby vegetables.

Nutrition Facts (per 2-tablespoon serving of sauce): 100 cal., 8 g total fat (5 g sat. fat), 26 mg chol., 141 mg sodium, 3 g carbo., 0 g fiber, 3 g pro. **Daily Values:** 7% vit. A, 1% vit. C, 5% calcium, 1% iron.

Baby vegetables

Diminutive baby vegetables are immature versions of regular varieties. The most commonly available baby vegetables are corn, zucchini, yellow squash, potatoes, carrots (not "baby-cut" carrots), artichokes, green beans (or haricots verts), and beets. Because baby vegetables are so sweet and tender, they don't need a lot of added flavorings. Serve them whole or halved (rather than sliced or diced) and, for the most part, au naturel. They are at their best when they are steamed and dressed with butter, salt, freshly ground pepper, and a freshly snipped herb—or, as in the recipe above, with a mild-tasting sauce.

VINEGARS TO EXPLORE

Vinegar adds zip to salads, marinades, sauces, and more. Sample these types to find your favorites.

Apple cider vinegar: Made from fermented apple cider, it has a strong bite with a faint apple flavor.

Distilled white vinegar: Made from distilled grain alcohol, it is strong and sour.

Wine vinegars: Made from red or white wine, champagne, or sherry, wine vinegars derive flavor from the type of wine used.

Malt vinegar: Made from malted barley, it has a faint malt flavor.

Balsamic vinegar: Made from white Trebbiano grape juice, it's aged for at least 10 years, giving it a distinctive dark brown color, syrupy body, and slight sweetness (see recipe, right).

Rice vinegar: Made from rice wine or sake, it has a subtly sweet taste and mild tang.

Flavored vinegars: Made by steeping herbs, fruits, or hot peppers in vinegar, the vinegars take on the flavors of these ingredients.

roasted vegetables
over salad greens

prep: 20 minutes   **roast:** 40 minutes   **makes:** 6 servings

¾ pound baby beets or 3 medium beets	½ teaspoon salt
¾ pound whole tiny new potatoes, halved	½ teaspoon coarsely ground pepper
¼ pound pearl onions, peeled	2 tablespoons balsamic vinegar
¼ cup olive oil	1 tablespoon snipped fresh chives
6 cloves garlic, minced	1 tablespoon water
1 tablespoon snipped fresh rosemary or basil	6 cups torn Boston or Bibb lettuce

1 Scrub beets; trim off stem and root ends. (If using medium beets, peel them and cut into 1-inch pieces.) Place beets, potatoes, and onions in a 13×9×2-inch baking pan.

2 In a small bowl combine 2 tablespoons of the olive oil, the garlic, rosemary or basil, salt, and pepper. Drizzle over vegetables in pan. Toss lightly to coat. Cover pan with foil and roast in a 375° oven for 30 minutes; uncover and continue roasting 10 to 20 minutes more or until vegetables are tender. Cool vegetables to room temperature; drain, reserving pan drippings.

3 For dressing, in a screw-top jar combine reserved pan drippings, the remaining 2 tablespoons oil, balsamic vinegar, chives, and water. Cover and shake well.

4 Divide lettuce among 6 salad plates. Top each with roasted vegetable mixture; drizzle with dressing. Serve immediately.

Nutrition Facts per serving: 172 cal., 9 g total fat (1 g sat. fat), 0 mg chol., 245 mg sodium, 20 g carbo., 3 g fiber, 3 g pro. **Daily Values:** 6% vit. A, 30% vit. C, 4% calcium, 7% iron.

66

Pasta, Grains, & Beans

If you're looking for a terrific dinnertime duo, it's hard to beat pasta and vegetables. They're versatile, taste great, and make an easy one-dish meal.

One way to streamline cooking pasta and vegetables in a recipe, such as Pasta with Green Beans & Goat Cheese (see recipe, right), is to add the fresh or frozen vegetables to the pasta-cooking water a few minutes before the pasta is done. For crisp-tender vegetables, this is usually between 3 and 8 minutes before the end of cooking. If the water stops boiling, bring it back to a rolling boil and set the cooking time from that point. Drain the vegetables and pasta together before adding the sauce, herbs, or other flavorings.

pasta with green beans
& goat cheese

prep: 15 minutes   ***cook:*** 13 minutes   ***makes:*** 6 servings

12 cups water
½ teaspoon salt
8 ounces dried linguine
1 9-ounce package frozen cut green beans
2 medium leeks, thinly sliced (about ⅔ cup)
½ cup chopped walnuts
2 tablespoons olive oil

1 tablespoon margarine or butter
1 tablespoon snipped fresh thyme
    or marjoram
4 ounces semisoft goat cheese
    (chèvre), crumbled
    Cracked black pepper

1 In a 4-quart Dutch oven bring water and salt to boiling. Add linguine; boil for 5 minutes. Add green beans. Continue boiling, uncovered, about 5 minutes more or until linguine is tender but still firm; drain in a colander.

2 In the same Dutch oven cook leeks and walnuts in hot olive oil and margarine or butter for 3 to 4 minutes or until leeks are tender and walnuts are lightly toasted.

3 Stir in thyme or marjoram. Stir in drained linguine and green beans; heat through.

4 Transfer pasta mixture to a serving platter. Sprinkle with goat cheese and pepper. Serve immediately.

Nutrition Facts per serving: 351 cal., 19 g total fat (5 g sat. fat), 15 mg chol., 125 mg sodium, 35 g carbo., 3 g fiber, 11 g pro. **Daily Values:** 12% vit. A, 10% vit. C, 10% calcium, 13% iron.

thai rice noodles

prep: 20 minutes   **cook:** 8 minutes   **makes:** 4 servings

12 ounces fresh rice noodles
     (rice ribbon noodles)
3 tablespoons cooking oil
12 ounces skinless, boneless chicken breast
     halves, cut into bite-size pieces
2 cloves garlic, minced
1 tablespoon minced fresh ginger

2 cups broccoli florets
2 carrots, cut into thin, bite-size pieces
     (1 cup)
1 small onion, cut into thin wedges (⅓ cup)
¼ cup oyster sauce
1 tablespoon brown sugar

1 Cut rice noodles into strips 1 inch wide and 3 to 4 inches long; set aside. In a large skillet heat 2 tablespoons of the oil for 1 minute over medium-high heat. Carefully add noodles; cook and stir for 3 to 4 minutes or until edges of noodles just begin to turn golden. Remove noodles from skillet; set aside.

2 Add remaining oil to skillet; add chicken, garlic, and ginger. Cook and stir for 2 to 3 minutes or until chicken is no longer pink. Stir in broccoli, carrots, and onion; cook and stir for 2 to 3 minutes more or until vegetables are crisp-tender. Stir in the oyster sauce, brown sugar, and noodles; heat through.

Nutrition Facts per serving: 341 cal., 12 g total fat (2 g sat. fat), 49 mg chol., 507 mg sodium, 37 g carbo., 2 g fiber, 22 g pro. **Daily Values:** 58% vit. A, 64% vit. C, 5% calcium, 9% iron.

VERSATILE RICE NOODLES

Asian-style noodles are being gobbled up with great enthusiasm, and most Asian markets, and many supermarkets, stock a wide variety of interesting types. One of the most popular is rice noodles. Made from rice flour and water, these noodles are sold in several forms.

The crisp, threadlike type, such as *py mee fun* from China and *banh pho* from Vietnam, is called by a variety of names in English. You'll find the noodles in both dried and fresh varieties labeled as thin rice sticks, rice vermicelli, or rice stick noodles. They are sold in Asian food stores and larger supermarkets.

Rice ribbon noodles, used in the recipe, left, are larger cousins to the thin rice sticks. Called *kui teow sen yai* in Thailand, the noodles are between ¼ and ½ inch wide and are sold fresh. Look for them in the refrigerator case of an Asian market.

ALL ABOUT DRIED TOMATOES

Dried tomatoes have an intense, rich flavor that is indispensable to many Italian dishes. Commercially dried tomatoes are sold in halves or pieces and can be plain or marinated in oil. Look for them in the produce section of the supermarket or with the canned tomato products.

When cherry tomatoes are plentiful, dry your own tomatoes for true fresh-from-the-garden flavor. Here's how:

Cut 1 pound of cherry tomatoes or roma tomatoes into halves or quarters. Place the tomatoes and 6 cloves garlic, crushed, in a 3-quart rectangular baking dish. Sprinkle with salt and pepper. Drizzle ½ cup olive oil over tomatoes. Sprinkle with 2 tablespoons snipped fresh thyme. Bake, uncovered, in a 250° oven for 2½ to 3 hours or until edges of tomatoes are slightly charred, stirring every 30 minutes. Cool; place in a nonmetal airtight container. Cover and refrigerate for up to 1 week. Makes about 1 cup.

pasta with eggplant & dried tomato pesto

prep: 25 minutes   *roast:* 25 minutes   *makes:* 4 servings

- 1 medium onion, cut into 8 wedges
- 2 tablespoons olive oil
- 1 medium eggplant (about 1 pound), halved lengthwise
- 6 ounces dried rigatoni, penne, or fusilli
- 1 ⅓-cup portion Dried Tomato Pesto

- ¼ teaspoon coarsely ground pepper
  Salt
- 2 tablespoons crumbled semisoft goat cheese (chèvre) or feta cheese (optional)
  Fresh basil (optional)

1 Place onion wedges in a large shallow baking pan; brush with 1 tablespoon of the olive oil. Roast in a 425° oven for 10 minutes; stir. Brush eggplant with remaining olive oil. Place eggplant in pan, cut side down. Roast 15 minutes more or until onion is golden brown and eggplant is tender.

2 Meanwhile, cook pasta according to package directions; drain. Add one ⅓-cup portion Dried Tomato Pesto and the pepper to pasta; toss gently to coat. Transfer pasta to a warm serving dish; keep warm.

3 Cut roasted eggplant into ½-inch slices. Toss eggplant and roasted onion wedges with pasta. Season to taste with salt. If desired, top with cheese and basil.

Nutrition Facts per serving: 370 cal., 19 g total fat (3 g sat. fat), 0 mg chol., 112 mg sodium, 43 g carbo., 4 g fiber, 8 g pro. **Daily Values:** 1% vit. A, 16% vit. C, 2% calcium, 16% iron.

Dried Tomato Pesto: Drain ¾ cup oil-packed dried tomatoes, reserving oil. Add enough olive oil to measure ½ cup; set aside. Place drained tomatoes, ¼ cup pine nuts or slivered almonds, ¼ cup snipped fresh basil, ½ teaspoon salt, and 8 cloves garlic, chopped, in a food processor bowl. Cover and process until finely chopped. With machine running, gradually add the reserved oil, processing until almost smooth. Divide pesto into thirds. Refrigerate or freeze unused portions. Makes about three ⅓-cup portions.

cheese ravioli with
mixed mushroom sauce

prep: 20 minutes   *cook:* 20 minutes   *makes:* 6 servings

1 ounce dried chanterelle mushrooms
    (about 2 cups)
1 ounce dried porcini or oyster mushrooms
    (about 1⅓ cups)
2 cups hot water
¼ cup chopped shallots
1 tablespoon snipped fresh sage leaves
    or 1 teaspoon rubbed dried sage

¼ teaspoon coarsely ground black pepper
2 tablespoons butter or margarine
½ cup dry sherry or chicken broth
1 tablespoon cornstarch
½ teaspoon salt
2 9-ounce packages refrigerated
    cheese-filled ravioli, cooked and drained

1 Place dried mushrooms in a bowl; cover with the hot water. Let stand for 15 minutes. Line a strainer with cheesecloth, a coffee filter, or a white paper towel. Strain mushrooms, reserving liquid (see tip, right). Remove and discard mushroom stems; cut mushrooms into bite-size pieces.

2 In a medium saucepan cook shallots, sage, and pepper in hot butter or margarine over medium heat about 3 minutes or until shallots are tender.

3 Add mushrooms and reserved soaking liquid. Bring to boiling; reduce heat. Simmer, covered, for 15 minutes. Combine dry sherry or chicken broth and cornstarch; add to mushroom mixture along with salt. Cook and stir until thickened and bubbly. Cook and stir for 2 minutes more. Serve over hot cooked ravioli.

Nutrition Facts per serving: 254 cal., 8 g total fat (5 g sat. fat), 34 mg chol., 426 mg sodium, 32 g carbo., 2 g fiber, 9 g pro. **Daily Values:** 6% vit. A, 1% vit. C, 10% calcium, 6% iron.

FLAVORING WITH DRIED MUSHROOMS

Dried mushrooms are a surefire way to add a rich, earthy, aromatic flavor to recipes. You also can use the soaking liquid to add even more flavor to dishes.

Most dried mushrooms need to be covered with hot water, broth, or wine and allowed to stand about 15 minutes before they're ready to use. Once the mushrooms have soaked, strain the liquid through a strainer lined with cheesecloth, paper towels, or a coffee filter to remove any grit (see photo, above). Use the strained liquid to make risotto, as a substitute for stock in soup, or to make a sauce for pasta as in Cheese Ravioli with Mixed Mushroom Sauce (see recipe, left).

It used to be an olive was green or black. Now there are more than 75 varieties. Here's a sampling (from top, above): **Nyon:** black, dry-roasted, tender, slightly bitter. **Niçoise:** black, brine-cured, fruity, juicy but not oily. **Arbequina:** green, brine-cured, slightly bitter. **Picholine:** green, brine-cured, meaty, crunchy, slightly citrusy. **Thasos:** black, somewhat dry, salt-cured, mellow, woodsy flavor. **Cerignola:** green, huge, brine-cured, mild, lemon-apple flavor. **Kalamata:** greenish black, brine-cured, pungent, lingering flavor.

fusilli with arugula, ## tomatoes, & olives

prep: 25 minutes   *cook:* 5 minutes   *makes:* 4 servings

8 ounces dried fusilli	2 medium plum tomatoes, chopped
3 cloves garlic, minced	1 cup pitted niçoise or kalamata olives, halved
¼ teaspoon crushed red pepper	
2 tablespoons olive oil	2 tablespoons snipped fresh parsley
3 to 4 cups torn arugula	¼ cup grated Parmesan cheese
¼ teaspoon salt	

1 Cook pasta according to package directions. Drain and keep warm.

2 Meanwhile, in a large skillet cook garlic and red pepper in hot olive oil for 3 to 4 minutes or until garlic is tender. Stir in arugula and salt. Cook and stir over medium heat just until arugula begins to wilt. Stir in tomatoes, olives, and parsley; heat through. Toss with hot cooked pasta. Sprinkle with Parmesan cheese.

Nutrition Facts per serving: 379 cal., 14 g total fat (2 g sat. fat), 5 mg chol., 636 mg sodium, 51 g carbo., 4 g fiber, 11 g pro. **Daily Values:** 8% vit. A, 14% vit. C, 10% calcium, 17% iron.

The incredible olive

After 6,000 years of cultivation, olives are more popular than ever—and for good reason. This versatile fruit can be stewed with meats and vegetables, whirled with garlic and oil into a rich tapenade, stirred into risotto, or tossed with salads or pasta.

Most olives are cured in a saltwater brine, but some varieties are dry-salt-cured, oil-cured, wine-cured, or dry-roasted. Salt- and dry-cured olives are wrinkled, soft, and leathery. Brine-cured, oil-cured, and wine-cured olives are plump and moist. Olives range in size from small to colossal depending on the variety. You can purchase green olives unpitted or pitted and stuffed with pimientos, anchovies, whole almonds, or tiny onions. Black olives are available unpitted, pitted, sliced, and chopped.

creamy tomato pasta
with pine nuts

prep: 20 minutes   **cook:** 16 minutes   **makes:** 4 servings

1 9-ounce package refrigerated linguine
3 ounces pancetta or bacon, finely chopped
2 cups sliced fresh mushrooms
½ cup pine nuts
1 tablespoon butter or margarine
1½ cups half-and-half or light cream
¼ teaspoon coarsely ground black pepper
2 medium tomatoes or 4 plum tomatoes, peeled, seeded, and chopped (about 1¾ cups)
½ cup freshly grated Parmesan cheese
Coarsely ground black pepper (optional)
Freshly grated Parmesan cheese (optional)

1 Cook linguine according to package directions. Drain and keep warm.

2 Meanwhile, in a large skillet cook and stir pancetta or bacon just until golden. Remove from skillet; drain fat. In same skillet cook mushrooms and pine nuts in hot butter or margarine until mushrooms are tender and pine nuts are golden. Return pancetta or bacon to skillet. Stir in half-and-half or light cream and the ¼ teaspoon pepper. Bring to boiling; reduce heat. Boil gently, uncovered, about 7 minutes over medium heat or until mixture thickens slightly. Stir in chopped tomatoes.

3 Toss hot cooked pasta with the ½ cup Parmesan cheese. Add to tomato mixture; toss lightly to coat. If desired, sprinkle with additional pepper and cheese.

Nutrition Facts per serving: 537 cal., 32 g total fat (11 g sat. fat), 67 mg chol., 338 mg sodium, 46 g carbo., 1 g fiber, 23 g pro. **Daily Values:** 19% vit. A, 26% vit. C, 19% calcium, 25% iron.

Choosing Parmesan cheese

All things considered, most Italian food fanciers—when pressed for their opinion of the world's best cheese—would take Parmesan cheese with them on a desert island.

This pale yellow hard cheese is made from cow's milk and has a sharp, salty taste. It's available in both domestic and imported versions in chunked, shredded, and grated forms. The flavor of Parmesan ranges from mild to robust depending on how long it's been aged. Domestic Parmesan is usually milder than imported types, but it's also more economical. The granddaddy of all Parmesan cheeses is Parmigiano-Reggiano. It only comes from the Italian provinces of Reggio-Emilia and Parma. It's expensive, but its buttery, nutty flavor is incredible. When purchasing Parmesan cheese, choose the type that fits your taste and your budget. For freshest flavor, buy chunk cheese and shred or grate only what you need at one time.

black & red beans
ranchero

prep: 15 minutes **stand:** 1 hour **cook:** 1 hour **makes:** 6 servings

1 cup dry red beans or dry
  red kidney beans
1 cup dry black beans
8 cups water
6 slices bacon
1 cup chopped onion
3 cloves garlic, minced
2 14½-ounce cans chicken broth

2½ cups water
2 to 3 teaspoons chopped, drained chipotle
  peppers in adobo sauce
2 teaspoons dried epazote leaves
  or 1 teaspoon dried oregano, crushed
1 cup chopped tomato
¼ cup snipped fresh cilantro

1 Rinse dry beans. In a large saucepan or Dutch oven combine beans and water. Bring to boiling; reduce heat. Simmer for 2 minutes. Remove from heat. Cover and let stand for 1 hour. (Or, place beans in water in saucepan. Cover and let soak in a cool place overnight.) Drain and rinse beans.

2 In the same large saucepan or Dutch oven cook bacon until crisp. Drain, reserving 1 tablespoon drippings in saucepan. Crumble bacon and set aside. Cook onion and garlic in hot bacon drippings over medium heat about 5 minutes or until tender. Stir in drained beans, chicken broth, the 2½ cups water, drained chipotle peppers, and epazote or oregano. Bring to boiling; reduce heat. Simmer, covered, for 1 to 1½ hours or until beans are tender, stirring occasionally.

3 Stir in crumbled bacon, chopped tomato, and cilantro; heat through.

Nutrition Facts per serving: 310 cal., 7 g total fat (2 g sat. fat), 7 mg chol., 576 mg sodium, 44 g carbo., 10 g fiber, 19 g pro. **Daily Values:** 7% vit. A, 16% vit. C, 9% calcium, 22% iron.

VARIETIES OF DRIED BEANS

Beans add lots of texture, color, and flavor to recipes. Besides the traditional red beans and black beans used in Black & Red Beans Ranchero (see recipe, left), there is a cornucopia of other beans to incorporate into your cooking.
Adzuki beans are russet-colored and have a soft texture and nutty, slightly sweet flavor.
Anasazi beans have white markings on a red-brown background that fades to dark pink after cooking. They have a mild, sweet flavor.
Cannellini beans—also known as white kidney beans—are large, white, and smooth-textured with a nutty flavor.
Cranberry beans are so called because of their deep pink color. Although they lose their color during cooking, they have a rich, nutty flavor and are a good substitute for pinto beans.
Fava beans—also called broad beans—are a staple in Middle Eastern and Italian cooking. Large, with light brown skin, they have a bold flavor.

QUICK WAYS WITH DRIED BEANS

Take your choice of these two shortcuts and you can more easily make that bean dish you've been craving.

Quick-soak method: In a large saucepan combine 1 pound dried beans with 6 to 8 cups hot water (or 3 cups water for each 1 cup beans). Heat the water to boiling and cook for 2 minutes. Remove beans from heat, cover, and let stand 1 hour. Drain and rinse. Simmer the beans in fresh water for 1½ to 2 hours or until tender. Drain and use.

Make-ahead freezer method: Cook a big batch of dried beans according to package directions until just tender. Drain, cool, and place in freezer bags or containers in 1¾-cup portions (1¾ cups cooked beans equal a 15-ounce can of beans). Label and freeze the beans for up to 3 months. To use, place the beans (thawed or frozen) in a saucepan with ½ cup water for each 1¾ cups of beans. Simmer, covered, over low heat until heated through. Drain and use.

cuban-style
black beans & rice

prep: 30 minutes   *stand:* 1 hour   *cook:* 1½ hours   *makes:* 4 servings

1½ cups dry black beans
 4 cups water
 1 small onion, halved
 2 bay leaves
 2 cups chopped onions
 1 to 2 fresh jalapeño peppers, seeded and finely chopped
 3 tablespoons cooking oil or olive oil
 4 cloves garlic, minced

 2 teaspoons ground cumin
 2 teaspoons finely shredded lime peel
 ¾ teaspoon salt
 ¼ teaspoon pepper
    Hot cooked brown rice
    Fresh cilantro sprigs (optional)
    Fresh jalapeño pepper slices (optional)
    Lime wedges (optional)

1 Rinse dry beans. To soak beans, see quick-soak method, left. (Or, place beans in water in saucepan. Cover and let soak in a cool place overnight.) Drain and rinse beans.

2 Return beans to saucepan or Dutch oven. Add 4 cups of water, onion halves, and bay leaves. Bring to boiling; reduce heat. Simmer, covered, for 1¼ to 1½ hours or until beans are tender. Remove and discard onion halves and bay leaves. Remove about ½ cup of the beans; mash them and return them to bean mixture in saucepan.

3 In a large skillet cook the 2 cups chopped onions and jalapeño peppers in hot oil over medium heat about 8 minutes or until onions are tender. Stir in garlic, cumin, lime peel, salt, and pepper; cook and stir for 1 to 2 minutes more.

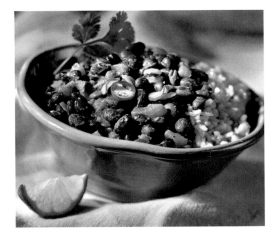

4 Stir the onion mixture into the bean mixture. Bring to boiling; reduce heat. Simmer, uncovered, for 5 to 10 minutes or until mixture thickens slightly.

5 Serve bean mixture with hot cooked rice. If desired, garnish with cilantro and serve with jalapeño slices and lime wedges.

Nutrition Facts per serving: 451 cal., 12 g total fat (2 g sat. fat), 0 mg chol., 408 mg sodium, 70 g carbo., 4 g fiber, 18 g pro. **Daily Values:** 19% vit. C, 8% calcium, 40% iron.

indian lentils & spinach

prep: 15 minutes   *cook:* 34 minutes   *makes:* 6 servings

1 cup chopped red sweet pepper
½ cup chopped onion
2 cloves garlic, minced
½ teaspoon curry powder
2 tablespoons butter or margarine
1½ cups dry green or brown lentils, rinsed
    and drained
1 14½-ounce can beef broth or
    vegetable broth

1¼ cups water
¼ teaspoon pepper
6 cups baby spinach, torn
   Salt
   Pepper
2 tablespoons snipped fresh mint (optional)

1 In a large saucepan cook sweet pepper, onion, garlic, and curry powder in hot butter or margarine for 2 to 3 minutes or until vegetables are just tender.

2 Stir in lentils, beef or vegetable broth, water, and pepper. Bring to boiling; reduce heat. Simmer, covered, about 30 minutes or until lentils are tender and most of the liquid is absorbed.

3 Stir in spinach; cook about 2 minutes more or until spinach is wilted. Season to taste with salt and pepper. If desired, serve with mint.

Nutrition Facts per serving: 163 cal., 4 g total fat (2 g sat. fat), 11 mg chol., 272 mg sodium, 23 g carbo., 5 g fiber, 9 g pro. **Daily Values:** 36% vit. A, 83% vit. C, 7% calcium, 28% iron.

TYPES OF LENTILS

Lentils are a favorite food in France, the Middle East, and India where they are used in soups, stews, and other main dishes. There are three common types: the brown lentil, which actually has a greenish brown coat and a yellow interior; the red lentil; and the yellow lentil. In food specialty stores, more exotic varieties, such as green, white, or black, also are available.

In the United States, the brown lentil is the most common type and is most often used in recipes such as Indian Lentils & Spinach (see recipe, left). If you wish to substitute one type of lentil for another, you may need to adjust the cooking time. If you're using yellow lentils, the cooking time will be the same as for brown lentils. For the red varieties, which are smaller, you'll need to reduce the time significantly. For example, to use red lentils in Indian Lentils & Spinach, test for doneness after 5 to 10 minutes of simmering. For other types, check the package directions for cooking times.

basmati rice pilaf

prep: 20 minutes   **cook:** 29 minutes   **makes:** 6 servings

½ cup chopped onion
⅓ cup slivered almonds
2 tablespoons butter or margarine
1 cup basmati rice, uncooked
½ cup finely chopped carrot
⅓ cup currants or chopped dried
    tart red cherries

1 teaspoon finely shredded orange peel
¼ teaspoon ground cinnamon
¼ teaspoon black pepper
⅛ teaspoon crushed red pepper
1 14½-ounce can chicken broth
¼ cup water

1 In a medium saucepan cook onion and almonds over medium heat in hot butter or margarine about 5 minutes or until onion is tender and almonds are golden. Stir in uncooked rice. Cook and stir for 4 minutes. Stir in carrot, currants or dried cherries, orange peel, cinnamon, black pepper, and red pepper.

2 Carefully stir chicken broth and water into saucepan. Bring to boiling; reduce heat. Simmer, covered, about 20 minutes or until liquid is absorbed and rice is tender.

Nutrition Facts per serving: 232 cal., 8 g total fat (3 g sat. fat), 11 mg chol., 268 mg sodium, 35 g carbo., 2 g fiber, 6 g pro. **Daily Values:** 30% vit. A, 2% vit. C, 3% calcium, 14% iron.

Rainbow of rices

Rice is the most popular grain in the world, and it comes in several forms.

- **Brown rice** only has the hull removed. The bran layers left on the grain give it a tan color and a nutty flavor with a slightly chewy texture.
- **White or polished rice** is milled to remove both the hull and the bran layers. It's mild, delicately flavored, and comes in several varieties (see tip, right).
- **Precooked** (quick-cooking) rice is available in both white and brown varieties and cooks in just a few minutes.
- **Parboiled** (sometimes called converted) rice is treated by a steam-pressure process before milling to make the white cooked grain extra fluffy.
- **Wild rice** is used like rice but isn't rice at all; it's the long, dark brown or black, nutty-flavored seed of a marsh grass.

   In addition, there are a host of **colored rices.** These include Himalayan Red, Chinese Black, Colusari Red, Black Japonica, and Purple Thai, now available for cooks who want to go beyond basic white or brown.

THE LONG & SHORT OF RICE

When cooking white rice for recipes, you can choose from three types. Here's how to pick the right one for your needs:

Short-grain rice is high in starch, making it stickier than other rices. It is most often used in Asian cooking, Spanish paella, and risotto (see recipe, page 82). One prized short-grain rice is Arborio rice—a mainstay for risotto.

Medium-grain rice is slightly sticky. It cooks up tender and plump with a mild flavor and can be used in a variety of dishes.

Long-grain white rice is the most common rice used in America. It has a neutral taste and firm texture, and remains separate and fluffy when cooked. Long-grain rices such as jasmine and basmati are aromatic rices known for their fragrances. Both are nice paired with stir-fry dishes and other Asian- and Indian-style foods or used in pilafs (see recipe, left).

risotto with leeks
& roasted asparagus

prep: 20 minutes   ***cook:*** 25 minutes   ***makes:*** 4 servings

³/₄ pound asparagus spears, trimmed
2 tablespoons olive oil
 Salt
 Pepper
1½ cups sliced leeks
1 cup Arborio rice, uncooked

3 cups chicken broth
⅓ cup freshly grated Parmesan cheese
2 tablespoons snipped fresh parsley
½ teaspoon finely shredded lemon peel
1 tablespoon lemon juice
¼ teaspoon coarsely ground pepper

1 Brush asparagus spears with
1 tablespoon of the olive oil. Arrange
spears in a single layer on a baking sheet;
sprinkle lightly with salt and pepper. Bake,
uncovered, in a 450° oven about 10 minutes
or until crisp-tender. When cool enough to
handle, cut asparagus into 2-inch pieces;
set aside.

2 Meanwhile, in a large saucepan cook
leeks in remaining olive oil until tender.
Stir in uncooked rice. Cook and stir over
medium heat about 5 minutes or until rice
begins to turn golden brown.

3 In another saucepan bring broth to
boiling; reduce heat and continue
simmering broth while making risotto.

Slowly add 1 cup of the broth to the rice
mixture, stirring constantly. Continue to
cook and stir over medium heat until liquid
is absorbed. Add another ½ cup of the
broth to the rice mixture, stirring
constantly. Continue to cook and stir until
liquid is absorbed. Continue adding broth,
½ cup at a time, stirring constantly until all
the broth has been absorbed. (This should
take about 20 minutes total.)

4 Stir in roasted asparagus pieces,
Parmesan cheese, parsley, lemon peel,
lemon juice, and pepper.

Nutrition Facts per serving: 333 cal., 11 g total fat
(3 g sat. fat), 7 mg chol., 755 mg sodium, 44 g carbo.,
2 g fiber, 13 g pro. **Daily Values:** 4% vit. A, 35% vit. C,
16% calcium, 20% iron.

More flavorful rice
Rice dishes make excellent companions to many meat entrées. To boost the flavor
of any kind of rice, replace the water when making the rice with chicken broth
(which comes in several variations, including roasted garlic and Italian herbs),
beef broth, vegetable broth, or homemade soup stock (see recipe, page 30).

southwest
hominy skillet

prep: 20 minutes   *cook:* 10 minutes   *makes:* 6 servings

- 1 to 2 fresh poblano peppers, seeded and chopped
- ½ cup chopped onion
- 2 cloves garlic, minced
- 1 teaspoon chili powder
- ½ teaspoon ground cumin

- 2 tablespoons olive oil
- 2 14½-ounce cans hominy, drained
- 1 cup chopped zucchini
- 4 plum tomatoes, chopped
- 3 tablespoons snipped fresh cilantro
- ¼ teaspoon salt

1 In a large skillet cook poblano peppers, onion, garlic, chili powder, and cumin in hot olive oil over medium-high heat for 3 minutes, stirring frequently. Stir in the drained hominy and the zucchini.

2 Cook and stir for 5 minutes more. Stir in tomatoes, cilantro, and salt; cook about 2 minutes more or until heated through.

Nutrition Facts per serving: 133 cal., 6 g total fat (1 g sat. fat), 0 mg chol., 296 mg sodium, 19 g carbo., 1 g fiber, 2 g pro. **Daily Values:** 5% vit. A, 68% vit. C, 2% calcium, 8% iron.

FRESH SNIPPED HERBS

In nearly every dish featuring herbs, fresh is best. Here's how to prepare fresh herbs for use in cooking:

Herbs with delicate stems, such as cilantro, parsley, basil, and mint, can simply be snipped— stems and all—in a small bowl with a pair of clean kitchen shears (see photo, above). This is often much faster and neater than chopping the herbs on a cutting board.

Herbs with woodier stems, such as thyme, oregano, and particularly rosemary, should be stripped from their stems before using. Hold the stem in one hand, and—starting at the top of the stem—strip off the leaves by running the fingers of your other hand firmly down the stem.

HEARTY BARLEY

You're missing out if you haven't tried barley. Its toothsome texture and nutty flavor make it a great choice for pilaf, barley "risotto," or for adding to soups and casseroles. Look for barley in these forms:

Pearl barley has the outer hull removed and has been polished or "pearled." It is sold in regular or quick-cooking forms.

Scotch or **pot barley** is less processed than pearl barley. It requires a long soaking period before cooking. Look for it in health food stores.

Barley flakes are similar to rolled oats, but thicker and chewier. Use in homemade granola and in baked goods.

To heighten barley's nutty flavor, take an extra, easy step—toast it before cooking. In a heavy, dry pan over low heat, cook barley about 10 minutes, stirring often, until golden brown.

risotto-style barley & vegetables

start to finish: 30 minutes   ***makes:*** 4 servings

⅔ cup thinly sliced zucchini	1 14½-ounce can reduced-sodium chicken broth
⅓ cup chopped onion	¼ cup evaporated milk, half-and-half, or light cream
⅓ cup chopped carrot	Salt
¼ teaspoon dried rosemary, crushed	Pepper
⅛ teaspoon pepper	
1 tablespoon olive oil or cooking oil	
⅔ cup quick-cooking barley	

1 In a medium saucepan cook zucchini, onion, carrot, rosemary, and pepper in hot oil until vegetables are just tender; stir in the barley.

2 Meanwhile, in a small saucepan heat chicken broth until simmering. Carefully stir 1 cup of the hot broth into the barley mixture. Cook and stir over medium heat until liquid is absorbed. Add remaining broth, ½ cup at a time, cooking and stirring until broth is absorbed. (This will take 15 to 20 minutes total.) Stir in evaporated milk, half-and-half, or light cream; cook and stir 2 minutes more. Season to taste with salt and pepper.

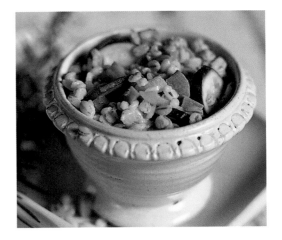

Nutrition Facts per serving: 188 cal., 6 g total fat (1 g sat. fat), 5 mg chol., 317 mg sodium, 29 g carbo., 3 g fiber, 6 g pro. **Daily Values:** 28% vit. A, 3% vit. C, 4% calcium, 4% iron.

Eggs & Cheese

85

MAKING A GREAT FRITTATA

The wonderful thing about frittatas is you can tailor them to please many tastes. Be creative and use the basic egg mixture (see recipe, right), but branch out with the other ingredients. Here are just some of the options you can select: cooked meat, poultry, seafood, cheeses, fresh and dried herbs, olives, garlic, and vegetables.

Grate, shred, chop, or slice into bite-size pieces all ingredients, and well-drain any ingredients that come in a juice or brine, such as olives. If you're using vegetables, you may want to precook items such as zucchini, carrots, potatoes, broccoli, or mushrooms (see step 1, right).

To add even more flavor, substitute chicken, beef, or vegetable broth for the milk normally used to make a frittata. Add a topper, such as a spoonful of sour cream, salsa, or heated spaghetti sauce.

holiday frittata

prep: 15 minutes   *cook:* 12 minutes   *makes:* 6 servings

1 cup fresh or frozen broccoli florets
½ of a large red sweet pepper, seeded and thinly sliced
¼ cup chopped onion
½ teaspoon dried Italian seasoning, crushed
¼ teaspoon salt
⅛ teaspoon pepper

1 tablespoon cooking oil
10 beaten eggs or 2½ cups refrigerated or frozen egg product, thawed
2 tablespoons milk
2 tablespoons finely shredded Parmesan cheese
Curly endive (optional)

1 In a 10-inch skillet cook broccoli, sweet pepper, onion, Italian seasoning, salt, and pepper in hot oil over medium heat for 4 to 5 minutes or until vegetables are crisp-tender.

2 In a medium bowl combine eggs or egg product and milk. Pour over vegetable mixture. As eggs begin to set, run a spatula around edge of skillet, lifting egg mixture to allow uncooked portions to flow underneath. Continue cooking and lifting edges until eggs are nearly set (surface will be moist).

3 Remove skillet from heat; sprinkle with cheese. Cover; let stand for 3 to 4 minutes or until set. If desired, garnish with curly endive. To serve, cut frittata into wedges.

Nutrition Facts per serving: 168 cal., 11 g total fat (3 g sat. fat), 357 mg chol., 230 mg sodium, 4 g carbo., 1 g fiber, 12 g pro. **Daily Values:** 24% vit. A, 47% vit. C, 6% calcium, 10% iron.

blue cheese
& broccoli soufflé

prep: 25 minutes   **bake:** 35 minutes   **makes:** 4 servings

4   egg yolks
¼   cup margarine or butter
¼   cup all-purpose flour
⅛   teaspoon salt
     Dash ground red pepper
     Dash dry mustard
1   cup milk

1   cup finely chopped cooked broccoli
     florets, drained
½   cup crumbled blue cheese or finely
     shredded cheddar cheese (2 ounces)
4   egg whites
½   teaspoon cream of tartar

1 Attach a foil collar to a 1½-quart soufflé dish. (For collar, measure enough foil to go around the dish plus a 2- to 3-inch overlap. Fold the foil into thirds lengthwise. Lightly butter one side of foil.) With the buttered side in, position foil around the soufflé dish, letting collar extend 2 inches above top of dish. Fasten foil with masking tape; set aside.

2 In a medium bowl use a fork to lightly beat the egg yolks; set aside. In a medium saucepan melt the margarine or butter over medium-high heat. Stir in flour, salt, red pepper, and mustard. Stir in the milk. Cook and stir until thickened and bubbly. Cook and stir for 1 to 2 minutes more. Remove from heat.

3 Add the cooked broccoli and the blue cheese or cheddar cheese to the milk

mixture, stirring until the cheese is melted. Slowly add the broccoli mixture to the egg yolks, stirring constantly. Cool slightly.

4 In a large bowl beat the egg whites and cream of tartar with an electric mixer on high speed until stiff peaks form (tips stand straight). Gradually pour the yolk mixture over the beaten egg whites, folding to combine.

5 Pour the egg mixture into the ungreased soufflé dish. Bake in a 350° oven for 35 to 40 minutes or until the soufflé jiggles when gently shaken. Test soufflé for doneness while it's still in the oven. Serve soufflé immediately.

Nutrition Facts per serving: 296 cal., 22 g total fat (7 g sat. fat), 228 mg chol., 501 mg sodium, 12 g carbo., 2 g fiber, 13 g pro. **Daily Values:** 58% vit. A, 49% vit. C, 16% calcium, 8% iron.

Start your soufflé ahead
A soufflé may be made a short time ahead. Prepare the egg mixture up to the point at which you pour it into the soufflé dish. The soufflé will hold at this stage, covered and refrigerated, for up to 2 hours before baking.

SOUFFLÉ MAGIC

In French, "soufflé" means "puff." Nearly every step in making a soufflé is to either increase its puff or protect it from falling. These tips will help you achieve this.

Use a collar. Because a soufflé often increases in volume two to three times, a soufflé dish needs a collar to hold in the mixture as it bakes and expands.

Remember the acid. A small amount of acid, often cream of tartar, helps prevent a soufflé from collapsing. Adding too much acid can interfere with coagulation of the egg proteins during baking though, so follow your recipe instructions carefully.

Beat the egg whites to stiff peaks. The air that is beaten into the whites heats and expands during baking, making the soufflé rise.

Gently fold the egg yolk mixture into the egg whites. Use a large rubber spatula and a down-up-and-over motion. Make sure the whites are well incorporated, but don't stir too much or the soufflé won't rise very high.

Keep the oven door closed. Opening the door during the first 20 to 25 minutes of baking may cause the soufflé to fall because of the sudden influx of cold air.

french omelet

start to finish: 7 minutes   **makes:** 1 serving

2 eggs	Dash pepper
1 tablespoon water	Nonstick cooking spray
⅛ teaspoon salt	

1 In a bowl combine eggs, water, salt, and pepper. Using a fork, beat until combined but not frothy. Coat with cooking spray an unheated 8- or 10-inch nonstick skillet with flared sides.

2 Add egg mixture to skillet; cook over medium heat. As eggs set, run a spatula around the edge of the skillet, lifting eggs so uncooked portion flows underneath (see photo, right). When eggs are set but still shiny, remove from heat. Fold omelet in half. Transfer to a warm plate.

Nutrition Facts per serving: 152 cal., 11 g total fat (3 g sat. fat), 426 mg chol., 393 mg sodium, 1 g carbo., 0 g fiber, 13 g pro. **Daily Values:** 19% vit. A, 4% calcium, 9% iron.

Low-Fat Omelet: Prepare as above, except use 1 whole egg and 2 egg whites.

Mushroom Omelet: Prepare as at left, except, for filling, cook ⅓ cup sliced fresh mushrooms in 1 tablespoon margarine or butter until tender. When eggs are set but still shiny, spoon filling across center of omelet. Fold sides of omelet over cooked mushrooms.

Cheese Omelet: Prepare as at left except omit salt. When eggs are set but still shiny, sprinkle ¼ cup shredded cheddar, Swiss, or Monterey Jack cheese across center of omelet. Fold sides of omelet over cheese.

Fruit Omelet: Prepare as at left, except omit pepper, and when eggs are set but still shiny, spread 2 tablespoons dairy sour cream or yogurt across center of omelet. Fold sides of omelet over sour cream. To serve, top with ¼ cup halved strawberries; sliced, peeled peaches; or blueberries. Sprinkle with 1 tablespoon brown sugar.

Egg substitutes

Refrigerated or frozen egg substitutes are easy to use, readily available, and enable anyone on a cholesterol-restricted diet to enjoy great-tasting egg dishes. These products are based mostly on egg whites, contain less fat than whole eggs, and have no cholesterol. Use ¼ cup of either the refrigerated or thawed frozen egg product for each whole egg in scrambled egg dishes, omelets, quiches, and stratas. To replace hard-cooked eggs in salads and other recipes, cook the egg product as you would cook an omelet and cut it into bite-size pieces.

DEMYSTIFYING THE OMELET

Making an omelet doesn't have to be tricky. Follow these tips and you'll be filling and folding an omelet like a chef in no time.

- Use an 8- to 10-inch nonstick omelet pan for a two-egg omelet. It has sloped sides to help you slide out the finished omelet.
- Coat the omelet pan with nonstick cooking spray or melt butter in the pan. Heat pan until a drop of water sizzles.
- Cook the omelet over medium heat. As the eggs set, lift their edge with a spatula to allow the uncooked egg on the top to flow underneath (see photo, above).
- When the eggs are set but still shiny, spoon filling ingredients across center of omelet. Fold sides of omelet over filling and slide omelet from pan.

You don't need fancy cooking gadgets to perfectly poach eggs. Here are some tips:

- Use the freshest eggs possible; they will hold their shape better in the water.
- Bring 2 to 3 inches of water to boiling in a skillet. Reduce the heat to a very gentle simmer (bubbles should just begin to break the surface).
- Break 1 egg into a measuring or custard cup. Carefully slide the egg into the simmering water, holding the lip of the cup as close to the water as possible (see photo, above). Repeat with remaining eggs, spacing them evenly in the skillet.
- Lift the eggs from the pan with a slotted spoon and drain either in the spoon or on paper towels.

poached eggs
on polenta

prep: 35 minutes   ***chill:*** 1 hour   ***cook:*** 23 minutes   ***makes:*** 6 servings

1½ cups water
1 tablespoon butter or margarine
1½ cups milk
1 cup yellow cornmeal
½ cup freshly shredded Parmesan cheese
1 cup finely chopped onion
4 cloves garlic, minced (2 teaspoons)
2 tablespoons olive oil
1¾ pounds plum tomatoes, seeded and chopped (4 cups)
¼ cup snipped fresh basil
½ teaspoon salt
5 cups water
¼ cup vinegar
⅛ teaspoon salt
6 eggs
⅓ cup freshly shredded Parmesan cheese
Freshly ground black pepper

1 To make polenta, combine the 1½ cups water and the butter or margarine in a large saucepan. Bring to a simmer over medium heat. Combine milk and cornmeal; slowly add to simmering mixture while stirring constantly. Reduce heat to low. Cook for 10 to 15 minutes or until mixture is very thick, stirring occasionally. Remove from heat and stir in the ½ cup Parmesan cheese. Spread polenta in a lightly greased 9×5×3-inch loaf pan. Cool, then cover and chill at least 1 hour. Before serving, remove polenta from pan and cut into 12 slices. Arrange slices on baking sheet; set aside.

2 For sauce, in a large skillet cook onion and garlic in hot oil over medium heat for 5 minutes or until tender. Stir in tomatoes. Cook, uncovered, for 5 minutes more. Remove from heat; stir in basil and the ½ teaspoon salt. Cover and keep warm.

3 Broil polenta 4 inches from the heat for 4 to 5 minutes on each side or until golden brown. Keep warm.

4 Meanwhile, to poach eggs, lightly grease a 12-inch skillet. Add the 5 cups water, the vinegar, and ⅛ teaspoon salt. Bring to boiling; reduce heat to simmering. Add eggs (see tip, left). Simmer eggs, uncovered, for 3 to 5 minutes or until the whites are completely set and the yolks begin to thicken but are not hard. Remove eggs with a slotted spoon.

5 To serve, arrange 2 polenta slices on each serving plate. Top with sauce and a poached egg. Sprinkle with the ⅓ cup Parmesan cheese and ground black pepper.

Nutrition Facts per serving: 350 cal., 18 g total fat (7 g sat. fat), 237 mg chol., 546 mg sodium, 31 g carbo., 4 g fiber, 17 g pro. **Daily Values:** 29% vit. A, 43% vit. C, 29% calcium, 14% iron.

savory cheesecake tarts

prep: 50 minutes   **chill:** 30 minutes   **bake:** 12 minutes   **makes:** 8 servings

1½ cups all-purpose flour
¼ teaspoon salt
⅓ cup butter, chilled and cut up
2 tablespoons shortening
3 to 4 tablespoons cold water
1 8-ounce package cream cheese, softened
1 tablespoon all-purpose flour
2 eggs

2 teaspoons lemon juice
¼ teaspoon pepper
½ cup grated dry Monterey Jack cheese
    or Parmesan cheese
¼ cup finely chopped leek or green onions
2 tablespoons snipped fresh parsley
1 tablespoon snipped fresh basil
2 teaspoons snipped fresh thyme

1 For crust, combine the 1½ cups flour and the salt in a large bowl. Using a pastry blender, cut in butter and shortening until mixture resembles coarse crumbs. Sprinkle 1 tablespoon of the water over part of the mixture; gently toss with a fork. Push moistened dough to the side of the bowl. Repeat moistening dough, using 1 tablespoon of the water at a time, until all of the dough is moistened. Form dough into a ball; wrap in plastic wrap. Refrigerate dough at least 30 minutes.

2 For eight 3- to 3½-inch tart pans, divide dough into 8 pieces. On a lightly floured surface, roll each piece of dough into a 5-inch circle. Fit dough circles into tart pans and trim pastry even with edge of pans. Place on a large baking sheet; set aside. (Or, for twelve 2½-inch muffin cups, divide dough into 12 portions. On a lightly floured surface, roll each portion into a 4-inch circle and press evenly onto bottom and up sides of muffin cups; set aside.)

3 For filling, in a medium bowl, beat cream cheese and the 1 tablespoon flour with an electric mixer on medium speed until smooth. Beat in eggs, lemon juice, and pepper. Stir in cheese, leek or green onions, parsley, basil, and thyme. Divide filling evenly among crusts.

4 Bake tarts in a 375° oven for 12 to 15 minutes, or until centers appear nearly set when shaken. Serve warm.

Nutrition Facts per serving: 330 cal., 24 g total fat (14 g sat. fat), 111 mg chol., 372 mg sodium, 19 g carbo., 1 g fiber, 9 g pro. **Daily Values:** 23% vit. A, 4% vit. C, 13% calcium, 10% iron.

TART PAN PRIMER

Tart pans come in an array of sizes and shapes. Savory Cheesecake Tarts (see recipe, left) call for individual-size round tart pans for a personalized presentation. Larger-diameter round, rectangular, and square tart pans also are available.

For most recipes, tart pans with removable bottoms are easier to use because they allow you to quickly and neatly transfer a baked tart to a serving plate. Cutting a large tart into serving-size pieces also is easier.

Although nonstick tart pans are available, this type of pan isn't essential because most tart pastries contain a great deal of butter, so they usually don't stick to a nontreated pan.

Fondue is back! A craze in the '60s, cheese fondue is having renewed popularity today. Here are some of the secrets to a great fondue:

- Tossing flour with the shredded or cubed cheese helps keep it from sticking together and provides a little thickening for the fondue.
- The most common problem in making fondue is having the cheese melt into one great lump or into a series of strings that float in the liquid. An acid in the recipe helps break down the cheese proteins so this clumping doesn't occur. Swiss-Onion Fondue (see recipe, right) uses white wine, white wine vinegar, and brandy—all of which contain acid. If the recipe you're using doesn't contain an acidic ingredient, squeeze a little fresh lemon juice over the shredded or cubed cheese before adding it to the fondue pot.
- To ensure a smooth fondue, add the cheese a little at a time, minimizing the chances the cheese will clump.

swiss-onion fondue

prep: 15 minutes   *cook:* 15 minutes   *makes:* 6 servings

2 tablespoons butter	1 pound Swiss cheese, shredded (4 cups)
1½ cups chopped onions	2 tablespoons all-purpose flour
½ cup dry white wine	1 tablespoon brandy or Cognac
¾ cup beef broth	½ teaspoon freshly ground pepper
2 tablespoons white wine vinegar	Toasted French bread cubes

1 In a large saucepan melt butter over medium heat. Add onions; cook for 15 to 20 minutes or until brown and caramelized, stirring occasionally. (If onions brown too quickly, reduce heat slightly.) Stir in wine, beef broth, and vinegar. Bring to boiling; reduce heat to medium-low.

2 In a medium bowl combine cheese and flour; toss to coat cheese. Add cheese mixture to onion mixture, a handful at a time, stirring after each addition until cheese is melted. Stir in brandy or Cognac and pepper. Do not boil.

3 Transfer hot cheese mixture to a fondue pot; keep warm. Serve the fondue immediately with toasted French bread cubes.

Nutrition Facts per serving: 369 cal., 25 g total fat (15 g sat. fat), 80 mg chol., 323 mg sodium, 8 g carbo., 1 g fiber, 23 g pro. **Daily Values:** 23% vit. A, 4% vit. C, 74% calcium, 3% iron.

Storing cheese

Airtight packaging is the key to storing cheese. If cheese is exposed to even a little bit of air, it dries out. If a cheese has a rind, leave it on during storage to help keep the cheese fresh. Wrap cheese tightly in plastic wrap; then seal it in a plastic bag or a container with an airtight lid. Store the cheese in the refrigerator. If a hard or firm cheese develops mold, cut off about 1 inch around the moldy area. If a soft cheese—such as feta, ricotta, cream, or cottage cheese—develops mold, discard the cheese.

PREBAKING A PIE OR TART CRUST

Prebaking a pie or tart crust without the filling (called blind baking) makes for a delightfully crisp crust. It is a necessity to prevent a soggy bottom crust in some recipes, such as Egg & Sausage Quiche (see recipe, right), or when an ingredient, such as fresh strawberries or raspberries, will not be cooked.

To prebake a crust, firmly press a double thickness of foil over the dough in the pie or tart pan, closely following the contours of the pan. As long as the foil is firmly in place, there is no need to fill the crust with pie weights or dry beans. Bake the crust until it is approximately half done. Remove the foil and continue baking to brown the crust.

egg & sausage quiche

prep: 30 minutes   *bake:* 35 minutes   *stand:* 10 minutes   *makes:* 8 servings

1   recipe Pastry for Single-Crust Pie (see page 58)
8   ounces ground turkey sausage or bulk pork sausage
1   tablespoon margarine or butter
1   cup chopped vegetables (such as asparagus, onion, green sweet pepper, and/or broccoli)
¾   cup shredded Swiss cheese (3 ounces)
¾   cup shredded cheddar cheese (3 ounces)
1   tablespoon all-purpose flour
3   beaten eggs
1½ cups milk, half-and-half, or light cream
⅛   teaspoon ground black pepper

1 On a lightly floured surface, roll pastry from center to edges into a circle about 12 inches in diameter. Line a 9-inch pie plate with the pastry; flute edges. Do not prick. Line pastry shell with a double thickness of foil. Bake pastry in a 450° oven for 8 minutes. Remove foil. Bake 5 minutes more. Remove from oven. Reduce oven temperature to 325°.

2 Meanwhile, in a medium skillet cook sausage until brown; drain well. In a small saucepan melt margarine or butter over medium heat; add vegetables and cook for 3 to 5 minutes or until tender. In a medium bowl toss together Swiss cheese, cheddar cheese, and flour.

3 Sprinkle cooked vegetables in bottom of hot baked pastry shell. Top with cooked sausage and cheese mixture. In a small bowl combine beaten eggs, milk or cream, and pepper; pour over mixture in pastry shell. Bake in the 325° oven for 35 to 40 minutes or until a knife inserted in center comes out clean. Let stand 10 minutes before serving.

Nutrition Facts per serving: 351 cal., 23 g total fat (9 g sat. fat), 115 mg chol., 443 mg sodium, 18 g carbo., 1 g fiber, 18 g pro. **Daily Values:** 10% vit. A, 7% vit. C, 25% calcium, 11% iron.

Lower-Fat Version: Omit the margarine or butter and cook the vegetables in a small amount of boiling water for 3 to 5 minutes or until crisp-tender. Use reduced-fat Swiss and cheddar cheeses and fat-free milk instead of regular cheeses and milk. Substitute refrigerated or frozen egg product, thawed, for the whole eggs.

Sandwiches

dried tomato
burgers

prep: 20 minutes   **grill:** 12 minutes   **makes:** 4 servings

1 pound lean ground beef
1 tablespoon finely chopped oil-packed
    dried tomatoes, drained
1 teaspoon finely shredded lemon
    peel or lime peel
½ teaspoon salt
¼ teaspoon pepper

¼ cup light mayonnaise or salad dressing
2 tablespoons snipped fresh basil
1 fresh jalapeño pepper, seeded
    and finely chopped
4 onion hamburger buns, split and toasted
1 cup lightly packed arugula or
    spinach leaves

1 In a medium bowl combine ground beef, drained tomatoes, lemon or lime peel, salt, and pepper; mix well. Shape into four ½-inch-thick patties. Grill patties on the rack of an uncovered grill directly over medium heat for 12 to 16 minutes or until a thermometer inserted in the centers of patties registers 160°, turning once.

2 Meanwhile, in a small bowl combine mayonnaise or salad dressing, basil, and jalapeño pepper; mix well. Set aside.

3 For the last 1 to 2 minutes of grilling, place buns, cut sides down, on grill rack to toast. Serve burgers on buns with mayonnaise mixture and arugula or spinach leaves.

Nutrition Facts per serving: 450 cal., 20 g total fat (6 g sat. fat), 71 mg chol., 784 mg sodium, 40 g carbo., 2 g fiber, 26 g pro. **Daily Values:** 1% vit. A, 13% vit. C, 6% calcium, 25% iron.

beef & sweet onion
sandwiches

start to finish: 20 minutes   **makes:** 4 servings

12 ounces boneless beef sirloin or top round
       steak, cut 1 inch thick
½ teaspoon coarsely ground black pepper
2 teaspoons cooking oil
1 medium sweet onion (such as Vidalia or
       Walla Walla), sliced
2 tablespoons Dijon-style mustard

½ of a 7-ounce jar roasted red sweet peppers,
       drained (about ½ cup)
8 1-inch-thick slices sourdough or marbled
       rye bread
1½ cups torn packaged prewashed spinach or
       other salad greens

1 Trim fat from steak. Sprinkle both
sides of steak with black pepper; press
in lightly. In a large skillet cook steak in hot
oil over medium-high heat about 8 minutes
or until slightly pink in center, turning
once. Remove from skillet; keep warm. Add
onion to drippings in skillet. (Add more oil,
if necessary.) Cook and stir about 5 minutes
or until onion is crisp-tender. Stir in
mustard; remove from heat.

2 Meanwhile, cut drained roasted sweet
peppers into ½-inch-wide strips. Toast
bread, if desired, and shred spinach.

3 Just before serving, cut steak into bite-
size strips. To serve, top 4 bread slices
with spinach, steak strips, roasted pepper
strips, onion mixture, and remaining
bread slices.

Nutrition Facts per serving: 335 cal., 12 g total fat
(4 g sat. fat), 57 mg chol., 553 mg sodium, 30 g carbo.,
1 g fiber, 25 g pro. **Daily Values:** 23% vit. A, 96% vit. C,
5% calcium, 28% iron.

SWEET AND JUICY ONIONS

All onions are not created equal—some are sweeter than others. The onions called for in Beef & Sweet Onion Sandwiches are milder, sweeter, and less pungent than common yellow and white onions. Sweet onions generally have thin, light outer skins, a high water content, and a high sugar content. They bruise easily and are fragile, so they have a fairly short storage life.

This group of naturally sweet onions, available April through August, includes Vidalia, Walla Walla, Maui, Texas Spring Sweet, Imperial Sweet, and Carzalia Sweet varieties. During the winter months, some additional sweet varieties, such as Oso Sweet and Rio Sweet, often are imported from South America.

smoked turkey dagwood
with chile mayonnaise

start to finish: 25 minutes   ***makes:*** 4 servings

½ cup mayonnaise or salad dressing

2 tablespoons snipped fresh cilantro

1 fresh jalapeño pepper, seeded
     and finely chopped

½ teaspoon ground cumin

1 avocado, seeded, peeled, and thinly sliced

1 tablespoon lime juice

8 ½-inch slices sourdough bread, toasted

16 thin slices smoked turkey (about 8 ounces)

8 slices tomato

8 slices peppered bacon, crisp-cooked
     and drained

1 For chile mayonnaise, in a small bowl combine mayonnaise or salad dressing, cilantro, jalapeño pepper, and cumin. Cover and chill for up to 2 days ahead, if you wish.

2 In a small bowl toss avocado slices with lime juice; set aside.

3 To assemble, spread chile mayonnaise evenly over toasted bread slices. On 4 of the bread slices layer turkey, tomato, avocado, and bacon. Top with remaining bread slices. Serve immediately.

Nutrition Facts per serving: 560 cal., 40 g total fat (8 g sat. fat), 56 mg chol., 1,245 mg sodium, 33 g carbo., 2 g fiber, 21 g pro. **Daily Values:** 7% vit. A, 34% vit. C, 4% calcium, 20% iron.

The right avocado

If you're after neat little cubes or slices of avocado, choose firm fruits—not rock-hard ones—that give a little under gentle pressure. If you plan to mash the avocado to make guacamole, choose fruits that feel soft to your fingers. If you want to shop ahead, buy very firm avocados. Stored at room temperature, they'll ripen in 3 to 4 days. Speed ripening by placing avocados in a brown paper bag or in a fruit ripening bowl. When they're ripe, put them in the refrigerator and use within a few days.

SEEDING AVOCADOS THE EASY WAY

A cut and a twist are all that's between you and an avocado's delicious flesh.

Use a sharp knife to cut the avocado lengthwise through the flesh and to the seed. Separate the halves by placing one hand on each side of the avocado and twisting in opposite directions.

To remove the seed, tap it with the blade of a sharp knife. When the blade catches in the seed, rotate the knife to lift out the seed (see photo, above). Use a knife or vegetable peeler to remove the skin from the flesh. Or, if the flesh is soft, scoop it out of the skin with a spoon.

updated tuna melt

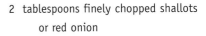

start to finish: 22 minutes   ***makes:*** 4 servings

12 ounces fresh or frozen tuna steaks, ¾ to 1 inch thick	2 tablespoons finely chopped shallots or red onion
¼ cup balsamic vinegar	4 slices provolone cheese (3 ounces total)
2 tablespoons honey	8 ½-inch slices sourdough or crusty Italian bread, toasted
¼ cup mayonnaise or salad dressing	

1 Thaw fish, if frozen. Rinse fish; pat dry. Cut tuna into 4 serving-size pieces, if necessary. Set tuna aside. In a small saucepan bring the balsamic vinegar to boiling; reduce heat. Simmer, uncovered, for 3 to 4 minutes or until vinegar is reduced by half (about 2 tablespoons).

2 In a small bowl stir together 1 tablespoon of the reduced vinegar and 1 tablespoon of the honey; cover and set aside to brush over tuna. Stir remaining vinegar and honey into mayonnaise or salad dressing. Add shallots or onion to mayonnaise or salad dressing mixture; stir until combined. Cover and chill.

3 In a grill with a cover, arrange medium-hot coals around a drip pan. Test for medium heat above pan. Place tuna on the grill rack directly over drip pan. Cover and grill until tuna flakes easily when tested with a fork, turning tuna once and brushing with the vinegar-honey mixture halfway through grilling time. (Allow 6 to 9 minutes for ¾-inch steaks and 8 to 12 minutes for 1-inch steaks.) Top tuna with cheese slices. Cover and grill about 1 minute more or until cheese is melted.

4 Spread the mayonnaise or salad dressing mixture on one side of each toast slice. Place 4 toast slices, spread sides up, on 4 dinner plates. Top with tuna and remaining toast slices, spread sides down.

Nutrition Facts per serving: 489 cal., 22 g total fat (6 g sat. fat), 51 mg chol., 601 mg sodium, 40 g carbo., 2 g fiber, 30 g pro. **Daily Values:** 56% vit. A, 1% vit. C, 21% calcium, 13% iron.

Grill marks without the grill

Give sandwiches made with toasted bread, such as the one above, a picture-perfect appearance with dark, hot-off-the-grill marks. Butter the bread on both sides. To toast the bread, heat a stove-top griddle pan with raised ribs over high heat. Place the bread on the hot griddle pan. Use a spatula to press the bread against the hot ribs to mark the bread. Turn the slices and repeat on the second side (see photo, left).

roast beef & turkey
with rémoulade

start to finish: 20 minutes   *makes:* 6 servings

½ cup mayonnaise or salad dressing
1 tablespoon snipped parsley
2 teaspoons drained capers
2 teaspoons finely chopped sweet
      or dill pickle (gherkin)
2 teaspoons anchovy paste (optional)
1 small clove garlic, minced
½ teaspoon Dijon-style mustard

⅛ teaspoon dried tarragon, crushed
⅛ teaspoon pepper
1 10-inch round focaccia bread
      (about 16 ounces)
2 large or 4 small romaine lettuce leaves
1 medium tomato, thinly sliced
6 to 8 ounces sliced roast beef
6 to 8 ounces sliced smoked turkey

1 For rémoulade, in a medium bowl stir
together mayonnaise or salad dressing;
parsley; capers; pickle; anchovy paste, if
desired; garlic; mustard; tarragon; and
pepper. Set aside. Slice the focaccia bread in
half horizontally with a long serrated knife.

2 Spread cut surfaces of bread halves
with rémoulade. Layer lettuce, tomato,
beef, and turkey on bottom half of bread.
Replace top; cut into wedges to serve.

Nutrition Facts per serving: 431 cal., 22 g total fat
(5 g sat. fat), 51 mg chol., 462 mg sodium, 39 g carbo.,
4 g fiber, 22 g pro. **Daily Values:** 8% vit. A, 15% vit. C,
88% calcium, 2% iron.

Slicing flatbreads
Large, irregularly shaped focaccia and other flatbreads
are a refreshing change of pace from perfectly shaped
sandwich breads. To slice them horizontally for
sandwiches, use a long, thin serrated knife. Holding
your hand flat (see photo, left), gently press on the top
of the bread to hold it in place while you carefully
slice the bread in half.

BRING ON THE RÉMOULADE

Rémoulade is a sharp,
sweet-salty sauce that's a
super complement to cold
meats and fish. Flavored with
a medley of mayonnaise,
mustard, anchovies, capers,
pickles, and herbs, rémoulade
will keep for several days in the
refrigerator—if it lasts that long.

Double the recipe at left, and
keep it on hand to use as a
spread for cold-cut sandwiches,
to team with crab cakes, or as
a cocktail sauce for cooked
lobster, shrimp, or crab. It also
tastes great as a dip for carrots,
celery, broccoli florets, or other
fresh vegetables.

101

CARAMELIZING ONIONS

Caramelized onions make a deliciously mellow topper for burgers, such as the recipe, right, or a flavorful side dish for meats, poultry, or fish.

To caramelize enough onions for 4 to 6 servings, thinly slice 2 large onions. Cook them, covered, in a skillet in 2 tablespoons hot margarine or butter over medium-low heat for 13 to 15 minutes or until the onions are tender. (To make sure the steam stays trapped in the skillet and helps cook the onions during this stage of cooking, uncover the skillet only occasionally to stir the onions.)

Uncover the skillet and add 4 teaspoons brown sugar and ¼ teaspoon salt. Cook and stir over medium-high heat for 5 to 6 minutes or until the onions are golden. It's important to stir continuously so the onions don't stick. Also, don't overcook the onions or they may burn and take on an off-flavor.

grilled burgers
with caramelized onions

prep: 15 minutes   ***grill:*** 12 minutes   ***makes:*** 4 servings

1   pound lean ground beef
2   tablespoons honey mustard
½   teaspoon salt
1   teaspoon coarsely ground black pepper
2   large sweet onions (such as Vidalia or Walla Walla), halved lengthwise and thinly sliced

2   tablespoons margarine or butter
4   teaspoons brown sugar
¼   teaspoon salt
2   tablespoons balsamic vinegar
4   onion hamburger buns, split and toasted

1 In a medium bowl combine beef, honey mustard, and the ½ teaspoon salt; mix lightly until combined. Shape beef mixture into four ½-inch-thick patties. Sprinkle both sides of hamburger patties with pepper; press in lightly.

2 Grill patties on the rack of an uncovered grill directly over medium heat for 12 to 16 minutes or until a thermometer inserted in the centers of patties registers 160°, turning once. (Or, broil on the unheated rack of a broiler pan, 4 inches from the heat, for 12 to 16 minutes or until a thermometer inserted in the centers of patties registers 160°, turning once.)

3 Meanwhile, in a large skillet caramelize onions using the margarine or butter, brown sugar, and the ¼ teaspoon salt (see tip, left). Cook and stir over medium-high heat for 5 to 6 minutes or until onions are golden. Remove from heat. Add vinegar; stir to scrape up browned bits from bottom of skillet.

4 Serve burgers on toasted buns topped with the caramelized onions.

Nutrition Facts per serving: 476 cal., 23 g total fat (7 g sat. fat), 61 mg chol., 834 mg sodium, 40 g carbo., 3 g fiber, 26 g pro. **Daily Values:** 6% vit. A, 8% vit. C, 10% calcium, 22% iron.

sautéed onion
& tomato sandwiches

start to finish: 20 minutes   ***makes:*** 4 servings

2 medium onions, sliced
1 teaspoon olive oil
8 slices hearty whole grain bread
    (toasted, if desired)
   Honey mustard
3 small red and/or yellow tomatoes,
    thinly sliced (see tip, right)

4 lettuce leaves, shredded
    Small basil leaves
4 ounces spreadable Brie cheese
    or soft-style cream cheese

1 In a large skillet cook onion slices in hot oil over medium-high heat for 5 to 7 minutes or until tender and just starting to brown. Remove the skillet from heat; cool onions slightly.

2 To assemble, lightly spread one side of 4 bread slices with honey mustard. Top with cooked onion, tomato slices, and lettuce. Sprinkle with basil leaves. Spread one side of each of the 4 remaining bread slices with Brie or cream cheese; place on sandwiches, spread side down.

Nutrition Facts per serving: 287 cal., 12 g total fat (6 g sat. fat), 28 mg chol., 490 mg sodium, 35 g carbo., 1 g fiber, 12 g pro. **Daily Values:** 8% vit. A, 16% vit. C, 8% calcium, 15% iron.

TOP TOMATOES

Thanks to Mother Nature's savvy planning, there's a tomato for every culinary need.

Hearty **common tomatoes,** including the supersize beefsteak varieties, are ideal for sandwiches, salads, stir-frying, or other cooking. They're juicy and firm-textured and are often available in red, yellow, and orange (see photo, left).

Plum (sometimes labeled **roma**) tomatoes make great sauces. Drop these beauties into a pot to simmer into a velvety sauce.

Tiny **cherry** and **grape** varieties grow in hues of red, orange, and yellow and boast a big, sweet taste. They're perfect for snacking out of hand or tossing into salads.

PIZZA ON THE GRILL

To add to the wonderful "outdoor" flavor of Grilled Chicken and Vegetable Pizza (see recipe, right), try finishing off the pizza on the grill.

After the chicken and vegetables are grilled, cooled, and cut into bite-size pieces, oil the grill rack. Carefully slide 1 of the dough circles onto the rack of the uncovered grill directly over medium-hot coals.

Grill for 1 to 2 minutes or until dough is puffed in some places and starting to become firm. When the dough is just starting to char on the underside, turn the crust.

Top with half of the mozzarella cheese, half of the chicken, and half of the vegetables. Grill for 1 to 2 minutes more or until cheese is melted and crust is crisp.

Remove pizza from grill. Repeat with remaining dough, cheese, chicken, and vegetables.

grilled chicken & vegetable pizza

prep: 45 minutes   ***marinate:*** 1 hour   ***bake:*** 22 minutes   ***makes:*** 6 servings

- 12 ounces skinless boneless chicken breast halves
- 3 plum tomatoes, halved
- 2 small zucchini, halved lengthwise
- 1 medium red onion, cut into $\frac{1}{2}$-inch slices
- $\frac{1}{2}$ cup bottled Italian salad dressing or vinaigrette salad dressing
- 1 16-ounce package hot roll mix
- 1 $4\frac{1}{2}$-ounce can chopped pitted ripe olives, drained
- $\frac{1}{2}$ cup shredded Parmesan cheese (2 ounces)
- 2 cups shredded mozzarella cheese (8 ounces)

1 Place chicken breast halves, tomatoes, zucchini, and onion in a plastic bag set in a shallow dish. Pour salad dressing over chicken and vegetables; seal bag. Marinate in the refrigerator for 1 to 6 hours, turning bag occasionally.

2 Meanwhile, for crust, prepare hot roll mix according to package directions for pizza dough, adding drained olives and Parmesan cheese to the flour mixture.

3 Drain chicken and vegetables, discarding marinade. Grill chicken and vegetables on the rack of an uncovered grill directly over medium heat or until chicken is tender and no longer pink and vegetables are crisp-tender, turning once. (Allow 12 to 15 minutes for chicken, 12 to 14 minutes for onion slices, 5 to 6 minutes for zucchini, and 3 to 4 minutes for tomatoes.) Cool about 5 minutes. Cut into bite-size pieces.

4 Grease two 12-inch pizza pans. On a lightly floured surface, roll each half of dough into a 12-inch circle. Transfer to pans; build up edges slightly. Bake in a 425° oven for 12 minutes or until browned.

5 Top crusts with mozzarella cheese, chicken, and vegetables. Bake for 10 to 15 minutes more or until cheese is melted.

Nutrition Facts per serving: 514 cal., 24 g total fat (9 g sat. fat), 66 mg chol., 682 mg sodium, 47 g carbo., 3 g fiber, 29 g pro. **Daily Values:** 14% vit. A, 12% vit. C, 29% calcium, 24% iron.

Fish & Seafood

Some fish, such as the trout in Grilled Trout with Cilantro & Lime (see recipe, right), are fragile and may break into pieces when you turn them on the grill. Sidestep the problem with a grill basket.

Inexpensive and invaluable, a grill basket can be adjusted to hold foods of varying thickness. When it's time to flip the food on the grill, flip the basket instead. Greasing or oiling the basket before grilling helps prevent the food from sticking. To keep from burning yourself as you turn the grill basket, use an oven mitt to hold the basket's metal handle.

grilled trout with
cilantro & lime

prep: 10 minutes   **grill:** 8 minutes   **makes:** 4 servings

4   8- to 10-ounce fresh or frozen dressed trout, heads removed
3   tablespoons lime juice
2   tablespoons olive oil
2   tablespoons snipped fresh cilantro or parsley

½   teaspoon kosher salt
¼   teaspoon cracked black pepper
    Lime wedges

1 Thaw fish, if frozen. Rinse fish; pat dry. In a small bowl combine lime juice and olive oil; brush inside and outside of each fish with the lime juice mixture. Sprinkle insides of each fish cavity evenly with cilantro or parsley, salt, and pepper.

2 Place fish in a well-greased grill basket. Grill trout on the rack of an uncovered grill directly over medium coals for 8 to 12 minutes or until fish flakes easily when tested with a fork, turning basket once halfway through grilling. (Or, preheat a well-greased grill pan on the rack of an uncovered grill over medium heat for 5 minutes. Place fish in preheated pan. Grill for 8 to 12 minutes or until fish flakes easily when tested with a fork, turning fish once halfway through grilling.) Serve trout with lime wedges.

Nutrition Facts per serving: 376 cal., 19 g total fat (4 g sat. fat), 133 mg chol., 372 mg sodium, 1 g carbo., 0 g fiber, 47 g pro. **Daily Values:** 19% vit. A, 16% vit. C, 16% calcium, 4% iron.

ginger-marinated
sea bass

prep: 15 minutes   **marinate:** 1 hour   **broil:** 8 minutes   **makes:** 4 servings

4   fresh or frozen sea bass or halibut steaks, cut
      1 inch thick (1½ to 1¾ pounds total)
¼   cup teriyaki sauce
2   tablespoons lemon juice
1   tablespoon grated fresh ginger

2   teaspoons brown sugar
2   cloves garlic, minced
⅛   teaspoon ground red pepper
      Fresh cilantro (optional)

1 Thaw fish, if frozen. Rinse fish; pat dry. Place fish in a shallow, non-metallic dish. For marinade, combine teriyaki sauce, lemon juice, ginger, brown sugar, garlic, and red pepper. Pour over fish; turn fish to coat. Cover and marinate in the refrigerator for 1 to 2 hours, turning fish occasionally.

2 Drain fish, reserving marinade. Place fish on the greased unheated rack of a broiler pan. Broil 4 inches from heat for 5 minutes. Using a wide spatula, carefully turn fish over. Brush with marinade. Broil 3 to 7 minutes more or until fish flakes easily with a fork. Discard any remaining marinade. If desired, sprinkle with cilantro.

Nutrition Facts per serving: 179 cal., 3 g total fat (1 g sat. fat), 71 mg chol., 462 mg sodium, 3 g carbo., 0 g fiber, 32 g pro. **Daily Values:** 8% vit. A, 9% vit. C, 1% calcium, 4% iron.

FISH AT ITS FRESHEST

There are definite signs that fish is fresh. Fresh fish should have a mild scent and moist flesh, and appear freshly cut. Don't purchase fish that has a strong, fishy odor. Whole fish should have bright, bulging eyes and bright red or pink gills. Frozen fish should meet the fresh-smell test and have taut packaging with no evidence of ice or blood.

Fresh fish is best used right away. Or, you can store it for up to two days in the coldest part of the refrigerator. Frozen fish will keep in its original wrapping, frozen at 0° or lower, for up to 3 months.

107

smoked salmon
with apple glaze

prep: 15 minutes   **marinate:** 1 hour   **smoke:** 1¼ hours   **makes:** 4 servings

2 12-ounce fresh or frozen salmon fillets
¾ cup frozen apple juice concentrate, thawed
1 tablespoon snipped fresh rosemary
     or 1 teaspoon dried rosemary, crushed

½ teaspoon coarsely ground black pepper
¼ teaspoon salt
4 to 6 alder or pecan wood chunks
2 tablespoons apple jelly, melted

1 Thaw fish, if frozen. Rinse fish; pat dry. Place fish in a shallow, non-metallic dish. For marinade, in a small bowl combine thawed apple juice concentrate, rosemary, pepper, and salt. Reserve ¼ cup of the marinade. Pour remaining marinade over fish; turn fish to coat. Cover and marinate in the refrigerator for 1 to 2 hours. At least 1 hour before smoking, soak wood chunks in enough water to cover. Drain wood chunks. Drain fish, discarding marinade.

2 *If using a smoker,* arrange preheated coals, drained wood chunks, and water pan according to manufacturer's directions. Pour about 1 inch of water into water pan. Place fish on grill rack over water pan. Cover and smoke for 1¼ to 1½ hours or until fish flakes easily when tested with a fork, brushing with the reserved marinade after 1 hour.

3 *If using a charcoal grill,* arrange preheated coals around drip pan. Test for medium heat above the pan. Place wood chunks over the coals. Pour about 1 inch of water into the pan. Measure thickness of fish. Place fish on grill rack over pan. Cover and grill fish for 4 to 6 minutes per ½ inch of thickness or until fish flakes with a fork, basting with reserved marinade after 6 minutes.

4 Just before serving, drizzle fish with melted apple jelly.

Nutrition Facts per serving: 311 cal., 6 g total fat (1 g sat. fat), 88 mg chol., 276 mg sodium, 29 g carbo., 0 g fiber, 34 g pro. **Daily Values:** 6% vit. A, 2% vit. C, 4% calcium, 11% iron.

Help with fish prep

Conserve time and energy by asking your fish market to bone and skin your fish purchases before you take them home. Most fish markets will skin fish free of charge, and nearly all will remove the bones at no cost as well. Just ask! There's no reason to pass up an experienced helping hand.

THE INGREDIENT IS WOOD

Add a woodsy smoke flavor to your grilled, smoked, and barbecued specialties by adding hardwood to your fire. You'll find hardwood chips and chunks in cookware shops and some supermarkets.

Which varieties should you choose? Hickory is a favorite for all types of foods because it yields an intense, sweet flavor. Many say pecan is a smoother version of hickory with a fruity quality. Delicate, light alder is often paired with salmon and other fish (see recipe, left). Mesquite lends sweetness to beef, pork, poultry, and fish. Apple, orange, and cherry woods impart a lighter smoky sweetness that complements poultry and fish nicely.

Hardwood chips work best for quick-cooking foods; the chunks are better suited to larger items. Soak both the chips and the chunks in water for an hour before using so they will smoke rather than burn.

WHEN IS THE FISH DONE?

Whether you're grilling, baking, or poaching fish, estimate the cooking time with this simple technique. Stand a ruler against the thickest part of the fish. Allow 4 to 6 minutes of cooking time for each half inch of fish. Doing the math, half-inch pieces should cook for 4 to 6 minutes; 1-inch pieces will need 8 to 12 minutes, and so on. Tuck under any thin edges so the whole piece is an even thickness.

To test for doneness, slip a fork into the thickest part of the fish and give it a gentle twist. If the fish flakes easily and its color is opaque, it's ready to eat. If it doesn't flake easily or the color is still translucent, continue cooking.

spicy red snapper with mango salsa

prep: 20 minutes   **bake:** 4 to 6 minutes   **makes:** 4 servings

1 pound fresh or frozen red snapper fillets
1 tablespoon lime juice
1 tablespoon water
1 teaspoon paprika
$\frac{1}{2}$ teaspoon salt
$\frac{1}{4}$ teaspoon ground ginger
$\frac{1}{4}$ teaspoon ground allspice
$\frac{1}{4}$ teaspoon black pepper
1 recipe Mango Salsa
Lime wedges (optional)

1 Thaw fish, if frozen. Rinse fish; pat dry. Cut fish into 4 serving-size pieces. Measure thickness of fish. In a small bowl combine lime juice and water; brush onto fish. In another small bowl combine paprika, salt, ginger, allspice, and pepper. Use your fingers to rub the spice mixture onto the fish.

2 Arrange the fish in a shallow baking pan. Bake, uncovered, in a 450° oven until fish flakes easily when tested with a fork. (Allow 4 to 6 minutes for each $\frac{1}{2}$ inch of thickness.)

3 To serve, brush fish with pan juices. Serve with Mango Salsa. If desired, garnish with lime wedges.

Mango Salsa: In a medium bowl combine 1 mango, peeled, seeded, and chopped (about $1\frac{1}{2}$ cups); 1 medium red sweet pepper, finely chopped; $\frac{1}{4}$ cup thinly sliced green onions;

1 fresh Scotch bonnet (or habañero) or hot green chile pepper, seeded and finely chopped; 3 tablespoons olive oil; $\frac{1}{2}$ teaspoon finely shredded lime peel; 2 tablespoons lime juice; 1 tablespoon vinegar; $\frac{1}{4}$ teaspoon salt; and $\frac{1}{4}$ teaspoon pepper. Makes about 2 cups.

Nutrition Facts per serving: 260 cal., 13 g total fat (2 g sat. fat), 41 mg chol., 536 mg sodium, 13 g carbo., 2 g fiber, 24 g pro. **Daily Values:** 46% vit. A, 131% vit. C, 4% calcium, 7% iron.

110

wasabi-glazed whitefish
with vegetable slaw

prep: 15 minutes   **grill:** 6 minutes   **makes:** 4 servings

- 4 4-ounce fresh white-fleshed skinless fish fillets*, about ¾ inch thick
- 2 tablespoons light soy sauce
- ¼ teaspoon wasabi powder or 1 tablespoon prepared horseradish
- 1 teaspoon toasted sesame oil

- ½ teaspoon sugar
- 1 medium zucchini, coarsely shredded
- 1 cup sliced radishes
- 1 cup fresh pea pods
- 3 tablespoons snipped fresh chives
- 3 tablespoons rice vinegar

1 Rinse fish; pat dry. In a small bowl combine soy sauce, wasabi powder or horseradish, ½ teaspoon of the sesame oil, and ¼ teaspoon of the sugar. Brush soy mixture over fish.

2 Grill fish on the lightly greased rack of an uncovered grill directly over medium heat for 6 to 9 minutes or until fish flakes easily when tested with a fork, turning after 4 minutes.

3 Meanwhile, for vegetable slaw, in a medium bowl combine the zucchini, radishes, pea pods, and 2 tablespoons of the chives. Stir together the remaining sesame oil, remaining sugar, and the vinegar. Drizzle over the zucchini mixture; toss to combine. Sprinkle remaining chives over fish. Immediately serve fish on top of vegetable slaw.

Nutrition Facts per serving: 141 cal., 3 g total fat (1 g sat. fat), 60 mg chol., 363 mg sodium, 6 g carbo., 1 g fiber, 24 g pro. **Daily Values:** 3% vit. A, 46% vit. C, 3% calcium, 10% iron.

*Note: Use whitefish, sea bass, orange roughy, or other similar fish fillets.

WASABI & OTHER ASIAN FLAVORS

Wasabi is a Japanese horseradish condiment with head-clearing heat—at least when used in heavy doses. It has a very distinctive, pale lime-green color and is available in two forms: a paste in a tube or a fine powder in a small tin or bottle. When wasabi is stirred into soy sauce, as in Wasabi-Glazed Whitefish (see recipe, left), its flavor is toned down a bit, offering a zingy flavor accent to the fish. The wasabi and soy sauce combination also is a classic accompaniment to sushi.

Some other interesting Asian products include:

Rice vinegar: A vinegar with subtle tang and slightly sweet flavor. There are Chinese and Japanese versions. Seasoned rice vinegar is a sweeter version often used for sushi rice.

Tamari: A slightly thicker, mellower cousin to soy sauce.

Hoisin sauce: A sweet, tongue-tingling blend of fermented soybeans, molasses, vinegar, mustard, sesame seeds, garlic, and chiles.

CRISPY DEEP-FAT FRYING

The trick to producing crispy deep-fried foods is no trick at all. Just keep the fat at a constant high temperature. This is best done by using a heavy, flat-bottomed pan and a deep-fat thermometer to monitor the oil temperature. To ensure crispiness:

- Heat cooking oil to the temperature listed in your recipe, typically 365° to 375°. You'll need enough oil in the pan to cover the food you're frying.
- To avoid a pasty coating, dip the food in the batter and wait for the excess to drain off.
- Cook in small batches and add the food slowly. Avoid crowding; freely bubbling fat makes for a crispy crust.
- Watch the oil temperature and don't let it drop below the temperature specified.
- Stir the food several times to ensure even cooking.
- After frying, drain the food on paper towels. Keep finished batches warm in a 300° oven while you finish frying.

pecan-cornmeal fried catfish

prep: 20 minutes   *fry:* 4 minutes per batch   *makes:* 6 servings

1½ pounds fresh or frozen catfish fillets
¾ cup ground pecans or peanuts
⅔ cup yellow cornmeal
¾ teaspoon salt
¼ teaspoon black pepper
¼ teaspoon ground red pepper
¼ cup milk
1 beaten egg
   Cooking oil for deep-fat frying

1 Thaw fish, if frozen. Rinse fish; pat dry. Cut fish into 6 serving-size pieces, if necessary.

2 In a shallow dish combine ground pecans or peanuts, cornmeal, salt, black pepper, and red pepper. In another shallow dish combine milk and egg.

3 Dip each fish portion in milk mixture; coat with the nut mixture.

4 Meanwhile, in a heavy large saucepan or deep fryer heat 2 inches of oil to 375° (see tip, left). Fry fish in hot oil, 1 or 2 pieces at a time, about 2 minutes on each side or until golden brown. Carefully remove with a slotted spoon; drain on paper towels. Keep warm in a 300° oven while frying remaining fish.

Nutrition Facts per serving: 397 cal., 28 g total fat (4 g sat. fat), 89 mg chol., 367 mg sodium, 15 g carbo., 2 g fiber, 21 g pro. **Daily Values:** 5% vit. A, 2% vit. C, 3% calcium, 9% iron.

VERSATILE, QUICK PAN-FRYING

When you want crispy fried fish without the big pot of bubbling fat, pull out a skillet and pan-fry the fish in a few tablespoons of oil.

You can pan-fry larger, fattier fish, such as tuna or swordfish, without a coating, but you may want to rub the fish with herbs or other seasonings for flavor.

To pan-fry smaller, more delicate fish, you'll need to add a coating. Pan-Fried Trout with Corn & Zucchini Relish (see recipe, right) uses a four-step process to help the coating stick. The fish is dipped in milk, then in flour, and again in milk before it is covered with a mixture of ground nuts, cornmeal, and onion salt (see step 2, right).

pan-fried trout with
corn & zucchini relish

prep: 20 minutes   *fry:* 8 minutes   *makes:* 4 servings

    1 pound fresh or frozen rainbow trout fillets
    ¼ cup milk
    ¼ cup all-purpose flour
    ⅓ cup ground hickory nuts or hazelnuts
        (filberts)
    ⅓ cup cornmeal
    ½ teaspoon onion salt
    ¼ cup cooking oil
        Corn & Zucchini Relish

1 Thaw fish, if frozen. Rinse fish; pat dry. Cut fish into 4 serving-size pieces, if necessary. Measure thickness of fish. Put milk in a shallow dish. Place flour in another shallow dish. In a third shallow dish combine ground nuts, cornmeal, and onion salt.

2 Dip each piece of fish in the milk, then in the flour. Dip again in the milk, then coat with the nut mixture. In a 12-inch skillet heat oil over medium heat. Add half of the fish fillets in a single layer. (If fillets have skin, fry skin side last.) Fry fish on one side until golden. Turn carefully. Fry until second side is golden and fish flakes easily when tested with a fork. (Allow 2 to 3 minutes per side for ½-inch-thick fillets.)

Drain on paper towels. Keep warm in a 300° oven while frying remaining fish. Serve fish with Corn & Zucchini Relish.

Corn & Zucchini Relish: In a bowl combine 1 cup fresh or frozen whole kernel corn; 1 medium zucchini, chopped; ¼ cup finely chopped red sweet pepper; ¼ cup vinegar; 3 tablespoons sugar; ½ teaspoon dried dillweed; ¼ teaspoon salt; and ¼ teaspoon dry mustard. Cover and chill at least 4 hours. Serve with a slotted spoon.

Nutrition Facts per serving: 504 cal., 27 g total fat (5 g sat. fat), 68 mg chol., 402 mg sodium, 38 g carbo., 4 g fiber, 29 g pro. **Daily Values:** 25% vit. A, 48% vit. C, 12% calcium, 11 % iron.

tarragon-chardonnay
poached salmon

prep: 15 minutes   **cook:** 8 minutes   **makes:** 4 servings

- 4 5- to 6-ounce fresh or frozen salmon steaks, 1 inch thick
- 1 cup Chardonnay or other dry white wine
- 1 medium red onion, cut into thin wedges
- 2 stalks celery, sliced
- 1 teaspoon dried tarragon, crushed
- ¼ teaspoon salt
- ¼ teaspoon coarsely ground black pepper

1 Thaw fish, if frozen. Rinse fish; pat dry. In a large skillet combine wine, onion, celery, tarragon, salt, and pepper. Bring to boiling; add fish steaks. Simmer, covered, for 8 to 12 minutes or until fish flakes easily when tested with a fork. Use a slotted spatula to transfer salmon and vegetables from cooking liquid* to a serving platter.

*Note: If desired, the cooking liquid may be strained and used in recipes calling for fish stock. Store in a covered container in the refrigerator for up to 3 days. Or, freeze for up to 1 month.

Nutrition Facts per serving: 421 cal., 23 g total fat (5 g sat. fat), 111 mg chol., 255 mg sodium, 3 g carbo., 1 g fiber, 39 g pro. **Daily Values:** 21% vit. A, 26% vit. C, 16% calcium, 11% iron.

A sea of salmon

Colorful, full-flavored, and versatile, salmon is a saltwater fish available in several varieties. Most types of salmon come from the Pacific Ocean. Chinook, or king, salmon is the finest and most expensive variety with flesh ranging from red to near white. The Pacific also offers coho, or silver, salmon, firmer, paler, and lower in fat than Chinook. Sockeye, or red, salmon is firm with a deep red flesh. Pink, or humpback, salmon is the smallest Pacific salmon and has a delicate flavor. Chum, or dog, salmon are nearly fat-free and have the palest flesh. The famous Atlantic salmon, most of which comes from Canada, has a high oil content and is pink to red or orange in color. You'll find canned salmon in both the low-fat pink or humpback variety and the sweet, firm sockeye or red salmon. Canned salmon is available with and without bones and skin.

SKINNING FISH

Although you can ask to have the skin removed when buying fish fresh, you also can do it yourself.

Start with a sharp, broad-bladed chef's knife. With your dominant hand, press the blade away from you and into the short end of the fish steak or fillet (where flesh meets the skin) at a 30-degree angle. Hold the skin with your other hand and gently pull the skin from beneath the angled blade while you hold the blade in place (see photo, above). The knife will slide along the flesh as you pull on the skin.

red snapper & vegetables en papillote

prep: 20 minutes   **cook:** 12 minutes   **makes:** 4 servings

4 6-ounce fresh or frozen red snapper fillets
   (with skin), ½ to ¾ inch thick
12 ounces whole tiny new potatoes
   or Yukon gold potatoes, quartered

2 cups broccoli florets
⅓ cup pesto
   Aluminum foil or parchment paper

1 Thaw fish, if frozen. Rinse fish; pat dry. If desired, remove and discard skin from fish (see tip, page 115); set fish aside.

2 In a microwave-safe medium bowl microwave potatoes, covered, on 100-percent power (high) for 5 to 7 minutes or until nearly tender, stirring once. Add broccoli and about half the pesto; toss to coat.

3 Tear off four 12-inch squares of aluminum foil or parchment paper. Divide vegetable mixture into 4 portions, placing 1 portion in the center of each square. Top each with a fish fillet, tucking under any thin edges of fillets. Spoon remaining pesto over fillets.

4 Bring up opposite edges of foil or parchment paper and seal with a double fold. Fold remaining edges together to enclose mixture, leaving space for steam to build. Place packets on a shallow baking sheet.

5 Bake in a 400° oven until fish flakes easily when tested with a fork (allow 12 minutes for ½-inch fillets and 15 minutes for ¾-inch fillets). To serve, carefully slit packets open with a knife.

Nutrition Facts per serving: 364 cal., 12 g total fat (2 g sat. fat), 66 mg chol., 270 mg sodium, 17 g carbo., 3 g fiber, 40 g pro. **Daily Values:** 14% vit. A, 93% vit. C, 13% calcium, 9% iron.

Citrus garnishes

Lemon or lime is a bright note when squeezed over fish, and it is equally good as a garnish. The colored part of citrus peel is filled with aromatic oils that perfume your dish and add to its presentation.

For a quick garnish, slice wedges of citrus fruits to serve alongside fish. Or, make citrus twists by cutting thin slices of orange, lemon, or lime. Make a cut from the center of each slice to its edge and twist the ends in opposite directions. Get creative by stacking a lemon and lime slice, cutting to the centers, and twisting.

You also can garnish plates with a few aromatic herb stems loosely tied with a citrus knot. Use a zester or vegetable peeler to remove a long length of peel for the knot.

ONE-PACK MEALS

Here's a healthful cooking technique borrowed from the French: cooking *en papillote*. En papillote refers to the technique of cooking food in parchment paper or foil. Foods such as fish and vegetables cook in their own flavorful juices without added fat. The technique is described in the recipe at left.

Cooking en papillote can be used for a variety of foods. To adapt the technique to your taste, experiment with combinations of fish (or meat or poultry), quick-cooking vegetables (such as sliced zucchini, grape tomatoes, thinly sliced carrots, sliced mushrooms, and sliced green onions), herbs, and a little broth or wine.

117

THE LOWDOWN ON SHRIMP

When buying fresh shrimp for recipes, such as Greek Leek & Shrimp Stir-Fry (see recipe, right), you'll need to buy 1½ pounds of raw shrimp in the shell for each pound of shelled shrimp you need. The price of shrimp per pound depends on the size—the bigger the shrimp, the higher the price and the fewer per pound.

To peel a fresh shrimp, start at the head end and use your fingers to peel back the shell. Gently pull on the tail portion of the shell and remove it. To devein a shrimp, use a sharp knife to make a shallow slit along its back from head to tail. Rinse under cold running water to remove the vein, using the tip of a knife to dislodge it, if necessary.

greek leek & shrimp
stir-fry

prep: 30 minutes   ***cook:*** 5 minutes   ***makes:*** 4 servings

1¼ pounds fresh or frozen, peeled, deveined shrimp	1 cup quick-cooking couscous
⅔ cup water	¼ teaspoon salt
⅓ cup lemon juice	1½ cups boiling water
2 teaspoons cornstarch	1 tablespoon olive oil
¾ teaspoon bouquet garni seasoning or dried oregano, crushed	4 medium leeks, thinly sliced
	½ cup crumbled feta cheese
	10 pitted kalamata olives, quartered

1 Thaw shrimp, if frozen. Rinse shrimp; pat dry. In a bowl combine the ⅔ cup water, lemon juice, cornstarch, and ¼ teaspoon of the bouquet garni seasoning or oregano. Set the lemon juice mixture aside.

2 In a bowl combine the couscous, remaining bouquet garni or oregano, and salt. Pour the 1½ cups boiling water over the couscous mixture. Let stand, covered, for 5 minutes. Fluff with a fork.

3 Meanwhile, pour olive oil into a wok or large skillet. Preheat over medium-high heat. Stir-fry leeks in hot oil for 2 to 3 minutes or until tender. Remove from wok or skillet; set aside.

4 Stir lemon juice mixture; add to wok or skillet. Bring to boiling; add shrimp. Cook and stir about 3 minutes or until shrimp are opaque. Stir in leeks and ¼ cup of the feta cheese. Serve shrimp mixture over couscous. Top with olives and remaining feta cheese.

Nutrition Facts per serving: 412 cal., 10 g total fat (3 g sat. fat), 230 mg chol., 609 mg sodium, 49 g carbo., 11 g fiber, 33 g pro. **Daily Values:** 11% vit. A, 28% vit. C, 14% calcium, 36% iron.

asian-flavored crab
& linguine toss

prep: 30 minutes   *cook:* 5 minutes   *makes:* 4 servings

8 ounces dried linguine
1½ pounds fresh or frozen cooked crab legs
1½ cups sliced fresh cremini or shiitake
     mushrooms
2 tablespoons minced fresh ginger
¼ teaspoon crushed red pepper (optional)

1 tablespoon peanut oil or vegetable oil
1½ cups fresh snow pea pods, strings
     and tips removed
4 green onions, cut into 1-inch pieces
¼ teaspoon salt
2 teaspoons toasted sesame oil

1 In a Dutch oven cook linguine according to package directions. Drain; return to Dutch oven and keep warm.

2 Meanwhile, use a nutcracker to crack each crab leg joint and remove meat (see tip, right). Coarsely chop crab meat. Set meat aside.

3 In a large nonstick skillet cook and stir mushrooms, ginger, and, if desired, red pepper in hot oil over medium-high heat for 2 minutes. Add pea pods; cook and stir 1 minute more. Add mushroom mixture to cooked linguine along with crab meat, green onions, and salt; toss to combine. Heat through. Drizzle with sesame oil; toss to coat.

Nutrition Facts per serving: 373 cal., 8 g total fat (1 g sat. fat), 85 mg chol., 399 mg sodium, 47 g carbo., 3 g fiber, 27 g pro. **Daily Values:** 1% vit. A, 30% vit. C, 12% calcium, 19% iron.

CRAB: CREAM OF THE CATCH

Crab, famous for its sweet, succulent meat, is available in a myriad of forms. You can purchase whole crabs live, cooked, or frozen. Legs and claws also are available cooked and frozen. Cooked crabmeat comes frozen, pasteurized (which requires refrigeration), or canned. Canned crab, in turn, is available as claw meat, lump meat, or flaked meat.

To make Asian-Flavored Crab & Linguine Toss (see recipe, left), look for cooked crab legs in your supermarket's fish case or at a seafood shop. With this form of crab, all you have to do is use a nutcracker to crack each leg joint and remove the meat with a cocktail fork.

119

pan-seared scallops
with lemon vinaigrette

prep: 20 minutes   **cook:** 6 minutes   **makes:** 4 servings

12 ounces fresh or frozen sea scallops
1 lemon
1 pound asparagus spears, cut into
      2-inch pieces
1 medium red onion, cut into wedges
3 tablespoons olive oil

Salt
Pepper
2 to 3 fresh basil sprigs
2 tablespoons fresh basil leaves, cut into
      strips (see tip, page 160) (optional)
Lemon wedges (optional)

1 Thaw scallops, if frozen. Rinse scallops; pat dry. Set scallops aside.

2 Score lemon into 4 lengthwise sections with a sharp knife; remove peel from lemon. Scrape off white portion from peel; discard. Cut peel into very thin strips; set aside. Squeeze 2 tablespoons juice from lemon (see tip, below); set juice aside.

3 In a large skillet cook asparagus and onion in 1 tablespoon of the hot oil for 2 to 3 minutes or until crisp-tender. Season to taste with salt and pepper. Transfer asparagus mixture to a serving platter; keep warm.

4 In the same skillet combine the reserved lemon peel, the remaining olive oil, and basil sprigs. Cook for

30 seconds to 1 minute or until heated through. Remove lemon peel and basil sprigs with a slotted spoon, reserving oil in skillet. Discard lemon peel and basil sprigs.

5 Cook scallops in the hot flavored oil for 3 to 5 minutes or until scallops turn opaque, turning once. Stir in the reserved lemon juice. Season to taste with salt and pepper.

6 Arrange scallops over asparagus mixture. If desired, garnish with strips of fresh basil and squeeze lemon juice over scallops.

Nutrition Facts per serving: 190 cal., 11 g total fat (1 g sat. fat), 28 mg chol., 147 mg sodium, 6 g carbo., 1 g fiber, 16 g pro. **Daily Values:** 2% vit. A, 36% vit. C, 3% calcium, 4% iron.

Get the juice

A heavy plastic or wood citrus reamer is all you need to quickly extract juice from lemons, limes, or oranges. Mechanical juicing appliances—if they're not top quality—will extract pith and bitter elements from fruit along with the juice. When using a citrus reamer, juice will flow more freely if you bring the fruit to room temperature, then roll it on a hard surface with your hand before extracting the juice.

PAN-SEARING FOR SPEED & FLAVOR

Pan-searing foods means quickly browning the food on all sides to create a crispy crust and moist interior. High heat is the key to this speedy technique.

Shrimp and scallops, such as those in the recipe at left, are ideal choices for pan-searing because they are small and cook quickly. This allows the insides to get completely done before the outsides burn from prolonged contact with high heat. Thin steaks, chops, and medallions of meat also can be pan-seared.

Slower-cooking foods, such as roasts, can get the same flavor benefits from pan-searing. After browning, however, the meat needs to finish cooking by another cooking method that uses a lower temperature, such as roasting or braising.

121

CLARIFIED BUTTER

To clarify butter, melt the butter over low heat in a heavy saucepan without stirring. When the butter is completely melted, you will see a clear, oily layer on top of a milky layer. Slowly pour the clear liquid into a dish, leaving the milky layer in the pan. The clear liquid is the clarified butter (see photo, above). Discard the milky liquid. The clarified butter will keep up to 1 month in the refrigerator.

Although best known as a dipping sauce for lobster (see recipe, right), clarified butter also can be heated to high temperatures without burning. That makes it a good choice when you want to sauté foods at high temperatures.

grilled lobster
with rosemary butter

prep: 15 minutes   *grill:* 12 minutes   *makes:* 4 servings

4 8-ounce frozen lobster tails	4 teaspoons finely shredded orange peel
2 teaspoons olive oil	2 rosemary sprigs
1/2 cup butter, preferably unsalted	1 medium orange, cut into wedges (optional)

1 Thaw lobster. Rinse lobster; pat dry. Place lobster, shell sides down, on a cutting board. To butterfly, with kitchen scissors cut each lobster in half lengthwise, cutting to but not through the back shell. Bend backward to crack back shell and expose the meat. Brush lobster meat with oil.

2 *If using a charcoal grill,* grill lobster, shell sides down, on the greased rack of an uncovered grill directly over medium coals for 12 to 15 minutes or until lobster meat is opaque and shells are bright red, turning once halfway through grilling. *(If using a gas grill,* preheat grill. Reduce heat to medium. Place lobster, shell sides down, on greased grill rack over heat. Cover and grill as above.)

3 While lobster is grilling, melt butter with orange peel and rosemary over very low heat without stirring; cool slightly. Pour the clear, oily layer through a fine sieve into a serving dish, discarding the milky layer, orange peel, and rosemary. Serve with lobster; store any remaining butter covered in refrigerator up to 1 month. If desired, serve lobster with orange wedges.

Nutrition Facts per serving: 346 cal., 27 g total fat (16 g sat. fat), 147 mg chol., 434 mg sodium, 1 g carbo., 0 g fiber, 24 g pro. **Daily Values:** 20% vit. A, 8% calcium, 3% iron.

Flavored clarified butters
The rich, tempting flavor of clarified butter can be enhanced by the addition of herbs, as in the recipe above. Create your own combinations by experimenting with other flavor additions, such as star anise, fennel seeds, fresh ginger, coriander seeds, peppercorns, and snipped fresh dill.

Poultry

123

Much has been said and written about handling poultry safely. It comes down to one principle: Keep it clean. That means your hands, and anything else the raw poultry touches. Here are some pointers for handling fresh poultry:

• Always wash your hands as well as any work surfaces and utensils that come in contact with raw poultry. Use hot soapy water to prevent spreading bacteria to other foods.

• When cutting raw poultry, use a plastic cutting board; because it can be put in the dishwasher, it's easier to clean and disinfect than a wooden one.

• Always use a clean plate for cooked poultry (never reuse the plate that held uncooked or partially cooked poultry).

maple-mustard-glazed
chicken & winter squash

prep: 30 minutes   *cook:* 50 minutes   *makes:* 6 servings

2½ to 3 pounds meaty chicken pieces (breasts, thighs, and drumsticks), skinned
2 tablespoons maple syrup
2 tablespoons whiskey or orange juice
1 tablespoon Dijon-style mustard
1 tablespoon snipped fresh parsley
½ teaspoon pepper

1 1½- to 2-pound butternut squash
2 tablespoons butter or margarine, softened
2 tablespoons chopped pecans, toasted
1 tablespoon brown sugar
1 tablespoon maple syrup
¼ teaspoon salt

1 Arrange chicken pieces in a single layer in a 2- or 3-quart rectangular baking dish.

2 In a small bowl combine the 2 tablespoons maple syrup, the whiskey or orange juice, mustard, parsley, and pepper. Brush maple-mustard glaze over chicken.

3 Peel squash, if desired. Cut into serving-size pieces, removing seeds. Place squash in a 2-quart casserole; cover. In a small bowl combine softened butter or margarine, pecans, brown sugar, 1 tablespoon maple syrup, and the salt; set aside.

4 Bake chicken, uncovered, and the squash, covered, in a 375° oven for 35 minutes. Spoon juices over chicken. Uncover squash and dot with butter mixture. Continue to bake chicken and squash, uncovered, about 15 minutes or until chicken is tender and no longer pink and squash is tender.

5 Serve chicken with squash, spooning maple-flavored pan juices over each.

Nutrition Facts per serving: 302 cal.,12 g total fat (4 g sat. fat), 88 mg chol., 227 mg sodium, 20 g carbo., 2 g fiber, 26 g pro. **Daily Values:** 144% vit. A, 30% vit. C, 7% calcium, 11% iron.

pesto chicken with grilled tomatoes

prep: 10 minutes   **grill:** 50 minutes   **makes:** 4 servings

1   tablespoon olive oil
4   cloves garlic, minced
6   plum tomatoes, halved lengthwise
1½ to 2 pounds meaty chicken pieces
    (breasts, thighs, and drumsticks)

3   tablespoons butter or margarine, softened
3   tablespoons prepared pesto
2   tablespoons chopped walnuts, toasted
2   tablespoons finely chopped kalamata olives
    (optional)

1 Combine olive oil and garlic. Lightly brush tomato halves and chicken pieces with oil mixture.

2 In a grill with a cover arrange medium-hot coals around a drip pan. Test for medium heat above the pan. Place chicken pieces, bone side down, on grill rack over pan. Cover and grill for 50 to 60 minutes or until chicken is tender and no longer pink. During the last 6 to 8 minutes of grilling, place the tomatoes, cut side down, directly over coals; turn once.

3 Meanwhile, combine butter or margarine, pesto, walnuts, and, if desired, olives. Cover and chill until serving time.

4 To serve, remove chicken from grill. Immediately spread pesto butter over chicken pieces and cut sides of tomatoes.

Nutrition Facts per serving: 407 cal., 30 g total fat (10 g sat. fat), 104 mg chol., 252 mg sodium, 7 g carbo., 1 g fiber, 28 g pro. **Daily Values:** 18% vit. A, 29% vit. C, 6% calcium, 10% iron.

Free-range chicken

A free-range chicken is a bird that's allowed to fly the coop. Factory-raised birds are generally allotted 1 square foot of space per bird. Free-range chickens are allowed more space indoors and are allowed to roam outdoors, too. They're also fed a special all-grain diet free of antibiotics, animal products, hormones, and growth-enhancers. The diet and extra movement mean the chicken grows more slowly than a factory-raised bird, making the meat leaner and giving it a deeper flavor and denser texture—and a higher price tag.

TYPES OF CHICKEN

A chicken's age determines its tenderness and also its best use.

Broiler-fryers are young, usually under 13 weeks old. They weigh between 2 and 5 pounds, but the average is about 3½ pounds. These birds are best broiled, grilled, fried, and stir-fried.

Roasters are a little older and bigger—usually 3 to 5 months old and weighing about 5 pounds. Although they can be cut up and used in many ways, roasting brings out their best.

Stewing hens are usually more than 10 months old and have stopped laying eggs. Weighing between 3 and 7 pounds, stewing hens are tougher than younger birds, but they are flavorful and delicious cooked with moist heat in soups and dishes such as chicken and dumplings.

roasted capon with
wild mushroom stuffing

prep: 30 minutes   **roast:** 1¾ hours   **stand:** 10 minutes   **makes:** 8 servings

8 ounces mixed wild mushrooms
   (cremini, shiitake, portobello), chopped
½ cup thinly sliced green onions
   or finely chopped shallots
¼ cup butter or margarine
8 cups sage-and-onion stuffing mix
½ cup coarsely chopped walnuts, toasted
⅔ to 1 cup chicken broth

1 5- to 7-pound capon
  Salt
2 tablespoons olive oil
2 tablespoons snipped fresh sage
1½ teaspoons coarsely ground black pepper
¼ cup chicken broth
2 teaspoons olive oil

1 For stuffing, in a medium saucepan cook mushrooms and green onions or shallots in butter or margarine until tender; remove from heat. Place stuffing mix and walnuts in a large bowl; add mushroom mixture. Add enough chicken broth to moisten, tossing lightly.

2 Season body cavity of capon with salt. In a small bowl combine the 2 tablespoons olive oil, the sage, and pepper. Slip your fingers between the skin and breast meat of the bird and between the skin and leg meat, forming pockets. Spoon the sage mixture into the pockets, rubbing with your fingers to evenly distribute the mixture. Lightly spoon mushroom stuffing into the body cavity, using no more than ¾ cup stuffing per pound of capon. (Place any remaining stuffing in casserole; cover and chill. If desired, before baking, add additional chicken broth to moisten.) Bake stuffing alongside capon the last 30 to 45 minutes of roasting or until heated through.

3 Tie the drumsticks securely to tail; twist wing tips under back. Place capon, breast side up, on a rack in a shallow roasting pan. Brush with the 2 teaspoons of oil. Insert a meat thermometer into the center of one of the inside thigh muscles. The thermometer should not touch the bone. Roast, uncovered, in a 325° oven for 1¾ to 2½ hours or until drumsticks move easily in their sockets, capon is no longer pink, and meat thermometer registers 180° to 185°.

4 Remove capon from oven. Cover and let stand 10 minutes before carving. Serve with stuffing.

Nutrition Facts per serving: 651 cal., 42 g total fat (12 g sat. fat), 136 mg chol., 761 mg sodium, 31 g carbo., 2 g fiber, 37 g pro. **Daily Values:** 11% vit. A, 7% vit. C, 8% calcium, 20% iron.

WHY A CAPON?

Capons are male chickens castrated at a young age and fed a special diet so they grow big—weighing between 4 and 10 pounds. They have delicately flavored, tender flesh and a lot of white meat. Although they cost more per pound than ordinary chicken, stuffed and roasted, as in the recipe, left, they're nice for a change of pace from regular chicken or turkey.

127

THE ELEMENTS OF STUFFING

For many stuffing fans, the only reason for the turkey at Thanksgiving is to hold the stuffing. Stuffing, or dressing as it also is called, requires three elements: a starch, such as bread, corn bread, rice, or potatoes; a liquid, such as broth, wine, or liquor (or a combination of these); and other additions that can include herbs, onions, dried or fresh fruits, sausage or other meats, or seafood, such as oysters, crab, or shrimp. If you want to create your own recipe, keep these proportions in mind:

• For every 1 cup of bread or other starch, you will need about 2 tablespoons of liquid, just enough to moisten the bread.

• For each pound of uncooked poultry, you will need about ³/₄ cup stuffing.

• If you just want stuffing, there's no requirement for a bird. Mediterranean Fig Dressing (see recipe, right) is baked in a 1-quart casserole.

mediterranean fig dressing

prep: 25 minutes   *bake:* 55 minutes   *makes:* 4 servings

¹/₂ cup coarsely chopped dried figs
1 tablespoon brandy or dry red or white wine
1¹/₂ cups pita bread rounds, cut into thin strips
1¹/₂ cups Italian bread cubes
2 cloves garlic, minced
3 tablespoons margarine or butter
1¹/₂ teaspoons snipped fresh rosemary or
¹/₄ teaspoon dried rosemary, crushed

1¹/₂ teaspoons snipped fresh thyme or
¹/₂ teaspoon dried thyme, crushed
¹/₂ cup chopped Spanish or yellow onion
¹/₄ cup chopped walnuts
¹/₂ to ²/₃ cup chicken broth
Fresh thyme sprigs (optional)

1 In a small bowl combine figs and brandy or wine; set aside. Place pita bread strips and Italian bread cubes in a shallow baking pan; set aside.

2 In a small skillet cook garlic in margarine or butter for 1 minute; reserve 1 tablespoon of the margarine mixture in skillet. Drizzle the remaining mixture over bread strips and cubes; sprinkle with rosemary and thyme. Bake in a 350° oven for 15 to 20 minutes or until bread is toasted, stirring once.

3 Meanwhile, in the small skillet cook onion in the reserved 1 tablespoon of margarine or butter mixture until tender; set aside. In a medium bowl combine bread cube mixture, undrained fig mixture, onion mixture, and walnuts. Add enough chicken broth to moisten, tossing lightly. Transfer stuffing to a lightly greased 1-quart casserole.

4 Bake, covered, in a 350° oven for 40 to 45 minutes or until heated through. If desired, garnish with fresh thyme sprigs.

Nutrition Facts per serving: 127 cal., 7 g total fat (1 g sat. fat), 0 mg chol., 179 mg sodium, 14 g carbo., 1 g fiber, 3 g pro. **Daily Values:** 5% vit. A, 2% vit. C, 3% calcium, 5% iron.

duck breast
with lime sauce

prep: 20 minutes   **grill:** 10 minutes   **makes:** 4 servings

½ cup currant jelly
¼ cup sweet or semidry white wine,
        such as Riesling or Sauternes
1 tablespoon raspberry vinegar, white
        balsamic vinegar, or vinegar
1 teaspoon finely shredded lime peel
1 tablespoon lime juice
¼ teaspoon grated fresh ginger

⅛ teaspoon salt
    Dash black pepper
1 tablespoon margarine or butter
2 teaspoons olive oil
4 skinless, boneless duck breasts or chicken
        breast halves (about 1 pound total)
    Mediterranean Fig Dressing (optional)

1 For sauce, in a small saucepan combine jelly, wine, vinegar, lime peel, lime juice, ginger, salt, and black pepper. Bring to boiling; reduce heat. Simmer, uncovered, about 12 minutes or until sauce is slightly thickened and reduced to ½ cup. Remove from heat; stir in margarine or butter. Transfer ¼ cup sauce to a small bowl for basting. Keep remaining sauce warm until ready to serve.

2 Meanwhile, brush oil over both sides of duck breasts. Grill duck on the rack of an uncovered grill directly over medium heat for 10 to 12 minutes or until tender and no pink remains, turning once and brushing with the ¼ cup sauce during the last 5 minutes of grilling. Serve the duck with the warm sauce and, if desired, Mediterranean Fig Dressing (see page 128).

Nutrition Facts per serving: 222 cal., 8 g total fat (2 g sat. fat), 22 mg chol., 124 mg sodium, 29 g carbo., 0 g fiber, 6 g pro. **Daily Values:** 4% vit. A, 5% vit. C, 1% calcium, 8% iron.

BUYING AND COOKING DUCK

Duck or duckling is known for its distinctive, earthy flavor and dark, moist meat. Most of the ducks sold in the supermarket are commercially raised and are between 3 and 6 pounds. Duck is available fresh and frozen, whole, or in packages of breasts only. When purchasing a duck, remember, the darker the flesh, the older the duck. Look for USDA Grade A duck with a plump, firm breast.

Domestic duck is fattier than its wild cousin and most other types of poultry. It has a thick layer of fat under the skin (which makes the meat incredibly moist). Prick the skin before you roast or grill a duck to allow the fat to escape.

turkey tender steaks
& sweet pepper-citrus salsa

prep: 15 minutes   *marinate:* 2 hours   *grill:* 12 minutes   *makes:* 6 servings

6 turkey breast tenderloin steaks, cut
   $\frac{1}{2}$ inch thick (about 1$\frac{1}{2}$ pounds total)*
$\frac{1}{3}$ cup olive oil
$\frac{1}{4}$ cup lemon juice
1 teaspoon finely shredded orange peel

$\frac{1}{4}$ cup orange juice
4 cloves garlic, minced
$\frac{1}{4}$ teaspoon salt
$\frac{1}{4}$ teaspoon pepper

1 Place turkey in a heavy plastic bag set in a shallow bowl.

2 For marinade, in a small bowl combine oil, lemon juice, orange peel, orange juice, garlic, salt, and pepper. Pour over turkey; seal bag. Marinate in the refrigerator 2 to 4 hours, turning occasionally.

3 Drain turkey, reserving marinade. Grill turkey on the rack of an uncovered grill directly over medium coals for 12 to 15 minutes or until turkey is tender and no longer pink, turning once halfway through grilling and brushing with marinade during the first 6 minutes of grilling. Serve with Sweet Pepper-Citrus Salsa.

Sweet Pepper-Citrus Salsa: In a small bowl combine one 7-ounce jar roasted red sweet peppers, drained and chopped; 1 orange, peeled, seeded, and cut up; 2 green onions, sliced; 2 tablespoons balsamic vinegar; and 1 tablespoon snipped fresh basil or 1 teaspoon dried basil, crushed. Cover and refrigerate salsa until serving time. Makes 1$\frac{1}{2}$ cups salsa.

Nutrition Facts with $\frac{1}{4}$ cup salsa: 222 cal.,
10 g total fat (2 g sat. fat), 50 mg chol.,
108 mg sodium, 10 g carbo., 2 g fiber, 22 g pro.
Daily Values: 22% vit. A, 132% vit. C, 13% iron.

*Note: Precut turkey breast tenderloin steaks are available in some areas. If you find only the large whole tenderloins, slice them horizontally into $\frac{1}{2}$-inch-thick steaks.

TURKEY STEAKS

Though there are not nearly as many types of turkey steak as there are beef steak, turkey steak is a toothsome, meaty, full-flavored cut of the bird that is as versatile as its bovine counterpart. Like beef steak, turkey steak is terrific grilled, broiled, and pan-fried.

Generally, you'll find two types of turkey steaks at the supermarket: breast steaks, which are $\frac{1}{2}$- to 1-inch-thick crosswise cuts from the turkey breast; and tenderloin steaks, which are lengthwise cuts from the turkey tenderloin, about $\frac{1}{2}$ inch thick.

131

Boneless chicken breast is a great candidate for stuffing because it can be easily flattened (see step 1, right) and goes well with a variety of fillings.

To stuff a chicken breast, place 2 to 3 tablespoons of filling in the center of each flattened chicken piece. Fold in the bottom and sides and roll up (see photo, above). Secure with wooden toothpicks.

Once you've made the recipe at right a few times, you may want to experiment with different fillings. Some of the nearly limitless combinations include mozzarella, prosciutto, and red peppers; feta cheese and fresh spinach; goat cheese and fresh herbs; wild rice and pistachios.

chicken stuffed with
smoked mozzarella

prep: 40 minutes   ***bake:*** 25 minutes   ***makes:*** 6 servings

6 skinless, boneless chicken breast halves (about 1½ pounds total)
   Salt
   Pepper
¼ cup finely chopped shallots or onions
1 clove garlic, minced
2 teaspoons olive oil

½ of a 10-ounce package frozen chopped spinach, thawed and well drained
3 tablespoons pine nuts or walnuts, toasted
¾ cup shredded smoked mozzarella cheese
¼ cup seasoned fine dry bread crumbs
¼ cup grated Parmesan cheese
1 tablespoon olive oil

1 Place 1 chicken breast half between 2 pieces of plastic wrap. Pound lightly with the flat side of a meat mallet into a rectangle about ⅛ inch thick. Remove plastic wrap. Season with salt and pepper. Repeat process with all chicken breasts.

2 For filling, in a medium skillet cook shallots or onions and garlic in the 2 teaspoons hot oil until tender. Remove from heat; stir in spinach, nuts, and smoked mozzarella.

3 In a shallow bowl combine bread crumbs and Parmesan cheese.

4 Fill each roll, using 2 to 3 tablespoons of filling (see tip, left).

5 Lightly brush each roll with the 1 tablespoon olive oil; coat with bread crumb mixture. Place rolls, seam side down, in a shallow baking pan. Bake, uncovered, in a 400° oven about 25 minutes or until chicken is tender and no longer pink. Remove toothpicks before serving.

Nutrition Facts per serving: 274 cal., 11 g total fat (3 g sat. fat), 77 mg chol., 368 mg sodium, 6 g carbo., 1 g fiber, 35 g pro. **Daily Values:** 39% vit. A, 6% vit. C, 18% calcium, 8% iron.

Roasted Cornish hens are great stuffed, of course, but for quicker cooking, butterfly them as called for in Citrus-Marinated Cornish Hen (see recipe, right). Butterflying simply means removing the backbone so the hen can be opened up like a book and laid flat (see photo, above). The greater surface area exposed when the birds are flat allows them to cook faster.

To butterfly a Cornish hen, place it back side up on a cutting board. Using poultry shears, cut closely along one side of the backbone. Repeat on the other side; discard backbone. Turn breast side up. Open the bird so the drumsticks point out. Press the breastbone firmly to flatten.

citrus-marinated
cornish hen

prep: 25 minutes   *marinate:* 2 hours   *roast:* 45 minutes   *makes:* 4 servings

2   1¼- to 1½-pound Cornish game hens
1   tablespoon finely shredded orange peel
¼   cup orange juice
2   tablespoons snipped fresh chives
2   tablespoons lime juice
1   teaspoon finely shredded lemon peel
2   tablespoons lemon juice
2   tablespoons rice vinegar

2   tablespoons minced fresh garlic
2   tablespoons olive oil
1   tablespoon snipped cilantro
1   tablespoon snipped fresh parsley
1   tablespoon grated fresh ginger
2   teaspoons sugar
¼   teaspoon salt
½   teaspoon pepper

1 Butterfly hens (see tip, left). Place butterflied hens in a plastic bag set in a large bowl; set aside.

2 For marinade, whisk together orange peel, orange juice, chives, lime juice, lemon peel, lemon juice, rice vinegar, garlic, olive oil, cilantro, parsley, ginger, sugar, salt, and pepper. Pour marinade over hens; seal bag. Marinate in the refrigerator for 2 to 4 hours, turning bag occasionally.

3 Drain hens; discard marinade. Place hens on a rack in a shallow roasting pan. Tuck wings under hens. Use a brush to evenly distribute any marinade solids that cling to the birds.

4 Roast, uncovered, in a 375° oven about 45 minutes or until hens are tender and no longer pink or until a meat thermometer inserted in the thigh registers 180°. (Thermometer should not touch bone.)

Nutrition Facts per serving: 756 cal., 49 g total fat (11 g sat. fat), 240 mg chol., 275 mg sodium, 6 g carbo., 0 g fiber, 73 g pro. **Daily Values:** 2% vit. A, 23% vit. C, 2% calcium, 2% iron.

roasted italian chicken

prep: 15 minutes   **roast:** 1¼ hours   **makes:** 6 servings

2 tablespoons balsamic vinegar

2 tablespoons olive oil

1 tablespoon lemon juice

3 cloves garlic, minced

½ teaspoon salt

½ teaspoon coarsely ground black pepper

1 tablespoon snipped fresh oregano or

    1 teaspoon dried oregano, crushed

1 tablespoon snipped fresh basil or

    1 teaspoon dried basil, crushed

1½ teaspoons snipped fresh thyme or

    ½ teaspoon dried thyme, crushed

1 3- to 3½-pound whole broiler-fryer chicken

1 In a small bowl whisk together vinegar, oil, lemon juice, garlic, salt, pepper, oregano, basil, and thyme. Set aside.

2 Place chicken, breast side up, on a rack in a shallow roasting pan. Tie legs to tail. Twist wing tips under back. Slip your fingers between the skin and the breast and leg meat of the chicken, forming a pocket. Spoon herb mixture into pocket (see photo, right).

3 Roast, uncovered, in a 375° oven for 1¼ to 1½ hours or until drumsticks move easily in their sockets, chicken is no longer pink, and a meat thermometer inserted into inside thigh muscle registers 180° (see tip, below). Remove chicken from oven. Cover with foil; let stand for 10 minutes before carving.

Nutrition Facts per serving: 266 cal., 17 g total fat (4 g sat. fat), 79 mg chol., 268 mg sodium, 2 g carbo., 0 g fiber, 25 g pro. **Daily Values:** 5% vit. A, 2% vit. C, 3% calcium, 8% iron.

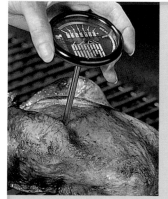

Judging when poultry is cooked

The safest way to determine the doneness of whole birds and other large pieces of poultry is to use a meat thermometer. You can choose from liquid-filled, instant-read, and digital thermometers.

    To use the thermometer, insert it into the thickest part of the bird, the inside thigh muscle (see photo, left). Don't let it touch any bones or fat. Take the bird out of the oven (or off the grill) when the thermometer reads 180°. Cover it with foil and let it stand 10 to 15 minutes before carving. During this time, the bird will continue to cook, so the internal temperature of the bird will rise about 5° to 185°.

USING AN UNDER-THE-SKIN RUB

Roasted chicken tastes even better if something flavorful, such as an herb, is placed under its skin. The under-the-skin rub used in Roasted Italian Chicken (see recipe, left), for example, adds a lot of flavor while working like a marinade.

    To get the herb mixture easily under the skin of the bird, lift the skin gently away from the breast right above the cavity (see recipe, left, and photo, above). You should have a nice, large pocket for tucking in the herb mixture with a spoon.

Fresh ginger adds a slightly hot, spicy flavor and fragrant aroma that are hard to resist. Working with it is easy.

To peel fresh ginger, cut off one end of the root and peel with a vegetable peeler, moving down the root (see photo, above).

If a recipe calls for grated fresh ginger, as in the recipe at right, the grater you use should have fine openings.

If a recipe calls for minced ginger, it's best to mince it by hand. If you try to mince ginger in a food processor, you'll end up with lots of unappetizing little strings and fibers. To mince the root, slice the peeled ginger with the grain (lengthwise) into thin sticks. Stack the sticks in a bundle and cut them finely.

lemongrass chicken & rice noodles

prep: 25 minutes   *grill:* 12 minutes   *makes:* 4 servings

¼ cup finely chopped green onions	¼ cup fish sauce
¼ cup finely chopped lemongrass	3 to 4 tablespoons fresh lime juice
1 tablespoon grated fresh ginger	2 tablespoons brown sugar
6 cloves garlic, minced	1 to 2 cloves garlic, minced
4 skinless, boneless chicken breast halves (about 1 pound total)	1 cup shredded carrots
8 ounces dried rice noodles	¼ cup coarsely snipped fresh cilantro
	¼ cup coarsely chopped peanuts

1 For rub, in a food processor bowl or blender container, combine green onions, lemongrass, ginger, and the 6 cloves garlic. Cover and process or blend with a few on-off turns until mixture forms a paste. Use your fingers to rub lemongrass-ginger paste evenly onto both sides of chicken breast halves.

2 Grill chicken on the rack of an uncovered grill directly over medium coals for 12 to 15 minutes or until chicken is tender and no longer pink, turning once halfway through grilling. Cut chicken into thin, diagonal slices. Set chicken aside.

3 Meanwhile, cook noodles in a large amount of boiling water for 3 to 4 minutes or until just tender; drain. In a medium bowl combine fish sauce, lime juice, brown sugar, and the 1 to 2 cloves garlic; stir until brown sugar dissolves. Add hot cooked noodles, carrots, cilantro, and peanuts; toss lightly to coat.

4 Arrange sliced chicken over hot noodle mixture. Serve immediately.

Nutrition Facts per serving: 431 cal., 6 g total fat (1 g sat. fat), 66 mg chol., 471 mg sodium, 63 g carbo., 2 g fiber, 30 g pro. **Daily Values:** 81% vit. A, 20% vit. C, 7% calcium, 18% iron.

Working with lemongrass

Lemongrass, a highly aromatic, lemon-flavored herb, is used in many Asian dishes, such as the one above. It has layers similar to a leek and should be treated the same. Trim the fibrous ends and slice what remains into 3- to 4-inch sections. Cut each section in half lengthwise, exposing the layers. Rinse the pieces under cold water to remove any grit and slice the lemongrass thinly.

MARINATING POULTRY

Marinating poultry not only makes the meat more tender, it adds wonderful flavor. Usually, a marinade consists of an acid, such as vinegar or lemon juice; seasonings; and cooking or olive oil. The acid acts as a tenderizer, the seasonings make the poultry flavorful, and the oil does a little bit of both.

Because marinades contain acid, they should always be placed in a ceramic, glass, or stainless-steel container—never aluminum. Better yet, use a big plastic bag to simplify cleanup and help ensure the marinade is evenly distributed.

Never marinate anything at room temperature longer than 30 minutes. If a recipe calls for longer marinating, place the food in the refrigerator. Turn the bag occasionally to distribute the marinade.

asian-style turkey
with fruit salsa

prep: 20 minutes   **marinate:** 4 hours   **broil:** 8 minutes   **makes:** 4 servings

1 pound turkey breast tenderloins or skinless, boneless chicken breast halves
¼ cup dry white wine
¼ cup orange juice
¼ cup soy sauce
2 tablespoons water

1 tablespoon rice vinegar
1 tablespoon cooking oil
1 teaspoon garlic powder
1 teaspoon ground ginger
   Fruit Salsa

1 Cut turkey or chicken lengthwise into thin strips. Place strips in a plastic bag set in a shallow bowl. For marinade, combine wine, orange juice, soy sauce, water, rice vinegar, oil, garlic powder, and ginger. Pour over meat strips; seal bag. Marinate in the refrigerator for 4 hours, turning bag occasionally.

2 Drain meat, discarding the marinade. Thread meat strips onto metal skewers accordion-style. Place on the unheated rack of a broiler pan. Broil 4 inches from heat for 8 to 10 minutes or until tender and no longer pink, turning once. Serve with Fruit Salsa.

Nutrition Facts per serving: 143 cal., 3 g total fat (1 g sat. fat), 50 mg chol., 390 mg sodium, 4 g carbo., 0 g fiber, 22 g pro. **Daily Values:** 21% vit. C, 1% calcium, 7% iron.

Fruit Salsa: In a medium bowl stir together 1 cup peeled, chopped papaya or mango; 1 cup chopped pineapple; ¼ cup finely chopped red onion; ¼ cup chopped sweet pepper; 3 tablespoons snipped fresh cilantro; 1 teaspoon finely shredded lime or lemon peel; 2 tablespoons lime or lemon juice; 2 to 4 teaspoons finely chopped jalapeño pepper;* and 1 teaspoon grated fresh ginger. Cover and chill salsa for 8 to 24 hours.

*Note: Hot peppers contain oils that can burn your eyes, lips, and skin, so protect yourself when working with the peppers by covering your hands with plastic bags or plastic or rubber gloves. Wash hands thoroughly before touching your eyes or face.

Safely using leftover marinades
If a recipe calls for leftover marinade to be served with the finished food, such as Mustard Chicken Barbecue, page 143, boil it thoroughly before you serve it. Boiling destroys any harmful bacteria that may have been transferred from the raw poultry or meat to the marinade.

thyme chicken marsala

prep: 25 minutes   **cook:** 13 minutes   **makes:** 2 servings

- 2 skinless, boneless chicken breast halves
- 1 tablespoon all-purpose flour
- 2 tablespoons olive oil
- 1 medium carrot, cut into thin strips
- 1 small red or yellow sweet pepper, cut into thin strips
- 2 cloves garlic, minced

- ¼ teaspoon salt
- ¼ teaspoon black pepper
- ⅓ cup dry Marsala
- 1 tablespoon snipped fresh thyme or ¼ teaspoon dried thyme, crushed
  Hot cooked linguine or other pasta (optional)

1 Place 1 chicken breast half between 2 pieces of plastic wrap. Pound lightly with the flat side of a meat mallet into a rectangle about ¼ inch thick. Remove plastic wrap. Repeat process with other breast. Coat breasts lightly with flour; shake off excess. Set aside.

2 In a large skillet heat 1 tablespoon of the oil. Add the carrot strips and cook for 3 minutes. Add the pepper strips, garlic, salt, and black pepper to the skillet. Cook and stir about 5 minutes or until crisp-tender. Arrange vegetable mixture on 2 dinner plates. Cover and keep warm.

3 In the same skillet heat the remaining 1 tablespoon oil over medium heat. Add chicken; cook for 2 to 3 minutes on each side until chicken is tender and no longer pink. Place chicken on top of vegetables. Keep warm.

4 Add the Marsala and thyme to the skillet. Cook and stir for 1 minute, scraping up any browned bits from skillet. Pour over chicken. If desired, serve with linguine or other pasta.

Nutrition Facts per serving: 311 cal., 17 g total fat (3 g sat. fat), 59 mg chol., 350 mg sodium, 10 g carbo., 2 g fiber, 23 g pro. **Daily Values:** 119% vit. A, 81% vit. C, 3% calcium, 11% iron.

CRUSHING DRIED HERBS

You'll get more flavor out of dried herbs if you crush them before adding them in recipes.

For the correct amount of herb, first measure it in a measuring spoon, then empty the spoon into your hand. Crush the herb with the fingers of your other hand to release the herb's flavor, and add it to the specified ingredients.

Some dried herbs, such as rosemary and thyme, are more easily crushed with a mortar and pestle—but if you don't have one, try crushing them with a wooden spoon against the inside of a bowl. This is not an ideal substitute for a mortar and pestle but should do in a pinch.

WHAT IS DREDGING?

The culinary technique known as dredging is a simple process of coating a piece of food that is to be fried—such as poultry, meat, or fish— with seasoned flour, cornmeal, or bread crumbs.

To make the dry mixture stick better, the pieces often are dipped first in liquid, such as buttermilk, milk, beaten eggs, or a mixture of eggs and milk. This also makes for a thicker, crunchier crust.

To keep your fingers from getting more coating on them than the food, use one hand for dipping the food in liquid and the other for dipping it in breading. Your dry hand can be used to sprinkle the breading onto the food (see photo, above).

almond chicken with
yogurt dipping sauce

prep: 15 minutes   ***cook:*** 10 minutes   ***makes:*** 6 servings

¼ cup all-purpose flour	½ cup milk
1 cup soft bread crumbs	1½ pounds skinless, boneless chicken
½ cup chopped almonds	breast halves
2 tablespoons snipped fresh cilantro	¼ cup cooking oil
1½ teaspoons curry powder	Yogurt Dipping Sauce
1 egg	

1 In a shallow dish place the flour. In another shallow dish, combine bread crumbs, almonds, cilantro, and curry powder; set aside. In another shallow dish beat together egg and milk; set aside.

2 Cut chicken, lengthwise, into 1-inch-wide strips. Coat strips with flour, dip in egg mixture, then coat with almond mixture. Heat oil in a large skillet. Carefully add strips to hot oil. Cook over medium heat for 10 to 12 minutes or until chicken is tender and no longer pink, turning once. Drain on paper towels. Serve with Yogurt Dipping Sauce.

Yogurt Dipping Sauce: Stir together one 8-ounce carton plain yogurt, 2 tablespoons snipped fresh cilantro, and 1 tablespoon honey. Use immediately or cover and chill in the refrigerator until needed.

Nutrition Facts per serving: 365 cal.,18 g total fat (3 g sat. fat), 105 mg chol., 150 mg sodium, 17 g carbo., 2 g fiber, 33 g pro. **Daily Values:** 59% vit. A, 5% vit. C, 15% calcium, 11% iron.

FRESH HERB EXCHANGE

The use of fresh herbs is one of the hallmarks of fresh-tasting, flavorful cooking. Although each herb has its own distinctive flavor, there's no culinary rule that says you can't substitute one for another. Here are some fresh herb alternates to try:

- **Sage:** savory, marjoram, rosemary.
- **Basil:** oregano, thyme.
- **Thyme:** basil, marjoram, oregano, savory.
- **Mint:** basil, marjoram, rosemary.
- **Rosemary:** thyme, tarragon, savory.
- **Cilantro:** parsley.

provençal chicken & herbed penne

start to finish: 25 minutes   *makes:* 4 servings

8 ounces dried tomato or garlic and herb-flavored penne pasta or plain penne pasta
4 medium skinless, boneless chicken breast halves (about 1 pound total)
1 medium zucchini, halved lengthwise
8 thick asparagus spears (8 to 10 ounces total), trimmed
3 tablespoons olive oil
1 tablespoon fines herbes or herbes de Provence, crushed (see tip, below)
$\frac{1}{2}$ teaspoon salt
1 tablespoon snipped fresh thyme
$\frac{1}{2}$ cup finely shredded Asiago or Pecorino Romano cheese
   Pepper

1 Cook pasta according to package directions. Meanwhile, brush chicken, zucchini, and asparagus with 1 tablespoon of the oil; sprinkle all sides with fines herbes or herbes de Provence and salt.

2 Place the chicken in the center of the lightly greased rack of an uncovered grill; place the zucchini and asparagus around chicken. Grill directly over medium heat for 12 to 15 minutes or until chicken is tender and no longer pink and vegetables are tender, turning once.

3 Transfer chicken and vegetables to cutting board; cool slightly. Cut chicken and zucchini into 1-inch cubes; slice asparagus into 1-inch-long pieces.

4 Drain pasta; return to saucepan. Add chicken, vegetables, remaining oil, and thyme to pasta; toss well. Divide among 4 dinner plates; top with cheese and season with pepper.

Nutrition Facts per serving: 480 cal., 17 g total fat (2 g sat. fat), 69 mg chol., 492 mg sodium, 45 g carbo., 4 g fiber, 35 g pro. **Daily Values:** 7% vit. A, 20% vit. C, 15% calcium, 17% iron.

Fines herbes & herbes de Provence

Fines herbes and *herbes de Provence*—both French herb blends—are interchangeable. Fines herbes is a quartet of chervil, chives, parsley, and tarragon. Herbes de Provence is a melange of basil, fennel, lavender, marjoram, rosemary, sage, savory, and thyme.

mustard chicken
barbecue

prep: 20 minutes   ***marinate:*** 4 hours   ***grill:*** 50 minutes   ***makes:*** 4 servings

- 4 whole chicken legs (thigh-drumstick piece);
    4 chicken drumsticks and 4 chicken
    thighs (about 3 pounds total); or
    4 chicken breast halves (about
    2 pounds total)
- 1/2 cup Dijon-style mustard

- 3 tablespoons vinegar
- 4 teaspoons Worcestershire sauce
- 1 teaspoon snipped fresh thyme
    or 1/8 teaspoon dried thyme, crushed
- 2 tablespoons light-flavored molasses

1 If desired, remove skin from chicken. Place chicken in a plastic bag set in a shallow dish; set aside.

2 For marinade, stir together mustard, vinegar, Worcestershire sauce, and thyme. Pour marinade over chicken; seal bag. Marinate in the refrigerator for 4 to 24 hours, turning bag occasionally.

3 Drain chicken, reserving marinade. Set aside 1/3 cup of the marinade for sauce.

4 In a grill with a cover arrange medium-hot coals around a drip pan. Test for medium heat above the pan (see tip, below).

Place the chicken pieces, bone side down, on the grill rack over drip pan. Cover and grill for 50 to 60 minutes or until tender and no longer pink, brushing occasionally with marinade up to the last 5 minutes of grilling.

5 Meanwhile, for sauce, in a small saucepan combine the reserved 1/3 cup marinade and the molasses. Bring to boiling; reduce heat. Simmer, covered, for 5 minutes. Pass sauce with chicken.

Nutrition Facts per serving: 327 cal., 17 g total fat (4 g sat. fat), 103 mg chol., 904 mg sodium, 10 g carbo., 0 g fiber, 31 g pro. **Daily Values:** 4% vit. A, 14% vit. C, 3% calcium, 15% iron.

How hot is hot?

Some foods need to be grilled hot and fast, some low and slow. The recipe will specify the heat you need. To gauge how hot the coals in your grill are, hold the palm of your hand a few inches over the center of the grill rack, where the food will cook. If you can hold your hand there 2 seconds or less, the coals are hot; 3 seconds, they are medium-hot; 4 seconds, they are medium; 5 seconds, they are medium-low; and 6 seconds, they are low. When grilling indirectly, hot coals will provide medium-hot heat and medium-hot coals will provide medium heat.

DIRECT VERSUS INDIRECT GRILLING

The great thing about grilling is you can tailor it to the type of food you have.

Direct grilling, which means positioning the food directly over the hot coals and cooking uncovered, is best suited to foods that are tender, small, or thin, and cook quickly.

Indirect grilling means placing food adjacent to rather than directly over the coals and grilling covered. This is the best method for whole birds, big cuts of meat, and whole vegetables.

For indirect grilling in a charcoal grill, heat the coals until they are covered with gray ash; then use long-handled tongs to position them around the edge of the grill. Position a drip pan in the center of the grill, directly under where the food will be placed (see photo, above).

143

MAKING PERFECT GRAVY

Gravy is the star of many great dishes, such as Maryland Fried Chicken (see recipe, right). Here are a few secrets to help you make sensational gravy:

• If you're making gravy for something that's been roasted or pan-fried, deglaze the pan (see tip, page 153) and use the drippings for extra flavor.

• For lump-free gravy, make sure the flour or cornstarch is thoroughly mixed with the fat or the cold liquid before cooking it.

• Cook and stir constantly (use a whisk) until the gravy boils and thickens.

• Browned bits of meat or poultry in gravy add lots of flavor—don't bother with straining them out.

• To finish gravy, season it to taste with salt and pepper and, if needed, thin it with a little broth, wine, or milk.

maryland fried chicken

prep: 25 minutes   **cook:** 55 minutes   **makes:** 6 servings

  1 beaten egg
  3 tablespoons milk
  1 cup finely crushed saltine crackers
       (28 crackers)
  1 teaspoon dried thyme, crushed
 $\frac{1}{2}$ teaspoon paprika
 $\frac{1}{8}$ teaspoon pepper

 $2\frac{1}{2}$ to 3 pounds meaty chicken pieces
       (breasts, thighs, and drumsticks)
  2 to 3 tablespoons cooking oil
  1 cup milk
     Cream Gravy
     Hot mashed potatoes (optional)
     Fresh thyme sprigs (optional)

1 In a small bowl combine the egg and the 3 tablespoons milk. In a shallow bowl combine crushed crackers, thyme, paprika, and pepper. Rinse chicken; pat dry. Dip chicken pieces, 1 at a time, in egg mixture, then roll in cracker mixture.

2 In a large skillet cook chicken, uncovered, in hot oil over medium heat for 10 to 15 minutes, turning occasionally to brown evenly. Remove chicken from skillet and drain fat. Return chicken to skillet.

3 Add the 1 cup milk to skillet. Reduce heat to medium-low; cover. Cook for 35 minutes. Uncover; cook for 10 minutes more or until chicken is tender and no longer pink. Drain on paper towels. Transfer chicken to a serving platter; cover and keep warm. Prepare Cream Gravy. If desired, serve with mashed potatoes and garnish with fresh thyme.

Nutrition Facts per serving: 409 cal., 23 g total fat (5 g sat. fat), 118 mg chol., 398 mg sodium, 17 g carbo., 1 g fiber, 30 g pro. **Daily Values:** 9% vit. A, 1% vit. C, 13% calcium, 13% iron.

Cream Gravy: Skim fat from drippings. Reserve 3 tablespoons of drippings in skillet. In a screw-top jar combine ¾ cup milk, 3 tablespoons all-purpose flour, ¼ teaspoon salt, and ⅛ teaspoon pepper; cover and shake well. Add to skillet. Stir in ¾ cup milk. Cook over medium heat, stirring constantly, until thickened and bubbly. Cook and stir for 1 minute more. (If desired, thin with additional milk.)

When a recipe such as Deep-Dish Chicken Pie (see recipe, right) calls for cooked chicken and you don't have any leftovers, stop by the supermarket and pick up a deli-roasted chicken (a cooked chicken yields 1½ to 2 cups of chopped meat). Or, if you prefer to cook chicken breasts at home, follow these steps.

To poach chicken breasts, place ¾ pound of skinless, boneless chicken breasts in a large skillet with 1½ cups water. Bring to boiling; reduce heat. Simmer, covered, for 12 to 14 minutes or until the chicken is tender and no longer pink. Drain well.

If you're chopping or shredding the chicken, you can do it while it's warm. But if you need even slices of chicken or cubed chicken, chill the chicken first. To quick-chill chicken, cover and place it in the freezer for 30 minutes.

deep-dish chicken pie

prep: 50 minutes   *bake:* 30 minutes   *cool:* 20 minutes   *makes:* 6 servings

Pastry Topper
3 medium leeks or 1 large onion, chopped
1 cup sliced fresh mushrooms
¾ cup sliced celery
½ cup chopped red sweet pepper
2 tablespoons margarine or butter
⅓ cup all-purpose flour
1 teaspoon poultry seasoning
¼ teaspoon salt
¼ teaspoon pepper
1½ cups chicken broth
1 cup half-and-half, light cream, or milk
2½ cups chopped cooked chicken
1 cup frozen peas
1 egg, beaten

1 On a lightly floured surface, roll Pastry Topper into a rectangle ⅛ inch thick and at least 13×9 inches. Trim to a 12×8-inch rectangle. Using a sharp knife, cut slits in pastry to allow steam to escape. If desired, use a small cookie cutter to cut shapes from pastry. Set aside.

2 In a large saucepan cook leeks or onion, mushrooms, celery, and sweet pepper in hot margarine or butter over medium heat for 4 to 5 minutes or until tender. Stir in flour, poultry seasoning, salt, and pepper. Add broth and half-and-half, light cream, or milk all at once. Cook and stir until thickened and bubbly. Stir in chicken and peas. Pour into a 2-quart rectangular baking dish.

3 Place pastry over the hot chicken mixture in dish; turn edges of pastry under and flute to top edges of dish. Brush with some of the beaten egg. If desired, place reserved pastry shapes on top of pastry. Brush again with egg.

4 Bake, uncovered, in a 400° oven for 30 to 35 minutes or until crust is golden brown. Cool 20 minutes before serving.

Nutrition Facts per serving: 470 cal., 26 g total fat (8 g sat. fat), 103 mg chol., 598 mg sodium, 33 g carbo., 3 g fiber, 25 g pro. **Daily Values:** 20% vit. A, 49% vit. C, 9% calcium, 18% iron.

Pastry Topper: In a medium bowl stir together 1¼ cups all-purpose flour and ¼ teaspoon salt. Using a pastry blender, cut in ⅓ cup shortening until pieces are the size of small peas. Sprinkle 1 tablespoon cold water over part of the mixture; gently toss with fork. Push moistened dough to side of bowl. Repeat with 3 to 4 tablespoons cold water, using 1 tablespoon at a time, until all dough is moistened. Form into a ball.

Beef, Pork, & Lamb

Whether you're cutting flank steak when it's raw (see photo, above) or after it's been cooked, as in the recipe, right, the best way to do it is across the grain. "Across the grain" means to cut across the fibers of the meat, rather than with them. Cutting across the fibers makes them shorter so the meat is easier to chew. For most flank steaks, this means slicing across the width of the steak rather than its length (see photo, above).

flank steak on tap

prep: 20 minutes   *marinate:* 4 hours   *grill:* 12 minutes   *makes:* 4 servings

1 large onion, thinly sliced	1 1¼- to 1½-pound beef flank steak
¾ cup beer	¼ teaspoon salt
3 tablespoons Worcestershire sauce	2 teaspoons cornstarch
2 tablespoons brown sugar	Snipped fresh parsley (optional)
3 cloves garlic, minced	Coarsely ground pepper (optional)
1 bay leaf	
¼ teaspoon coarsely ground pepper	

1 For marinade, in a small saucepan combine onion, beer, Worcestershire sauce, brown sugar, garlic, bay leaf, and the ¼ teaspoon pepper. Bring to boiling; reduce heat. Simmer, uncovered, for 4 to 5 minutes or until sugar is dissolved and onion and garlic are crisp-tender. Cool to room temperature.

2 Score both sides of steak (see tip, below). Place the steak in a plastic bag set in a shallow dish. Pour marinade over steak; seal bag. Marinate in refrigerator for 4 to 24 hours, turning occasionally.

3 Drain steak, reserving marinade. Remove bay leaf. Season steak with salt. Grill steak on the rack of an uncovered grill directly over medium heat to desired doneness, turning once. (Allow 12 to 14 minutes for medium doneness.)

4 Meanwhile, for sauce, in a small saucepan combine reserved marinade and cornstarch. Cook and stir over medium heat until thickened and bubbly. Cook and stir 2 minutes more.

5 To serve, thinly slice steak diagonally across the grain (see tip, left). Spoon sauce over steak. If desired, sprinkle with parsley and pepper.

Nutrition Facts per serving: 185 cal., 7 g total fat (3 g sat. fat), 44 mg chol., 221 mg sodium, 10 g carbo., 1 g fiber, 17 g pro. **Daily Values:** 25% vit. C, 2% calcium, 16% iron.

Scoring meat

Scoring meat, as in Flank Steak on Tap (see recipe, above), accomplishes two things: It makes the meat more tender, and it forms a decorative diamond pattern. To score a flank steak, cut the steak in a diamond pattern by making shallow diagonal cuts in two directions at 1-inch intervals. Don't cut too deeply or you'll lose flavorful moisture-imparting meat juices. Cut only about ⅛ inch into the surface of the meat; this depth is enough to allow the tenderizing marinade to penetrate the meat.

herbed strip steak
with balsamic sauce

prep: 10 minutes   *cook:* 12 minutes   *makes:* 4 servings

1	tablespoon cracked black pepper
1½	teaspoons dried basil, crushed
1½	teaspoons dried oregano, crushed
1	teaspoon garlic powder
2	boneless beef top loin (strip) steaks, cut ¾ inch thick (about 8 ounces each)

1	tablespoon olive oil
¼	cup balsamic vinegar
¼	cup beef broth
1	tablespoon butter or whipping cream
¼	cup snipped fresh parsley

1 In a small bowl combine black pepper, basil, oregano, and garlic powder. Use your fingers to rub the mixture onto both sides of the steaks.

2 In a heavy large skillet cook steaks in hot oil over medium heat until desired doneness, turning once. (Allow 8 to 11 minutes for medium-rare doneness and 12 to 14 minutes for medium doneness.) Remove steaks from skillet, reserving drippings in the skillet. Keep steak warm.

3 For sauce, carefully add vinegar and broth to the skillet, scraping up crusty browned bits. Bring to boiling. Boil gently, uncovered, about 4 minutes or until sauce is reduced by half. Remove from heat; stir in butter or whipping cream.

4 To serve, divide sauce among 4 dinner plates. Place a steak on top of sauce on each plate; sprinkle with parsley.

Nutrition Facts per serving: 346 cal., 26 g total fat (10 g sat. fat), 84 mg chol., 134 mg sodium, 5 g carbo., 0 g fiber, 23 g pro. **Daily Values:** 6% vit. A, 15% vit. C, 2% calcium, 26% iron.

WHAT IS A REDUCTION?

Reduction is aptly named. It's a technique that involves decreasing the volume of a liquid by boiling rapidly to cause evaporation. As the liquid evaporates, it thickens and intensifies in flavor. You can make a quick and easy sauce for meats and roasted vegetables by reducing stock or broth, wine, vinegar, or another liquid.

The amount of reduction needed in a recipe usually is specified in one of two ways. A recipe, such as the one, left, may tell you to reduce a liquid by a general amount—one-third or one-half, for example. Or, it may say to keep boiling until the liquid has reached a specific volume, such as ½ cup or 3 tablespoons. The size of the pan you use will affect the time it takes to reduce a liquid. A bigger pan has a larger surface area and results in faster evaporation. Be sure to use the pan size recommended in the recipe.

grilled beef tenderloin
with mediterranean relish

prep: 25 minutes ***grill:*** 35 minutes ***stand:*** 15 minutes ***makes:*** 10 servings

2 teaspoons dried oregano, crushed
2 teaspoons cracked black pepper
1½ teaspoons finely shredded lemon peel
3 cloves garlic, minced
1 3- to 4-pound center-cut beef tenderloin
2 Japanese eggplants, halved lengthwise
2 red or yellow sweet peppers, halved lengthwise and seeded
1 sweet onion (such as Walla Walla or Vidalia), cut into ½-inch slices

2 tablespoons olive oil
2 plum tomatoes, chopped
2 tablespoons chopped, pitted kalamata olives (see tip, left)
2 tablespoons snipped fresh basil
1 tablespoon balsamic vinegar
¼ to ½ teaspoon salt
⅛ teaspoon ground black pepper

1 In a small bowl combine oregano, cracked pepper, lemon peel, and 2 cloves of the garlic. Use your fingers to rub the mixture onto all sides of the meat.

2 In a grill with a cover, arrange hot coals around a drip pan. Test for medium-hot heat above the pan. Place meat on grill rack over drip pan. Brush eggplants, sweet peppers, and onion slices with olive oil. Arrange vegetables on edges of grill rack directly over coals. Cover and grill for 10 to 12 minutes or until vegetables are tender, turning once. Remove vegetables from grill; set aside. Cover grill and continue grilling meat for 25 to 35 minutes more or until a

meat thermometer inserted in the center registers 140° for medium-rare doneness. Cover; let stand for 15 minutes before slicing.

3 Meanwhile, for relish, coarsely chop grilled vegetables. In a medium bowl combine grilled vegetables, tomatoes, olives, basil, the remaining garlic, the vinegar, salt, and the ⅛ teaspoon ground black pepper. Serve beef with relish.

Nutrition Facts per serving: 240 cal., 12 g total fat (4 g sat. fat), 77 mg chol.,133 mg sodium, 6 g carbo., 2 g fiber, 27 g pro. **Daily Values:** 12% vit. A, 49% vit. C, 1% calcium, 25% iron.

WHAT IS DEMI-GLACE?

Demi-glace (DEHM-ee glahs) is a thick, intense, meat-flavored gel that is a wonderful foundation for soups and sauces. Meaning "half glaze" in French, classic demi-glace is a mixture of brown sauce and brown stock that has been concentrated.

Because making demi-glace is a great deal of work, you'll probably want to buy it already prepared at gourmet shops or through mail-order catalogs. It's available in veal-, chicken-, duck-, fish-, and vegetable-flavored varieties. To use prepared demi-glace, you'll need to reconstitute it with water, using the proportions on the package. For best results, whisk the demi-glace into the water until it dissolves (see photo, above).

pork loin with
shiitake demi-glace

prep: 15 minutes   ***roast:*** 1½ hours   ***stand:*** 15 minutes   ***makes:*** 8 servings

1 3- to 5-pound pork loin center rib roast, backbone loosened
2 teaspoons coarsely ground black pepper
1 teaspoon dried thyme, crushed
1 cup chopped leeks (white part only)
1 cup thinly sliced shiitake mushrooms (stems removed)

1 tablespoon olive oil
1 cup prepared demi-glace, reconstituted (see tip, left)
1 tablespoon rice vinegar
1 tablespoon soy sauce
½ teaspoon ground ginger
½ teaspoon dry mustard

1 Trim fat from meat. Combine black pepper and thyme; sprinkle over roast. Use your fingers to press onto meat. Place roast, rib side down, in a shallow roasting pan. Insert a meat thermometer into the center of the roast without touching bone. Roast in a 325° oven for 1½ to 2 hours or until thermometer registers 155°. Transfer meat to a serving platter. Cover with foil; let stand for 15 minutes. (The temperature of the meat will rise 5° during standing.)

2 Meanwhile, for sauce, in a medium saucepan cook leeks and mushrooms in hot olive oil until tender. Stir in demi-glace, vinegar, soy sauce, ginger, and mustard; heat through. Slice roast between ribs; serve immediately with sauce.

Nutrition Facts per serving: 382 cal., 23 g total fat (7 g sat. fat), 112 mg chol., 338 mg sodium, 4 g carbo., 0 g fiber, 37 g pro. **Daily Values:** 1% vit. A, 4% vit. C, 5% calcium, 10% iron.

tequila new york strip

prep: 30 minutes　　**cook:** 8 minutes　　**makes:** 8 servings

- 1 cup chopped roma tomatoes
- ⅓ cup chopped yellow onion
- ½ cup chopped red sweet pepper
- 1 fresh Anaheim or poblano pepper, seeded and finely chopped
- 1 small fresh jalapeño pepper, seeded and finely chopped
- 2 tablespoons snipped fresh cilantro

- 3 tablespoons lime juice
- 1 teaspoon kosher salt or ¾ teaspoon salt
- 4 1-inch-thick boneless beef top loin steaks (about 12 ounces each)
- 1 tablespoon cooking oil
- ¼ cup tequila
- 3 tablespoons butter or margarine

1 For salsa, in a medium bowl combine tomatoes, onion, sweet pepper, Anaheim or poblano pepper, and jalapeño pepper. Stir in cilantro and 1 tablespoon of the lime juice. Cover and chill up to 4 hours.

2 Use your fingers to rub kosher salt on 1 side of each steak. In a heavy 12-inch skillet cook steaks, salted sides down, in hot oil over medium heat until desired doneness, turning once (allow 8 to 11 minutes for medium-rare and 12 to 14 minutes for medium doneness). Transfer steaks to a serving platter, reserving drippings in skillet. Keep warm.

3 For sauce, add remaining 2 tablespoons lime juice and the tequila to skillet, scraping up any crusty browned bits. Stir in the butter or margarine, 1 tablespoon at a time, until melted. Serve sauce over steaks. Top with the salsa; serve immediately.

Nutrition Facts per serving: 479 cal., 35 g total fat (15 g sat. fat), 124 mg chol., 368 mg sodium, 4 g carbo., 1 g fiber, 33 g pro. **Daily Values:** 11% vit. A, 95% vit. C, 2% calcium, 16% iron.

WHAT IS DEGLAZING?

When a piece of meat is pan-seared to form a delicious crust, as in the recipe at left, there are often bits of crusty, flavorful meat and meat juices left in the pan. Deglazing is the process of adding liquid to the pan, then stirring and scraping the bottom of the pan to remove the browned bits (see photo, above). Once this is accomplished—usually in a matter of seconds—the mixture can be used as a starting point for a delicious gravy or sauce.

A word of caution: A great deal of steam forms when you add liquid to a hot pan. Stand back and keep your pouring hand as far away from the inside of the pan as possible.

153

chile pork ribs with
chipotle barbecue sauce

prep: 15 minutes   *grill:* 1¼ hours   *makes:* 4 servings

1 tablespoon cumin seeds, slightly crushed
2 tablespoons brown sugar
1 tablespoon chili powder
1 teaspoon paprika
½ teaspoon ground red pepper
¼ teaspoon cracked black pepper
3 to 4 pounds pork loin back ribs
    or meaty spareribs

1½ cups bottled barbecue sauce
¼ cup finely chopped onion
3 cloves garlic, minced
½ to 1 teaspoon finely chopped, drained
    chipotle pepper in adobo sauce

1 In a small skillet heat cumin seeds over low heat about 3 minutes or until toasted and fragrant, shaking skillet occasionally. Remove from heat; transfer to a small bowl. Stir in brown sugar, chili powder, paprika, red pepper, and black pepper. Use your fingers to rub mixture onto both sides of ribs.

2 In a grill with a cover, arrange medium-hot coals around a drip pan. Test for medium heat above the pan. Place ribs, bone side down, on grill rack over drip pan. Cover and grill for 1 hour, adding more coals as necessary.

3 Meanwhile, for sauce, in a medium saucepan combine barbecue sauce, onion, garlic, and drained chipotle pepper in adobo sauce. Bring to boiling; reduce heat. Simmer, covered, for 10 minutes.

4 Continue grilling ribs for 15 to 30 minutes more or until ribs are tender, brushing with sauce the last 20 minutes of grilling. To serve, heat and pass any remaining sauce.

Nutrition Facts per serving: 446 cal., 17 g total fat (5 g sat. fat), 99 mg chol., 883 mg sodium, 23 g carbo., 2 g fiber, 49 g pro. **Daily Values:** 21% vit. A, 17% vit. C, 7% calcium, 21% iron.

FLAVORFUL DRY RUBS

A dry rub can add a powerful flavor boost to a grilled, smoked, or roasted meat. The mixture is a blend of several different herbs and spices that is rubbed over or patted onto the surface of the meat before it's cooked. Dry rubs are well-known among barbecue enthusiasts, some of whom follow up the flavoring at the table with a sauce.

To maximize the flavor of a dry rub, toast the spices (usually only those spices in whole seed form) in a dry skillet over low heat for a few minutes (see step 1, left). Toasting spices intensifies them and gives them a pleasant, nutty flavor.

Using freshly cracked pepper is one of the secrets to good cooking. Once you've experienced its wonderful flavor, you'll use it often. To evenly crack peppercorns, as called for in the recipe, right, without finely crushing them, stay away from your pepper grinder. Even at the coarsest setting, a grinder grinds the peppercorns too finely.

The best way to crack peppercorns is with a rolling pin. Place them in a small plastic bag, squeeze out all the air, then seal it. Roll the pin over the peppercorns while pressing down firmly until you hear the peppercorns crack. Repeat until they're cracked to your satisfaction.

grilled beef filet
with portobello relish

prep: 15 minutes   *grill:* 15 minutes   *makes:* 4 servings

4 beef tenderloin steaks, cut 1 inch
   thick (about 1¼ pounds)
   Kosher salt
   Cracked black pepper
8 ounces fresh portobello mushrooms,
   stems removed
1 medium yellow onion, cut into
   ½-inch slices

4 roma tomatoes, halved lengthwise
3 tablespoons snipped fresh basil
2 tablespoons minced fresh garlic
2 tablespoons olive oil
1 teaspoon kosher salt
1 teaspoon cracked black pepper

1 Trim fat from steaks. Season steaks with salt and pepper. Grill steaks on the rack of an uncovered grill directly over medium heat until of desired doneness, turning once. (Allow 8 to 12 minutes for medium-rare and 12 to 15 minutes for medium doneness.)

2 Meanwhile, for relish, grill mushrooms, onion, and tomatoes directly over medium heat until tender, turning once halfway through grilling. Allow 15 minutes for onion and 10 minutes for mushrooms and tomatoes. Remove vegetables from grill.

3 Cut onion, mushrooms, and tomato halves into 1-inch pieces. In a medium bowl stir together basil, garlic, olive oil, the 1 teaspoon kosher salt, and the 1 teaspoon cracked black pepper; stir in grilled vegetables. To serve, spoon warm relish over steaks.

Nutrition Facts per serving: 329 cal., 18 g total fat (5 g sat. fat), 87 mg chol., 617 mg sodium, 9 g carbo., 2 g fiber, 33 g pro. **Daily Values:** 4% vit. A, 25% vit. C, 4% calcium, 26% iron.

Kosher salt
Kosher salt is a coarse salt with no additives. Besides being used in kosher cooking, it's preferred by many cooks because it has a light, flaky texture, clean taste, and less sodium than regular salt. It's ideal for use in salads and relishes, as in the recipe above. Look for it next to the regular salt in your supermarket.

italian beef braciola

prep: 25 minutes   ***bake:*** 1½ hours   ***makes:*** 6 servings

1   1¼- to 1½-pound beef flank steak
½   teaspoon pepper
½   cup seasoned fine dry bread crumbs
⅓   cup grated Romano cheese
⅓   cup snipped fresh Italian parsley
¼   pound sliced pancetta or 4 slices
        bacon, chopped
2   cloves garlic, minced
2   tablespoons olive oil

1   28-ounce can whole Italian-style
        tomatoes, cut up and undrained
1   6-ounce can tomato paste
¾   cup water
3   tablespoons chopped fresh basil or
        1½ teaspoons dried basil, crushed
12   ounces dried mostaccioli pasta
        Grated Romano cheese (optional)

1 To butterfly steak, make a lengthwise cut horizontally through steak, cutting to within ½ inch of opposite side (see top photo, right). Spread open; cover with plastic wrap. Working from the center to the edges, pound with flat side of meat mallet to even thickness (about a 12-inch square). Remove plastic wrap. Sprinkle pepper over entire cut surface; set aside.

2 For filling, combine bread crumbs, the ⅓ cup Romano cheese, parsley, pancetta or bacon, and garlic. Sprinkle the filling over the cut surface of the steak. Roll up so that grain runs lengthwise (see bottom photo, right). Tie in several places with heavy kitchen string. If necessary, cut roll in half to fit pan.

3 In a large oven-going skillet or Dutch oven brown meat on all sides in hot oil. Remove beef and set aside. (Pour off excess drippings.) Add undrained tomatoes to skillet, stirring to loosen browned bits in skillet. Stir in tomato paste, water, and basil. Return steak to pan. Cover and bake in a 325° oven for about 1½ hours or until steak is tender.

4 Meanwhile, cook pasta according to package directions; drain.

5 Remove string from steak. Cut steak into 1½-inch slices. Arrange steak slices over hot pasta; spoon some sauce over all. Pass remaining sauce. If desired, serve with additional Romano cheese.

Nutrition Facts per serving: 530 cal., 16 g total fat (5 g sat. fat), 45 mg chol., 651 mg sodium, 61 g carbo., 4 g fiber, 36 g pro. **Daily Values:** 20% vit. A, 49% vit. C, 12% calcium, 27% iron.

STUFFING FLANK STEAK

Butterflying is a useful technique for meat that is to be stuffed. The technique creates a thinner piece of meat that's more easily rolled up.

To butterfly and stuff a flank steak for Italian Beef Braciola (see recipe, left), follow the directions in steps 1 and 2 and refer to the photos, above. Be careful not to cut completely through the meat or you may wind up with two or three pieces of meat rather than one large, thin one.

157

SELECTING A GREAT STEAK

When you're hungry for a steak, here's some advice to help you decide what cut to buy:

The meat's location on the animal determines how tender the steak will be. The most tender steaks come from the rib and loin sections; the less tender cuts, such as round and flank steak, come from the leg, rump, and shoulder areas.

For the most tender grilled steaks, choose one of these cuts: boneless chuck mock tender, boneless chuck top blade, porterhouse, T-bone, rib, ribeye, sirloin, top sirloin, tenderloin, top loin (strip), or tri-tip.

A good all-purpose steak is the top loin or sirloin steak because it is one of the more tender steaks but won't break your pocketbook.

grilled steaks
with gorgonzola butter

prep: 15 minutes   *grill:* 8 minutes   *makes:* 8 servings

4 boneless beef top loin steaks,
      cut 1 inch thick (about 2 pounds total)
2 tablespoons crumbled Gorgonzola cheese
      or blue cheese
2 tablespoons soft-style cream cheese
      with onion and garlic
1 to 2 tablespoons butter, softened
1 tablespoon chopped pine nuts
      or walnuts, toasted
   Salt (optional)

1 Trim fat from steaks. Grill steaks on the rack of an uncovered grill directly over medium heat until of desired doneness, turning once halfway through grilling. (Allow 8 to 12 minutes for medium-rare doneness and 12 to 15 minutes for medium doneness.)

2 Meanwhile, for butter, stir together Gorgonzola cheese or blue cheese, cream cheese, butter, and nuts. Shape into a 1-inch-diameter log. Wrap in plastic wrap; chill.

3 If desired, season grilled steaks with salt. Cut steaks in half. To serve, cut butter into 8 slices. Place 1 slice of butter on each steak; serve immediately.

Nutrition Facts per serving: 268 cal., 19 g total fat (8 g sat. fat), 82 mg chol., 110 mg sodium, 0 g carbo., 0 g fiber, 23 g pro. **Daily Values:** 3% vit. A, 2% calcium, 11% iron.

Storing steak
You can store steak in the refrigerator for about 3 days after purchase if you remove the supermarket wrapping and rewrap the steak loosely in plastic wrap so it can breathe. Store the meat in the coldest part of your refrigerator. Placing it on a plate will help catch any juices that might drip out.

pizza-topped meat loaf

prep: 20 minutes   **bake:** 30 minutes   **makes:** 6 servings

1 beaten egg	3/4 pound lean ground beef
1 cup soft bread crumbs	1/2 pound bulk hot Italian sausage
1/2 cup milk	2 roma tomatoes, thinly sliced
2 cloves garlic, minced	1/2 cup shredded Italian blend cheese
2 tablespoons grated Parmesan cheese	or shredded mozzarella cheese
2 tablespoons snipped fresh Italian parsley	2 tablespoons fresh basil chiffonade
or parsley	(see tip, left)
1/8 teaspoon salt	

1 In a large bowl combine egg, bread crumbs, milk, garlic, Parmesan cheese, parsley, and salt. Add ground beef and Italian sausage; mix lightly (see tip, below). Shape meat mixture into a round loaf, 9 inches in diameter*. Transfer loaf to the unheated rack of a broiler pan or roasting pan with rack.

2 Bake in a 375° oven for 25 to 30 minutes or until a thermometer inserted into the middle of the loaf registers 160° and juices run clear. Remove from oven. Top with sliced tomatoes; sprinkle with cheese. Bake about 5 minutes more or until cheese is melted. Transfer to a serving platter; sprinkle with basil chiffonade. Cut into wedges to serve.

*Note: To shape meat loaf, line a 9-inch pie plate or round cake pan with plastic wrap and use to form. Turn meat loaf out onto rack of broiler pan or roasting pan with rack. Remove pan and plastic wrap.

Nutrition Facts per serving: 269 cal., 12 g total fat (7 g sat. fat), 103 mg chol., 482 mg sodium, 7 g carbo., 1 g fiber, 21 g pro. **Daily Values:** 6% vit. A, 10% vit. C, 11% calcium, 13% iron.

Meat loaf hints
The principle of more is better applies when you're making meat loaves or patties. Using more than one kind of ground meat, as in the recipe above, gives your finished dish a flavor boost. Another important secret for a moist, flavorful meat loaf is gentle handling. Overmixing or compressing ground meat will give it a texture that is too firm after cooking.

oyster-stuffed
pork chops

prep: 35 minutes　　***grill:*** 40 minutes　　***makes:*** 4 servings

4　cups apple wood chips
¼　cup finely chopped carrot
¼　cup finely chopped celery
¼　cup chopped green onions
1　tablespoon olive oil
¼　cup snipped fresh parsley
2　teaspoons dried sage, crushed
½　teaspoon kosher salt or ¼ teaspoon salt

¼　teaspoon pepper
½　cup fresh oysters in juice (about 10 oysters plus 2 tablespoons liquid)
2　tablespoons dry white wine
1½　cups dried bread cubes, coarsely crushed*
4　bone-in pork loin chops or pork rib chops, cut 1½ inches thick (about 3½ pounds total)

1 At least 1 hour before grilling, soak wood chips in enough water to cover.

2 For stuffing, in a medium skillet cook carrot, celery, and green onions in the hot olive oil until tender. Stir in the parsley, sage, salt, and pepper. Cook and stir for 1 minute more. Stir in the oysters and juice and wine. Bring to boiling; reduce heat. Simmer, uncovered, for 4 to 5 minutes or until oysters are plump and opaque and liquid almost evaporates. Cool slightly.

3 Transfer oyster mixture to a food processor bowl or blender container. Cover and blend or process with several on-off turns until oysters are finely chopped. Transfer to a medium bowl and stir in crushed bread cubes.

4 Trim fat from chops. Make a pocket in each chop by cutting horizontally from the fat side almost to the bone (see photo and tip, right). Spoon about ⅓ cup of the stuffing into each pocket. If necessary, secure openings with wooden toothpicks.

5 Drain wood chips. In a grill with a cover arrange medium-hot coals around a drip pan. Pour 1 inch of water into the pan. Test for medium heat above the pan. Sprinkle half of the wood chips over preheated coals. Place chops on grill rack over the pan. Cover and grill for 40 to 45 minutes or until chops are slightly pink in center and juices run clear. Add remaining wood chips halfway through grilling. Serve chops immediately.

*Note: To make dry bread cubes for stuffing, cut bread into ½-inch-square pieces. (You'll need 3 slices of bread for 1½ cups of dry cubes.) Spread in a single layer in a shallow baking pan. Bake in a 300° oven for 10 to 15 minutes or until dry, stirring twice; cool. (Bread will continue to dry and crisp as it cools.) Or, instead of baking, let bread cubes stand, loosely covered, at room temperature for 8 to 12 hours.

Nutrition Facts per serving: 644 cal., 22 g total fat (7 g sat. fat), 255 mg chol., 624 mg sodium, 12 g carbo., 1 g fiber, 91 g pro. **Daily Values:** 26% vit. A, 20% vit. C, 12% calcium, 29% iron.

CUTTING A POCKET IN PORK CHOPS

Making a pocket in a pork chop to hold as much stuffing as possible is easily done.

Use a sharp, pointed knife to make a slit in the fatty side of the chop.

Work the knife inside the chop, cutting almost to the other side (or to the bone) without cutting through it and widening the size of the original slit.

Spoon the stuffing into the pocket and use 1 or 2 wooden toothpicks to close the opening.

Peppercorns come in a variety of colors and intensities (see tip, below right). The peppercorns shown above are (from top)

Mixed peppercorns: a mix of different colors of whole peppercorns.

Pink peppercorns: pink berries with a slightly sweet flavor and a little bite.

White peppercorns: light-colored berries that are milder than black peppercorns.

Black peppercorns: dried peppercorn berries with an intense flavor.

Green peppercorns: soft, mild berries, often preserved in a brine.

Szechwan peppercorns: reddish brown berries with a bold flavor.

pork au poivre with
mustard & sage

prep: 15 minutes   *cook:* 14 minutes   *makes:* 4 servings

1 to 2 teaspoons whole black peppercorns
1 to 2 teaspoons whole pink peppercorns
1 to 2 teaspoons whole white peppercorns
4 6- to 8-ounce boneless pork loin chops, butterflied
2/3 cup whipping cream

3 tablespoons dry white wine
2 tablespoons Dijon-style mustard
2 tablespoons snipped fresh sage
1 tablespoon green peppercorns in brine, drained and rinsed

1 Coarsely crack the black, pink, and white peppercorns (see tip, page 156); stir together. Generously coat 1 side of each pork chop with peppercorn mixture; use your fingers to press onto meat.

2 In a 12-inch skillet cook chops, peppered sides down, over medium-high heat for 6 minutes. Turn chops and cook about 6 minutes more or until juices run clear (if chops brown too quickly, reduce heat slightly). Transfer chops to serving platter; keep warm. Scrape any burnt peppercorns from skillet and discard.

3 For sauce, add cream, wine, mustard, sage, and drained green peppercorns to skillet. Bring to boiling; reduce heat. Simmer, uncovered, for 2 minutes or until reduced to about 1/2 cup. Serve over chops.

Nutrition Facts per serving: 416 cal., 25 g total fat (13 g sat. fat), 148 mg chol., 128 mg sodium, 4 g carbo., 1 g fiber, 39 g pro. **Daily Values:** 18% vit. A, 2% vit. C, 7% calcium, 11% iron.

Pepper genealogy

Where do peppercorns come from? Three of the most popular types come from the pepper plant (*Piper nigrum*). Black peppercorns are berries from this plant that are picked before they're ripe and dried until they shrivel and turn dark. White peppercorns are the same berries that are allowed to ripen, then are dried and hulled to expose a white creamy core. Green peppercorns are immature pepper berries that are picked while they're still tender and are usually preserved in brine—although they can be packed in water, dried, or freeze-dried. Pink peppercorns aren't true pepper at all, but rather the dried berries of a variety of rose plant. Szechwan peppercorns come from an ash tree and have a tiny seed inside each berry. They have a distinctive flavor and aroma and often are used in Oriental dishes.

pork medallions
with fennel & pancetta

prep: 20 minutes   *cook:* 10 minutes   *makes:* 4 servings

- 1 12-ounce pork tenderloin
- ¼ cup all-purpose flour
-     Dash salt
-     Dash pepper
- 2 tablespoons olive oil
- 2 ounces pancetta or bacon, finely chopped
- 2 fennel bulbs, trimmed and cut crosswise into ¼-inch slices
- 1 small onion, thinly sliced
- 2 cloves garlic, minced
- 2 tablespoons lemon juice
- ½ cup whipping cream

1 Trim fat from meat. Cut meat crosswise into 1-inch slices. Place 1 slice between 2 pieces of plastic wrap. Pound lightly with the flat side of a meat mallet to ¼-inch thickness. Remove plastic wrap. Repeat with remaining slices.

2 In a shallow bowl combine flour, salt, and pepper; coat meat with flour mixture. In a heavy large skillet heat olive oil over high heat. Add meat, half at a time, and cook for 2 to 3 minutes or until meat is slightly pink in center, turning once. (Add more oil if necessary.) Remove meat from skillet.

3 In the same skillet cook pancetta or bacon over medium-high heat until crisp; add fennel, onion, and garlic. Cook for 3 to 5 minutes or until crisp-tender. Add lemon juice; stir in cream. Bring to boiling; return meat to pan. Cook until meat is heated through and sauce is slightly thickened.

4 To serve, transfer meat to a serving platter. Spoon sauce over meat.

Nutrition Facts per serving: 341 cal., 23 g total fat (10 g sat. fat), 105 mg chol., 175 mg sodium, 12 g carbo., 12 g fiber, 22 g pro. **Daily Values:** 13% vit. A, 19% vit. C, 4% calcium, 10% iron.

POUNDING MEAT

There are two reasons to pound meat. One is to make the meat more tender by breaking up connective tissue. The other is to flatten the meat so it can be cut into uniform portions and cooked in a shorter amount of time. In Pork Medallions with Fennel and Pancetta (see recipe, left), the pork tenderloin is pounded so it cooks quickly and evenly.

To pound meat, start by covering the meat with heavy plastic wrap to avoid messy splatters. Use the smooth side of a meat mallet to gently pound it to the desired thickness, being careful to keep the thickness even (see photo, above). If you're without a meat mallet, you can use the bottom of a heavy saucepan or a heavy rolling pin.

165

cranberry-chipotle
pork chops

prep: 5 minutes   *grill:* 35 minutes   *makes:* 4 servings

- 4 pork loin rib chops, cut 1¼ inches thick (about 3 pounds)
- 1 8-ounce can jellied cranberry sauce
- ⅓ cup apricot or peach preserves or apricot or peach spreadable fruit
- ¼ cup chopped onion
- 1 tablespoon lemon juice or cider vinegar
- 1 drained canned chipotle pepper in adobo sauce or 1 fresh jalapeño pepper, seeded and chopped

1 Trim fat from chops. In a grill with a cover, arrange medium-hot coals around a drip pan. Test for medium heat above pan. Place chops on the grill rack over drip pan. Cover and grill chops for 35 to 40 minutes or until juices run clear (internal temperature registers 160°), turning once.

2 Meanwhile, for sauce, in a small saucepan combine the cranberry sauce, preserves or spreadable fruit, onion, lemon juice or vinegar, and drained chipotle or jalapeño pepper. Bring to boiling, stirring constantly; reduce heat. Simmer, uncovered, for 5 minutes, stirring occasionally.

3 To serve, brush chops with sauce. Pass remaining sauce.

Nutrition Facts per serving: 449 cal., 14 g total fat (5 g sat. fat), 116 mg chol., 187 mg sodium, 42 g carbo., 1 g fiber, 36 g pro. **Daily Values:** 5% vit. A, 10% vit. C, 4% calcium, 9% iron.

To broil: Prepare sauce and pork chops as directed, except place pork chops on the unheated rack of a broiler pan. Broil chops 3 to 4 inches from the heat for 18 to 22 minutes or until chops are slightly pink in the center and juices run clear, turning once. Serve as above.

Broiling basics
Broiling is a good substitute for grilling when the weather doesn't cooperate. Here are two tips to make broiling easier:
- To help with cleanup, line the drip pan of your broiler pan with foil before you start. Then line the slotted rack of the boiler pan with foil. Cut slots through the foil to correspond with the slots or holes in the rack of the broiler pan; this way the fat and meat juices can drip through. During cooking, any food that sticks will stick to the foil. When you're finished cooking, just throw away the foil.
- Before turning on the broiler, make sure the food—not the broiler pan—is the distance from the heat source specified in your recipe. To do this, place the broiler pan with the food in place in the oven; use a ruler to measure the distance from the top of the food to the heat source.

USING A MEAT THERMOMETER IN STEAKS AND CHOPS

Steaks, chops, and burgers are tasty and can be prepared in a hurry—perfect for today's busy cooks. But even experienced cooks may wonder just how long to cook these meats. The best way to tell when a steak, chop, or burger is done is to check the internal temperature with an instant-read thermometer.

Instant-read thermometers measure a wide range of temperatures, typically from 0° to 220°, but they are not designed to stay in food during cooking. To test for doneness, remove the meat from the heat (grill, stovetop, or oven) and insert the thermometer into the thickest portion of the meat, not touching bone or the pan. For these thin meats, it's best to insert the thermometer horizontally (from the side) to make certain the end of the thermometer is securely in the thickest part of the meat.

rosemary-mustard
lamb roast

prep: 15 minutes   ***roast:*** 45 minutes   ***stand:*** 15 minutes   ***makes:*** 4 servings

2 1- to 1½-pound lamb rib roasts
     (6 to 8 ribs each)
¼ cup coarse-grain brown mustard
1 tablespoon snipped fresh rosemary

1 to 2 cloves garlic, minced
½ teaspoon pepper
¾ cup soft bread crumbs
¼ cup finely chopped pecans

1 Trim fat from meat. In a small bowl combine mustard, rosemary, garlic, and pepper; brush onto meat. Toss together bread crumbs and nuts. Use your fingers to gently press the crumb mixture onto the roasts on all sides.

2 Place the roasts on a rack in a shallow roasting pan. Insert a meat thermometer into the center of the meat without touching bone. Roast in a 325° oven until the thermometer registers 140° for medium-rare (45 minutes to 1 hour) or 155° for medium (1 to 1½ hours) doneness.

3 Cover with foil; let stand for 15 minutes before carving. (The temperature of the meat will rise 5° during standing.)

Nutrition Facts per serving: 269 cal., 16 g total fat (4 g sat. fat), 74 mg chol., 311 mg sodium, 7 g carbo., 1 g fiber, 25 g pro. **Daily Values:** 1% vit. C, 5% calcium, 15% iron.

FRENCHING A RACK OF LAMB

Frenching a rack of lamb (or a pork rib crown roast) makes for an eye-catching presentation. The technique involves removing the cartilage and fat between the rib bones so the clean bones are exposed.

If you have a good butcher, ask him or her to French your rack of lamb for you. If you would like to try the technique yourself, use a small, sharp knife to cut away any cartilage and fat. Then scrape the exposed bone clean, if necessary.

In Braised Lamb Shank Bordelaise (see recipe, right) the sauce is thickened with a paste made by stirring together softened butter and flour. This mixture, called beurre manié (burr mahn-YAY), a French term, has long been a secret weapon chefs use for thickening soups and sauces.

If a bouillabaisse needs more body or a white sauce just doesn't set up, a tablespoon of beurre manié might just do the trick. Beurre manié works because the butter protects the flour from clumping as it cooks, even at high temperatures. (Simply sprinkling in some flour would cause lumps.)

To have some beurre manié on hand for emergencies, mix up a batch (see step 4, right) and keep it in a tightly sealed container in the refrigerator for up to 2 weeks. Or, freeze beurre manié in tablespoon-size portions for up to 3 months.

braised lamb
shanks bordelaise

prep: 25 minutes   *bake:* 2 hours   *makes:* 8 servings

4 meaty lamb shanks (about 4 pounds total)	1½ cups sliced carrots
⅓ cup all-purpose flour	1 cup chopped onion
1 teaspoon salt	1 14½-ounce can beef broth
1 teaspoon onion powder	1 cup dry red wine
1 teaspoon pepper	2 tablespoons butter, softened
2 tablespoons cooking oil	2 tablespoons all-purpose flour
8 ounces cremini mushrooms, halved (3 cups)	

1 Trim fat from lamb shanks. Place the ⅓ cup flour, the salt, onion powder, and pepper in a plastic bag. Add shanks, 1 at a time, shaking to coat.

2 In an 8-quart Dutch oven brown the lamb shanks on all sides in the hot oil. Add mushrooms, carrots, onion, broth, and wine. Cover and bake (braise) in a 350° oven for 2 hours or until lamb is tender.

3 Use a slotted spoon to transfer lamb shanks and vegetables to a serving platter; keep warm.

4 For sauce, measure cooking liquid, reserving 2 cups. Discard remaining cooking liquid. Return reserved cooking liquid to Dutch oven. Stir together the softened butter or margarine and the 2 tablespoons flour; drop small amounts into the cooking liquid, whisking well between each addition until smooth. Cook and stir until slightly thickened and bubbly. Cook and stir for 1 minute more. To serve, ladle sauce over lamb shanks and vegetables.

Nutrition Facts per serving: 373 cal., 21 g total fat (8 g sat. fat), 113 mg chol., 582 mg sodium, 11 g carbo., 1 g fiber, 31 g pro. **Daily Values:** 75% vit. A, 4% vit. C, 4% calcium, 17% iron.

How to buy lamb shanks
Lamb shanks are one of the most flavorful cuts of lamb. For the best results in recipes such as Braised Lamb Shank Bordelaise (see recipe, above), you need to purchase top-quality meat. The guiding principle in purchasing lamb is the color. The older the animal, the darker the flesh. (Meat from older animals is tougher and has a stronger flavor.) Look for young lamb, which has bright-pink and finely grained flesh, creamy-white fat, and moist, porous pink bones.

Breads

171

crispy corn bread
with dried tomatoes

prep: 15 minutes   **bake:** 18 minutes   **cool:** 10 minutes   **makes:** 8 servings

1 tablespoon shortening
1¼ cups stone-ground or regular yellow
     cornmeal
¾ cup all-purpose flour
2 tablespoons sugar
2 teaspoons baking powder
½ teaspoon salt

½ teaspoon baking soda
2 beaten eggs
1 cup buttermilk
¼ cup cooking oil
2 tablespoons finely snipped dried
     tomatoes (not oil-packed)

1 Place shortening in a 9-inch cast-iron skillet in oven; preheat oven to 425°.

2 Meanwhile, in a large bowl stir together cornmeal, flour, sugar, baking powder, salt, and baking soda. Make a well in the center of cornmeal mixture; set aside.

3 In another bowl combine beaten eggs, buttermilk, cooking oil, and snipped tomatoes. Add all at once to cornmeal mixture. Stir until moistened.

4 Remove skillet from oven. Carefully pour batter into hot skillet, spreading evenly. Return skillet to oven. Bake for 18 to 20 minutes or until a wooden toothpick inserted near the center comes out clean. Cool in skillet on a wire rack. (For a crispier bottom crust, immediately loosen edges and use a wide metal spatula to slide corn bread onto a wire rack.) Cool for 10 minutes. Cut into wedges to serve.

Nutrition Facts per serving: 171 cal., 10 g total fat (2 g sat. fat), 54 mg chol., 390 mg sodium, 16 g carbo., 1 g fiber, 4 g pro. **Daily Values:** 3% vit. A, 1% vit. C, 10% calcium, 5% iron.

Stone-ground cornmeal

For a fuller-flavored, crunchier corn bread, buy stone-ground cornmeal rather than milled cornmeal. Stone-ground cornmeal has a coarser texture than milled cornmeal (which is ground to a flourlike texture between heavy steel rollers) because it still contains some of the corn hull and germ, giving it a nuttier texture and more fresh-corn flavor. If you can't find stone-ground cornmeal at your grocery store, try a health food store. Once you get it home, keep it fresh by storing the cornmeal in the refrigerator for up to 2 months or freezer for up to 1 year.

CRISPY CORN BREAD

Everyone has an opinion about what makes good corn bread, but a penchant for a crisp crust is almost universal. The secret to crispiness in corn bread lies in how you bake it.

For a crisp-crusted corn bread, bake it in an oven-going skillet, such as the cast-iron skillet called for in the recipe, left. Place the fat—butter, shortening, olive oil, or bacon drippings—in the pan. Place the pan in the oven as it preheats. Test the pan to see if it's ready by dropping a tiny amount of batter into it. If it sizzles, it's ready. Pour the batter into the skillet and bake.

Serve corn breads, such as the recipe, left, warm with butter or honey. If you like, use corn bread to make stuffing for poultry or to serve with beef or pork roasts.

FOCACCIA MADE EASY

Focaccia (foh-KAH-chee-uh) is a flat Italian yeast bread that often is baked with a variety of toppers, such as onions, herbs, olives, dried tomatoes, nuts, or cheese. Simple Focaccia (see recipe, right) eliminates a lot of the work of making focaccia because it starts with a hot-roll mix.

Serve focaccia as you would garlic bread. It's a great accompaniment to pasta dishes and soups. Cut in thin wedges, it also makes a tasty appetizer or snack.

When it comes to making sandwiches, focaccia is terrific, too. To cut focaccia for sandwiches, slice the rounds in half horizontally (see tip, page 101), then stack the two halves and cut them into wedges.

simple focaccia

prep: per package directions   *rise:* 30 minutes   *bake:* 15 minutes   *makes:* 12 servings

1   16-ounce package hot-roll mix
1   egg
2   tablespoons olive oil

1   tablespoon olive oil
    Coarse salt

1 Lightly grease a 15×10×1-inch baking pan, a 12- to 14-inch pizza pan, or two 9×1½-inch round baking pans. Set aside.

2 Prepare the hot-roll mix according to package directions for basic dough, using the 1 egg and substituting the 2 tablespoons oil for the margarine. Knead dough; allow to rest as directed. If using large baking pan, roll dough into a 15×10-inch rectangle. If using a pizza pan, roll dough into a 12-inch round. If using round baking pans, divide dough in half; roll into two 9-inch rounds. Place dough in prepared pan(s).

3 With fingertips, press indentations randomly in dough. Brush dough with the 1 tablespoon olive oil; sprinkle lightly with coarse salt. Cover; let rise in a warm place until nearly double (about 30 minutes).

4 Bake in a 375° oven for 15 to 20 minutes or until golden. Cool 10 minutes on wire rack(s). Remove from pan(s) and cool completely.

Nutrition Facts per serving: 176 cal., 4 g total fat (1 g sat. fat), 18 mg chol., 306 mg sodium, 29 g carbo., 0 g fiber, 6 g pro. **Daily Values:** 1% vit. A, 6% iron.

Parmesan & Pine Nut Focaccia: Prepare recipe as directed, except omit the 1 tablespoon olive oil and the coarse salt. After making indentations, brush the dough with mixture of 1 egg white and 1 tablespoon water. Sprinkle with ¼ cup pine nuts, pressing lightly into dough. Sprinkle with 2 tablespoons freshly grated Parmesan cheese. Bake as directed.

Lemon & Savory Focaccia: Prepare recipe as directed, except omit the coarse salt. Add ¼ cup coarsely chopped pitted ripe olives, 3 tablespoons snipped fresh savory, and 1 teaspoon finely shredded lemon peel to the dough along with the 2 tablespoons olive oil. Continue as directed.

Handy hot-roll mix
When you want yeast breads in a hurry, hot-roll mix can come to the rescue. With a little experimenting, you can shape the dough from this versatile mix into loaves, rolls, pizza crust, cinnamon rolls, breadsticks, or even pretzels. Prepare the dough according to package directions, then shape and bake according to your favorite recipe.

MIXING MUFFIN & QUICK BREAD BATTER

The trick to making tender and finely crumbed muffins and quickbreads is all in the measuring and mixing.

• Measuring ingredients accurately is vital for quickbreads because if the ingredient proportions aren't correct, the breads will fail. If there's too much liquid, quick breads may sink in the middle. Or, too much fat can make them coarsely textured.

• Proper mixing also is important for quick breads. If the batter is overmixed, quick breads will have peaked tops and tunnels inside. To avoid these problems, combine the dry ingredients in a bowl and make a well in the center. The well creates a large surface area for the dry ingredients so they can be moistened with a minimum of stirring. Use a rubber spatula because its wide blade will make you less prone to overmix. Stop mixing while the batter is still lumpy for further insurance your quick breads will turn out beautifully.

pumpkin-pecan muffins

prep: 20 minutes   ***bake:*** 20 minutes   ***cool:*** 5 minutes   ***makes:*** 12 to 14 muffins

⅓ cup packed brown sugar
2 tablespoons dairy sour cream
⅔ cup chopped pecans
2 cups all-purpose flour
2 teaspoons baking powder
1 teaspoon ground cinnamon
½ teaspoon baking soda
¼ teaspoon salt

¼ teaspoon ground nutmeg
⅛ teaspoon ground cloves
1 beaten egg
¾ cup buttermilk or sour milk
   (see tip, page 181)
¾ cup canned pumpkin
⅔ cup packed brown sugar
⅓ cup butter, melted

1 Grease twelve to fourteen 2½-inch muffin cups or line with paper bake cups; set aside. In a small bowl stir together the ⅓ cup brown sugar and sour cream; stir in pecans. Set aside.

2 In a medium bowl combine flour, baking powder, cinnamon, baking soda, salt, nutmeg, and cloves. Make a well in the center of flour mixture.

3 In another medium bowl combine egg, buttermilk or sour milk, pumpkin, the ⅔ cup brown sugar, and melted butter. Add pumpkin mixture all at once to the flour mixture. Stir until moistened (batter should be lumpy).

4 Spoon batter into prepared muffin cups, filling each almost full. Spoon about 2 teaspoons of the pecan mixture on top of each muffin. Bake in a 375° oven for 20 to 25 minutes. Cool in muffin cups on a wire rack for 5 minutes. Remove from muffin cups; serve warm.

Nutrition Facts per serving: 234 cal., 10 g total fat (4 g sat. fat), 33 mg chol., 237 mg sodium, 33 g carbo., 1 g fiber, 4 g pro. **Daily Values:** 40% vit. A, 1% vit. C, 8% calcium, 12% iron.

creamy caramel-nut rolls

prep: 20 minutes   **rise:** 30 minutes   **bake:** 20 minutes   **cool:** 5 minutes   **makes:** 20 to 24 rolls

- 1¼ cups sifted powdered sugar
- ½ cup whipping cream
- 1 cup coarsely chopped pecans
- 2 14- to 16-ounce loaves frozen sweet roll dough or white bread dough, thawed

- 3 tablespoons margarine or butter, melted
- ½ cup packed brown sugar
- 1 tablespoon ground cinnamon
- ¾ cup light or dark raisins (optional)

1 For topping, in a small bowl stir together powdered sugar and whipping cream. Divide evenly between two 9×1½-inch round baking pans. Sprinkle pecans evenly over sugar mixture.

2 On a lightly floured surface roll each loaf of dough into a 12×8-inch rectangle. Brush with melted margarine or butter.

3 In a small bowl stir together brown sugar and cinnamon; sprinkle over dough. If desired, top with raisins. Roll up rectangles, jelly-roll style, starting from a long side. Pinch seam and ends to seal. Cut each roll into 10 to 12 slices. Place slices, seam side down, on sugar mixture in pans. Cover with a towel. Let rise in a warm place until nearly double, about 30 minutes. (Or, cover and refrigerate overnight, as directed in the tip, right.) Puncture surface bubbles with a greased toothpick before baking.

4 Bake rolls, uncovered, in a 375° oven for 20 to 25 minutes or until golden brown. If necessary, cover rolls with foil the last 10 minutes of baking to prevent overbrowning. Cool in pans on a wire rack for 5 minutes. Invert onto a serving platter. Serve warm.

Nutrition Facts per serving: 233 cal., 10 g total fat (3 g sat. fat), 31 mg chol., 96 mg sodium, 32 g carbo., 1 g fiber, 4 g pro. **Daily Values:** 3% vit. A, 4% calcium, 8% iron.

Proofing yeast breads

Proofing (raising) a yeast bread correctly can mean the difference between success and failure. Proof dough in a draft-free area that's between 80° and 85°. One spot that's almost perfect is your oven. To use it for proofing, place the dough in an unheated oven on an upper rack. Place a large pan of hot water under the dough on the lower rack. Let the dough rise according to the directions in your recipe. In Creamy Caramel-Nut Rolls (see recipe, above), the shaped dough should rise until it is nearly doubled. Don't let the dough rise above the top of the pan because the rolls need room to rise more as they bake.

COOL-RISING ROLLS

Have you dismissed the idea of serving freshly baked rolls for breakfast or brunch because you don't want to get up before the crack of dawn to bake? With the cool-rise method for proofing yeast breads in the refrigerator, you can have your rolls and your sleep, too.

To make Creamy Caramel-Nut Rolls (see recipe, left) using the cool-rise method, prepare and shape the rolls as directed up to the point of rising. Cover the rolls with oiled waxed paper, then with plastic wrap. Refrigerate for up to 24 hours.

Before baking, let the chilled rolls stand, covered, for 20 minutes at room temperature. Puncture surface bubbles with a greased toothpick. Bake the rolls, uncovered, in a 375° oven for 25 to 30 minutes. If necessary, cover the rolls with foil the last 10 minutes of baking to prevent overbrowning. Cool and serve as directed.

dried cherry scones

prep: 30 minutes   ***bake:*** 10 minutes   ***cool:*** 10 minutes   ***makes:*** 12 scones

- ½ cup snipped dried sweet cherries or raisins
- 2 cups all-purpose flour
- 3 tablespoons brown sugar
- 2 teaspoons baking powder
- ½ teaspoon salt
- ½ teaspoon baking soda

- ¼ cup butter
- 1 teaspoon finely shredded orange peel
- 1 beaten egg yolk
- 1 8-ounce carton dairy sour cream
   Orange Glaze

1 In a small bowl pour enough boiling water over dried cherries or raisins to cover. Let stand for 5 minutes; drain well. In a large bowl combine flour, brown sugar, baking powder, salt, and baking soda. Using a pastry blender, cut in butter until mixture resembles coarse crumbs. Add drained cherries or raisins and orange peel; toss lightly to coat. Make a well in the center of the flour mixture; set aside.

2 In a small bowl combine egg yolk and sour cream. Add yolk mixture all at once to flour mixture. Using a fork, stir until combined (mixture may seem dry).

3 Turn dough out onto a lightly floured surface. Quickly knead dough by folding and gently pressing for 10 to 12 strokes or until dough is nearly smooth.

Pat or lightly roll dough into a 7-inch circle. Cut into 12 wedges.

4 Arrange wedges 1 inch apart on an ungreased baking sheet. Bake in a 400° oven for 10 to 12 minutes or until light brown. Cool on a wire rack for 10 minutes. Drizzle warm scones with Orange Glaze. Serve warm.

Nutrition Facts per serving: 214 cal., 9 g total fat (4 g sat. fat), 31 mg chol., 249 mg sodium, 32 g carbo., 1 g fiber, 3 g pro. **Daily Values:** 13% vit. A, 2% vit. C, 7% calcium, 7% iron.

Orange Glaze: In small bowl stir together 1 cup sifted powdered sugar, 1 tablespoon orange juice, and ¼ teaspoon vanilla. Stir in enough additional orange juice, 1 teaspoon at a time, to make of drizzling consistency.

GREAT SCONES

Scones, biscuit-like quick breads that originated in Scotland, are richer than ordinary biscuits because they often contain eggs, butter, and cream or sour cream.

To ensure light, tender, flaky scones, it's important the butter be in small pieces and be cold when it's added to the flour mixture. A pastry blender is handy for cutting in the butter (see recipe, left), but if you don't have one, freeze the butter and cut it using a coarse shredder. Here's how: Remove the paper from a half-stick of frozen butter. Using the paper to hold the end of the stick, shred the butter using a shredder with large openings. Immediately stir the shredded butter into the flour.

You also can use two knives, cutting with a crossing motion, to cut the butter into the flour.

179

MAKING PERFECT POPOVERS

An airy, crispy-on-the-outside, moist-on-the-inside popover is irresistible. The higher popovers rise, the better they are.

To ensure crisp, mile-high popovers, place the batter-filled pan in a hot preheated oven. After the popovers are baked and firm, remove them from the oven and pierce each one gently with a fork to allow the steam to escape (see recipe, right). This will help the popovers keep their shape.

If you want even crisper popovers, turn off the oven and return the pierced popovers to the oven for 5 or 10 minutes more or until they're the desired crispness.

mostly mushroom popovers

prep: 15 minutes   **bake:** 35 minutes   **makes:** 6 popovers

Nonstick cooking spray
1/3 cup dried mushrooms (such as shiitake or porcini)
1/2 teaspoon salt
1/4 teaspoon dried thyme leaves

1/8 teaspoon pepper
1 cup milk
2 beaten eggs
1 tablespoon cooking oil
1 cup all-purpose flour

1 Coat the cups of a popover pan or six 6-ounce custard cups with cooking spray. Place the custard cups on a 15×10×1-inch baking pan; set aside. In a small bowl pour boiling water over the dried mushrooms to cover; let stand for 5 minutes. Drain, pressing out the liquid. Finely chop mushrooms.

2 In a large bowl combine chopped mushrooms, salt, thyme, and pepper. Add milk, eggs, and oil. Beat with a rotary beater until combined. Add flour; beat just until mixture is smooth.

3 Fill prepared cups about half full with batter. Bake in a 400° oven for 35 to 40 minutes or until very firm. Remove from oven. Immediately pierce each popover gently with a fork to let steam escape. Remove popovers from cups; serve immediately.

Nutrition Facts per serving: 150 cal., 5 g total fat (1 g sat. fat), 74 mg chol., 219 mg sodium, 20 g carbo., 1 g fiber, 6 g pro. **Daily Values:** 5% vit. A, 5% calcium, 8% iron.

irish soda bread

prep: 20 minutes **bake:** 35 minutes **makes:** 8 servings

- 1 cup whole wheat flour
- 1 cup all-purpose flour
- 1 teaspoon baking powder
- ½ teaspoon baking soda
- ¼ teaspoon salt
- 3 tablespoons butter
- 2 beaten eggs
- ¾ cup buttermilk or sour milk
- 2 tablespoons brown sugar
- ⅓ cup dried tart red cherries or raisins

1 Grease a baking sheet; set aside. In a medium bowl combine whole wheat flour, all-purpose flour, baking powder, baking soda, and salt. Using a pastry blender, cut in butter until mixture resembles coarse crumbs. Make a well in the center of the flour mixture; set aside.

2 In a small bowl stir together 1 of the eggs, buttermilk or sour milk, brown sugar, and cherries or raisins. Add egg mixture all at once to flour mixture. Stir until moistened.

3 Turn dough out onto a lightly floured surface. Quickly knead dough by folding and gently pressing for 10 to 12 strokes or until dough is nearly smooth. Shape into a 6-inch round loaf. Cut a 4-inch cross, ½ inch deep, on the top. Place on prepared baking sheet. Brush with remaining egg. Bake in a 375° oven about 35 minutes or until golden. Serve warm.

Nutrition Facts per serving: 196 cal., 6 g total fat (3 g sat. fat), 66 mg chol., 276 mg sodium, 30 g carbo., 3 g fiber, 6 g pro. **Daily Values:** 9% vit. A, 7% calcium, 10% iron.

SPEEDY SODA BREADS

When you don't have time to make a yeast bread but still want homemade bread, soda bread is a delicious alternative. Irish Soda Bread (see recipe, left) takes only a fraction of the time necessary to make a standard yeast bread, yet it offers a hearty wheat flavor.

Instead of yeast, soda breads rely on baking soda, baking powder, or a combination of both for leavening—or rising power. Just like yeast, baking powder and baking soda create carbon dioxide gas, which makes bread rise.

Making sour milk

If you find yourself without buttermilk, make some sour milk to use instead. For each cup of sour milk needed, place 1 tablespoon lemon juice or vinegar in a glass measuring cup; add enough milk to make 1 cup total liquid (for the ¾ cup called for in the recipe above, use 2¼ teaspoons lemon juice or vinegar and add enough milk to make ¾ cup total liquid). Let the mixture stand 5 minutes before using it in your recipe.

PREPARING PANS FOR QUICK BREADS

To get quick breads and muffins out of their pans easily, prepare the pans before you pour in the batter. Grease the pans lightly but carefully, greasing the corners, too. For nicely rounded tops rather than ledges around the edge of your loaves or muffins, grease only the bottom of the pan and ½ inch up the sides. The batter will then cling to the sides of the pans instead of sliding down during baking.

Cool breads or muffins in the pans after they're baked so the steam that accumulates as the breads cool will help release the breads from the pans. Cool muffins 5 minutes and quick bread loaves 10 minutes before removing them.

praline-apple bread

prep: 20 minutes   **bake:** 55 minutes   **cool:** 10 minutes   **makes:** 18 servings

2	cups all-purpose flour
2	teaspoons baking powder
½	teaspoon baking soda
½	teaspoon salt
1	cup granulated sugar
1	8-ounce carton dairy sour cream

2	eggs
2	teaspoons vanilla
1¼	cups chopped, peeled tart apples
1	cup chopped pecans
¼	cup butter or margarine
¼	cup packed brown sugar

1 Grease a 9×5×3-inch loaf pan; set aside. In a bowl stir together flour, baking powder, baking soda, and salt.

2 In a large bowl beat together granulated sugar, sour cream, eggs, and vanilla with an electric mixer on low speed until combined. Beat on medium speed for 2 minutes. Add flour mixture to sour cream mixture, beating on low speed until combined. Stir in apples and ½ cup of the chopped pecans.

3 Spread batter into prepared pan. Sprinkle with the remaining chopped pecans; press lightly into batter. Bake in a 350° oven for 55 to 60 minutes or until a wooden toothpick inserted in center comes out clean. If necessary, cover bread loosely with foil the last 10 minutes of baking to prevent overbrowning. Cool bread in pan on a wire rack for 10 minutes. Remove bread from pan.

4 Meanwhile, in a small saucepan combine butter or margarine and brown sugar; cook and stir until mixture begins to boil. Reduce heat and boil gently for 1 minute. Drizzle top of bread with brown sugar mixture; cool.

Nutrition Facts per serving: 203 cal., 10 g total fat (4 g sat. fat), 36 mg chol., 175 mg sodium, 27 g carbo., 1 g fiber, 3 g pro. **Daily Values:** 6% vit. A, 5% calcium, 6% iron.

Desserts

Using vanilla beans instead of extract gives Vanilla Bean Ice Cream (see recipe, right)—and lots of other sweets—an intense vanilla flavor and brown confetti-like flecks.

Vanilla beans are easy to use. In this recipe, the bean is softened by heating it in the half-and-half mixture, which makes the pod easier to split open. But even a dry vanilla bean can be cut lengthwise with a paring knife. After it's open, scrape out the tiny seeds—they're loaded with flavor (see photo, above).

vanilla bean ice cream

prep: 35 minutes   ***chill:*** 4 hours   ***freeze:*** 40 minutes   ***ripen:*** 4 hours   ***makes:*** 6 servings

2½ cups half-and-half, light cream, or whole milk
¾ cup sugar

1 4- to 6-inch vanilla bean or 1 tablespoon vanilla extract*
1¼ cups whipping cream

1 In a large saucepan bring half-and-half, cream, or milk; sugar; and vanilla bean (if using) just to simmering, stirring constantly*.

2 Remove saucepan from heat. Remove vanilla bean; let cool. Using a paring knife, cut vanilla bean lengthwise. Scrape out seeds. Stir seeds or vanilla extract, if using, and whipping cream into half-and-half mixture. Cover and chill in the refrigerator about 4 hours. Freeze mixture in ice cream freezer according to

manufacturer's directions. Ripen 4 hours. (Ice cream will harden, melt slower, and develop a fuller flavor if you allow it to ripen for 4 hours in your home freezer.) Makes 1½ quarts.

Nutrition Facts per ½-cup serving: 205 cal., 15 g total fat (9 g sat. fat), 54 mg chol., 30 mg sodium, 16 g carbo., 0 g fiber, 2 g pro. **Daily Values:** 16% vit. A, 5% calcium.

*Note: Omit heating the half-and-half mixture if using vanilla extract.

Easy ice cream

If you love homemade ice cream, but want an easy way to make it, look for a fuss-free no-ice, no-salt ice cream maker. It has an insulated container that is placed in the freezer overnight. A liquid coolant inside the double insulated walls keeps the ice cream mixture chilled while the machine is cranked by hand or by electricity. These machines typically make up to 1½ quarts of ice cream.

blueberry-buttermilk
chess tart

prep: 30 minutes   ***chill:*** 30 minutes   ***bake:*** 30 minutes   ***makes:*** 8 servings

1/3 cup pecan pieces
1 cup all-purpose flour
3 tablespoons sugar
1/3 cup cold butter, cut up
1 beaten egg yolk
1 tablespoon water
1 1/4 cups sugar
1/3 cup buttermilk

3 tablespoons butter, melted and cooled
3 eggs
2 tablespoons cornmeal
2 teaspoons finely shredded lemon peel
  (see tip, page 206)
2 tablespoons lemon juice
1 teaspoon vanilla
2 cups blueberries

1 For crust, place pecan pieces in a food processor bowl with a steel blade. Cover and process until very fine, but dry (not oily) (see tip, page 198). Remove ground pecans; set aside. Add flour and the 3 tablespoons sugar to processor bowl; cover and process until just combined. Add cold butter; cover and process with several on/off turns until crumbly (see top photo, right). Combine egg yolk and water. With food processor running, add egg yolk mixture through the feed tube; process until just combined. Return ground pecans to processor bowl. Cover and process with two on/off turns. (Dough will resemble the dough pictured in bottom photo, right.)

2 Remove dough from bowl; gently knead dough into a ball. Cover with plastic wrap and chill in the refrigerator for 30 to 60 minutes or until dough is easy to handle.

3 On a lightly floured surface, use your hands to slightly flatten pastry dough. Roll dough from center to edges, forming a 12-inch circle. Wrap pastry around the rolling pin. Unroll pastry onto a 10-inch tart pan with a removable bottom. Ease pastry into the tart pan, being careful not to stretch it. Press pastry into the fluted sides of the tart pan; trim edges. Using the tines of a fork, prick bottom and sides of pastry generously. Line pastry shell with a double thickness of foil. Bake in a 450° oven for 10 minutes. Remove foil. Bake about 5 minutes more or until golden brown.

4 Meanwhile, for filling, in a food processor bowl or blender container combine the 1 1/4 cups sugar, buttermilk, melted butter, eggs, cornmeal, lemon peel, lemon juice, and vanilla. Cover and process or blend until smooth.

5 Spread blueberries evenly over bottom of tart shell; pour filling mixture over blueberries. Bake in a 350° oven for 30 to 35 minutes or until a knife inserted near center comes out clean.

Nutrition Facts per serving: 398 cal., 19 g total fat (9 g sat. fat), 141 mg chol., 167 mg sodium, 54 g carbo., 2 g fiber, 5 g pro. **Daily Values:** 17% vit. A, 12% vit. C, 4% calcium, 7% iron.

EASY FOOD PROCESSOR PASTRY

A food processor makes quick work of pie or tart pastry.

First use it to cut the butter into the flour until it's crumbly (see recipe, left, and top photo, above). Then rely on the processor to incorporate the egg yolk and water into the pastry until the flour is moistened and dough begins to cling together (see bottom photo, above). Be careful not to overprocess the pastry or it will be tough.

185

Chefs and veteran home cooks alike use caramelized sugar to add a deliciously rich flavor to desserts. This simple technique involves heating sugar until it melts and turns a coppery brown. You can spoon the hot golden liquid over baked custard, drizzle it over ice cream or other desserts (see recipe, page 205), or turn it into fanciful shards (see recipe, right).

Make the decorative shards by cooling the caramelized sugar mixture in a baking pan and tapping the cooled mixture with a spoon to make jagged pieces (see photo, above). Use the pieces as garnishes for sundaes, puddings, and parfaits. Or, finely crush the pieces and sprinkle them on the tops of cakes and tortes.

frozen caramel custard

prep: 60 minutes   **freeze:** 35 minutes   **makes:** 8 servings

$\frac{1}{3}$ cup granulated sugar	Dash salt
$\frac{1}{2}$ cup whipping cream	2 cups whipping cream
5 beaten egg yolks	$\frac{1}{2}$ cup packed brown sugar
1 cup milk	2 teaspoons vanilla
$\frac{1}{4}$ cup nonfat dry milk powder	Caramel Shards (optional)

1 For caramel, in a small heavy saucepan, cook the granulated sugar over medium-high heat until sugar begins to melt, shaking saucepan occasionally. *Do not stir.* Reduce heat to low and cook until sugar is melted and golden brown, stirring frequently with a wooden spoon. Remove saucepan from heat.

2 Carefully stir in the $\frac{1}{2}$ cup whipping cream. (If a large lump of syrup forms, place saucepan over low heat and stir occasionally until syrup lump dissolves. This may take 15 minutes.)

3 In a medium saucepan combine egg yolks, milk, dry milk powder, and salt. Cook over medium-low heat, stirring constantly, until mixture coats the back of a metal spoon. Remove from heat. Stir in the 2 cups whipping cream. Add caramel, brown sugar, and vanilla to saucepan, stirring until brown sugar dissolves.

4 Cool custard mixture by placing the saucepan in a bowl of ice water. Stir occasionally, adding more ice to water as necessary until mixture is completely cool. (Or, cover and chill in the refrigerator.) Freeze custard mixture in an ice-cream freezer according to the manufacturer's instructions. If desired, garnish ice cream with Caramel Shards.

Nutrition Facts per serving: 404 cal., 32 g total fat (19 g sat. fat), 238 mg chol., 83 mg sodium, 26 g carbo., 0 g fiber, 5 g pro. **Daily Values:** 41% vit. A, 1% vit. C, 14% calcium, 4% iron.

Caramel Shards: Butter baking sheet. (If desired, line the baking sheet with foil and butter the foil.) Set baking sheet aside. In a large heavy skillet cook $\frac{3}{4}$ cup granulated sugar over medium-high heat until sugar begins to melt, shaking skillet occasionally. Do not stir. Reduce heat to low. Cook and stir about 3 minutes more or until sugar is melted and coppery brown in color. Remove from heat. Stir in $\frac{1}{2}$ teaspoon hot water. Immediately pour mixture onto prepared baking sheet, spreading as thin as possible. Cool for 30 minutes. When cool, tap gently with a spoon to break into shards (see photo, left). Store tightly covered.

An apple that is great for eating
fresh may not be ideal for
cooking because heat breaks
down the texture of some
apples, making them mushy
and less flavorful. Here's a brief
look at the best ways to use
some of the most widely
available apples:
All-purpose apples (terrific
fresh or cooked): Crispin,
Criterion, Fuji, Golden
Delicious, Granny Smith,
Jonagold, Jonathan, Winesap
Snacking and salads: Cortland,
Empire, Gala, McIntosh,
Newtown Pippin, Northern Spy,
Red Delicious, Stayman
Baking and pies: Rome Beauty,
Braeburn, York Imperial

apple-cranberry pie

prep: 20 minutes   *bake:* 40 minutes   *makes:* 8 servings

1 pound baking apples, quartered and cored (3 medium)	1 egg
1 cup cranberries	½ cup all-purpose flour
¼ cup walnuts	½ cup butter, melted
½ cup sugar	⅓ cup sugar
¼ cup raisins	1½ teaspoons finely shredded orange peel
1 tablespoon finely shredded orange peel (see tip, page 206)	½ teaspoon vanilla
	⅛ teaspoon salt
	Several drops almond extract

1 Generously butter a 9-inch pie plate; set aside. Place unpeeled apples in a food processor bowl. Cover and process until coarsely chopped. Remove from bowl. Repeat with cranberries and walnuts, processing separately, until coarsely chopped. (Or, chop ingredients by hand.)

2 In a medium bowl combine apples, cranberries, walnuts, the ½ cup sugar, the raisins, and the 1 tablespoon orange peel. Spread mixture evenly in the bottom of pie plate; set aside.

3 For topping, in the food processor bowl or a mixing bowl combine egg, flour, melted butter, the ⅓ cup sugar, the 1½ teaspoons orange peel, vanilla, salt, and almond extract. Cover and process or beat with an electric mixer on medium speed until smooth. Spread batter evenly over fruit mixture.

4 Bake in a 350° oven about 40 minutes or until topping is brown and a wooden toothpick inserted in the center comes out clean. Cool slightly in pie plate on a wire rack. Serve warm.

Nutrition Facts per serving: 290 cal., 15 g total fat (8 g sat. fat), 57 mg chol., 159 mg sodium, 40 g carbo., 2 g fiber, 2 g pro. **Daily Values:** 12% vit. A, 9% vit. C, 1% calcium, 4% iron.

To make ahead: Bake pie as directed and cool completely. Cover with foil and refrigerate for up to 24 hours. To reheat, bake, covered, in a 350° oven about 20 minutes or until warm.

brownie pudding cake

prep: 15 minutes   *bake:* 30 minutes   *makes:* 4 servings

½ cup all-purpose flour
¼ cup sugar
3 tablespoons unsweetened cocoa powder
¾ teaspoon baking powder
¼ cup milk

1 tablespoon cooking oil
½ teaspoon vanilla
¼ cup chopped walnuts
⅓ cup sugar
¾ cup boiling water

1 In a medium bowl stir together flour, the ¼ cup sugar, 1 tablespoon of the cocoa powder, and the baking powder. Add milk, oil, and vanilla; stir until smooth. Stir in walnuts. Transfer batter to an ungreased 1-quart casserole.

2 Combine the remaining 2 tablespoons cocoa powder and the ⅓ cup sugar. Gradually stir in boiling water. Pour evenly over batter. Bake in a 350° oven about 30 minutes or until a wooden toothpick inserted near the center of the cake comes out clean. Serve warm.

Nutrition Facts per serving: 270 cal., 9 g total fat (1 g sat. fat), 1 mg chol., 78 mg sodium, 44 g carbo., 1 g fiber, 4 g pro. **Daily Values:** 1% vit. A, 11% calcium, 9% iron.

What about white chocolate?

White chocolate contains cocoa butter, sugar, and milk solids, and has a mild flavor that's unlike the darker chocolate products listed at right. Other products sometimes confused with white chocolate include white baking bars, white baking pieces, white candy coating, and white confectionery bars. Although these products are often used interchangeably with white chocolate, they do not contain any cocoa butter and legally can't be labeled chocolate in the United States.

TYPES OF CHOCOLATE

How many kinds of chocolate are there to love? Plenty. Here are the main types you'll find at the supermarket:

Unsweetened chocolate is pure chocolate and cocoa butter with no sugar added. It's used for baking and cooking rather than snacking.

Semisweet chocolate and **bittersweet chocolate** are at least 35 percent pure chocolate with added cocoa butter and sugar. They can be used interchangeably.

Sweet chocolate is at least 15 percent pure chocolate with added cocoa butter and sugar. Sweeter and milder than semisweet chocolate, it is used in cooking and baking.

Milk chocolate is at least 10 percent pure chocolate with added cocoa butter, sugar, and milk solids. It is creamier and milder than semisweet.

Unsweetened cocoa powder is pure chocolate with most of the cocoa butter removed. Dutch-process or European-style cocoa powder has been treated to neutralize acids, making it mellower in flavor.

fresh fruit napoleons

prep: 25 minutes   **cook:** 6 minutes   **makes:** 8 servings

½ of a 17¼-ounce package frozen
    puff pastry (1 sheet), thawed
1 tablespoon milk
1 tablespoon granulated sugar or coarse sugar
4 cups sliced strawberries, whole
    blueberries, whole raspberries,
    and/or whole blackberries

4 egg yolks
⅓ cup sweet Marsala or cream sherry
⅓ cup sugar
Dash salt
Sifted powdered sugar (optional)

1 Unfold pastry sheet on a lightly floured surface. Roll slightly to remove creases; trim edges. Cut into eight 5×2½-inch rectangles. Transfer rectangles to an ungreased baking sheet. Brush lightly with milk; sprinkle with the 1 tablespoon sugar. Bake in a 375° oven for 10 to 12 minutes or until golden. Cool on a wire rack.

2 Gently split rectangles into 2 layers. Place 1 layer on each of 8 dessert plates. Divide fruit evenly over the bottom layers; set aside.

3 For custard filling, in the top of a double boiler beat egg yolks and

Marsala or sherry until combined. Stir in the ⅓ cup sugar and salt. Place over but not touching boiling water. Beat with an electric mixer on high speed for 6 to 8 minutes or until mixture thickens and mounds and temperature reaches 160°.

4 Immediately spoon over fruit on plates; add tops. If desired, sprinkle with powdered sugar. Serve immediately.

Nutrition Facts per serving: 236 cal., 12 g total fat (1 g sat. fat), 106 mg chol., 139 mg sodium, 26 g carbo., 2 g fiber, 3 g pro. **Daily Values:** 5% vit. A, 68% vit. C, 2% calcium, 3% iron.

Timesaving filling options

When you don't have time to make the custard filling for Fresh Fruit Napoleons (see recipe, above), substitute purchased pudding from the deli, make instant pudding from a mix, or pick up a jar of lemon or orange curd.

WORKING WITH PUFF PASTRY

Because the results often look so spectacular, many cooks think working with frozen puff pastry is difficult. Actually, if you keep these hints in mind, you'll find puff pastry is a quick and easy way to make a dramatic dessert.

The main rule for working with puff pastry is to keep it cool. If the dough becomes too warm, it will soften, making it sticky and unmanageable. To ensure the dough stays chilled, roll it out one sheet at a time, keeping what you're not using wrapped tightly in plastic wrap in the refrigerator.

For perfect rectangles, use a ruler and pastry wheel or sharp knife to cut even pieces (see photo, above).

irish coffee meringues

prep: 25 minutes   **bake:** 1¼ hours   **chill:** 30 minutes   **makes:** 6 servings

2 egg whites
½ cup slivered almonds, toasted (see note, page 198)
⅔ cup sugar
½ teaspoon instant espresso coffee powder or 1 teaspoon instant coffee crystals
1 teaspoon vanilla

¼ teaspoon cream of tartar
Dash salt
1 cup whipping cream
1 tablespoon Irish cream liqueur or cold strong coffee
Unsweetened cocoa powder
Chocolate-covered coffee beans (optional)

1 For meringues, in a medium bowl let egg whites stand at room temperature for 30 minutes. Meanwhile, line an extra-large baking sheet with parchment paper or plain brown paper. Draw twelve 3×1½-inch ovals on paper about 2 inches apart; set aside.

2 Place almonds in a food processor bowl. Cover and process until finely ground, but dry (not oily); set aside.

3 In a small bowl, combine sugar and espresso powder or coffee crystals. Add vanilla, cream of tartar, and salt to the egg whites. Beat with an electric mixer on medium to high speed until soft peaks form (tips curl). Gradually add sugar mixture, 1 tablespoon at a time, beating about 5 minutes on high speed or until stiff peaks form (tips stand straight) and sugar is almost dissolved. Fold in ground almonds.

4 Using a spoon or spatula, spread meringue mixture over the ovals on the prepared baking sheet. Bake in a 300° oven for 15 minutes. Turn off oven. Let meringues dry in oven with door closed for 1 hour. (Do not open oven.)*

5 For filling, in a chilled medium bowl combine the whipping cream and the Irish cream liqueur or cold coffee. Beat with an electric mixer on low speed until soft peaks form (tips curl).

6 To assemble, place 1 meringue on a dessert plate, flat side down. Spoon about ¼ cup of the filling over meringue. Top with another meringue, flat side down; press gently until filling spreads to edges. Repeat with remaining meringues and filling, making 6 stacks. Cover and refrigerate for 30 to 60 minutes. Cover and chill remaining whipped cream mixture.

7 To serve, sift cocoa powder over meringues. If desired, garnish with chocolate-covered coffee beans.

*Note: If you like, prepare the meringues ahead and store them in an airtight container for up to a week.

Nutrition Facts per serving: 304 cal., 21 g total fat (10 g sat. fat), 55 mg chol., 61 mg sodium, 26 g carbo., 1 g fiber, 4 g pro. **Daily Values:** 17% vit. A, 6% calcium, 3% iron.

Phyllo, often used in Greek cooking, consists of paper-thin sheets of dough. When baked, it becomes a delicate pastry.

Phyllo dries out easily because it is so thin. The secret to success with phyllo is keeping the dough moist. Start by thawing the phyllo while it is still wrapped. If you're only using half of the package, roll up the remaining sheets, wrap them tightly in plastic wrap, and return them to the freezer. As you prepare a recipe, keep the dough moist by covering it with plastic wrap.

Triangles (see recipe, right) are a typical way to shape phyllo. To make triangles, cut the dough into strips, place the filling at one end, and fold as shown in the photo, above.

194

fruit- & nut-filled
phyllo triangles

prep: 30 minutes   ***bake:*** 12 minutes   ***makes:*** 24 servings

1	cup walnuts
¼	cup sugar
1	teaspoon finely shredded lemon peel (see tip, page 206)
1	teaspoon ground cinnamon
½	teaspoon ground nutmeg

½	cup mixed dried fruit bits
3	tablespoons rum or apple juice
3	tablespoons honey
12	sheets (18×14 inches) frozen phyllo dough, thawed
⅔	cup butter or margarine, melted

1 For filling, place walnuts and sugar in a food processor bowl or blender container. Cover and process or blend until walnuts are finely ground, but dry (not oily). In a small bowl combine walnut mixture, lemon peel, cinnamon, and nutmeg; set aside.

2 In a small saucepan combine fruit bits, rum or apple juice, and honey. Bring to boiling over medium heat; reduce heat. Simmer, uncovered, about 8 minutes or until most of the liquid is absorbed. Add fruit mixture to walnut mixture; stir just until combined.

3 Place 1 sheet of phyllo dough on a cutting board or other flat surface. (Keep remaining phyllo covered with plastic wrap to prevent it from becoming dry and brittle.) Lightly brush the sheet with some of the melted butter. Place another phyllo sheet on top; brush with butter. Repeat with two more phyllo sheets. Cut layered sheets crosswise into 8 equal strips. Place about 2 teaspoons of filling 1 inch from an end of each dough strip. To fold into a triangle, bring a corner over filling so it is even with the other side of the strip (see photo, left). Continue folding strip in a triangular shape. Repeat process with remaining phyllo sheets, butter, and filling to make a total of 24 triangles.

4 Place filled triangles on a lightly greased baking sheet; brush tops with remaining melted butter. Bake in a 400° oven for 12 to 14 minutes or until triangles are golden brown. Transfer to a wire rack; cool slightly. Serve warm.

Nutrition Facts per serving: 138 cal., 9 g total fat (4 g sat. fat), 15 mg chol., 102 mg sodium, 12 g carbo., 1 g fiber, 2 g pro. **Daily Values:** 6% vit. A, 1% vit. C, 1% calcium, 3% iron.

coffee cheesecake

prep: 20 minutes   ***bake:*** 45 minutes   ***cool:*** 1¾ hours   ***chill:*** 4 hours   ***makes:*** 16 servings

½ cup graham cracker crumbs	1 cup sugar
½ cup chocolate cookie crumbs	3 tablespoons all-purpose flour
½ cup ground hazelnuts or almonds	1 teaspoon vanilla
3 tablespoons sugar	3 slightly beaten eggs
¼ cup butter, melted	¼ cup coffee-flavored liqueur
3 8-ounce packages cream cheese, softened	or cooled espresso coffee

1 Generously grease the bottom and sides of an 8-inch springform pan; set aside. For crust, in a bowl combine cracker crumbs, cookie crumbs, nuts, and the 3 tablespoons sugar. Stir in melted butter. Press crumb mixture firmly onto bottom and 2 inches up the side of prepared pan. Set aside.

2 For filling, in a large bowl beat cream cheese, the 1 cup sugar, the flour, and vanilla with an electric mixer on medium to high speed until fluffy, scraping sides of bowl as necessary. Stir in eggs and liqueur or coffee until just combined. Pour filling into crust-lined pan.

3 Place in a shallow baking pan in the oven. Bake in a 375° oven for 45 to 50 minutes or until center appears nearly set when gently shaken.

4 Cool in springform pan on wire rack for 15 minutes. Loosen sides of cake from pan and cool 30 minutes more. Remove sides from pan; cool 1 hour. Cover and chill in the refrigerator at least 4 hours or up to 24 hours before serving.

Nutrition Facts per serving: 419 cal., 30 g total fat (16 g sat. fat), 127 mg chol., 286 mg sodium, 30 g carbo., 1 g fiber, 7 g pro. **Daily Values:** 28% vit. A, 7% calcium, 7% iron.

Cheesecake cooling & unmolding

The best way to remove the sides of a springform pan from a cheesecake is to first cool the baked cheesecake for 15 minutes on a wire rack. Loosen the crust from the side of the pan with a very thin knife or flexible metal spatula; this helps prevent the cheesecake from cracking as it cools. Then let it cool for 30 minutes more. To remove the pan's sides, set the cooled cake on a large canister and release the clasp on the side of the pan, allowing the sides to drop down around the canister (see photo, left). Cool the cake another hour before chilling.

PERFECT CHEESECAKE

For heavenly cheesecake with the silkiest texture and a smooth, unblemished top, beat or stir the filling gently, especially after adding the eggs. Overzealous beating incorporates a lot of air, which is great for a soufflé, but not for a cheesecake. Too much air causes a cheesecake to puff and fall, creating a crack.

Trying to decipher when a cheesecake is done can be difficult. Inserting a knife in the center doesn't work and will cause a crack. The best way to tell if a cheesecake is done is to gently shake it. If it looks nearly set and only a small circle in the center jiggles, it's done. The center will firm up during cooling. Cheesecakes made with sour cream will jiggle a little more and have a larger soft spot in the center than regular cheesecake.

GRINDING NUTS

Many sweets call for ground nuts. When grinding nuts, you need to take some extra care or you may wind up with nut butter. Here's a trick:

If you're using a blender or food processor, add 1 tablespoon of the sugar or flour from the recipe for each cup of nuts. (It helps absorb some of the oil.) Use a quick start-and-stop motion for better control over the fineness of the nuts. For best results, grind the nuts in small batches.

brown sugar-hazelnut cooled

prep: 40 minutes   *chill:* 4 hours   *bake:* 10 minutes   *makes:* 60 cookies

½	cup shortening	
½	cup butter	
1¼	cups packed brown sugar	
½	teaspoon baking soda	
¼	teaspoon salt	

1	egg
1	teaspoon vanilla
2½	cups all-purpose flour
¾	cup toasted ground hazelnuts or pecans*

1 In a large bowl beat shortening and butter with an electric mixer on medium to high speed for 30 seconds. Add the brown sugar, baking soda, and salt. Beat until combined. Beat in egg and vanilla until combined. Beat in as much of the flour as you can. Using a wooden spoon, stir in any remaining flour and the ground nuts.

2 On waxed paper shape dough into two 10-inch rolls. Wrap each roll in waxed paper or plastic wrap. Chill in the refrigerator for at least 4 hours or up to 48 hours or until firm enough to slice.

3 Using a thin-bladed knife, cut dough into ¼-inch-thick slices. Place slices 1 inch apart on ungreased cookie sheets.

4 Bake in a 375° oven for 10 minutes or until edges are firm. Transfer the cookies to a wire rack and let cool.

Note: To toast nuts, spread them in a single layer in a shallow baking pan. Bake in a 350° oven for 5 to 10 minutes or until light golden brown, watching carefully and stirring once or twice. If desired, remove the skins from the hazelnuts by placing the warm nuts on a kitchen towel and rubbing the nuts until the skins come loose.

Nutrition Facts per cookie: 70 cal., 4 g total fat (1 g sat. fat), 8 mg chol., 37 mg sodium, 7 g carbo., 0 g fiber, 1 g pro. **Daily Values:** 1% vit. A, 2% iron.

peanut-sesame marbled brownies

prep: 20 minutes   **bake:** 30 minutes   **makes:** 48 bars

8 ounces semisweet chocolate	3 eggs
¾ cup butter	2 tablespoons milk
¼ cup creamy peanut butter	1 teaspoon vanilla
¼ cup tahini (sesame butter)	2 cups all-purpose flour
¾ cup packed brown sugar	½ cup coarsely chopped unsalted peanuts
½ cup granulated sugar	2 tablespoons sesame seeds
2 teaspoons baking powder	

1 In a small saucepan melt the chocolate and ¼ cup of the butter over low heat until smooth. Set aside to cool slightly.

2 In a large bowl beat the remaining ½ cup butter, the peanut butter, and tahini with an electric mixer on medium speed until combined. Add brown sugar, granulated sugar, and baking powder; beat until combined. Beat in the eggs, milk, and vanilla. Beat in as much of the flour as you can. Using a wooden spoon, stir in any remaining flour.

3 Spread half of the peanut butter batter into the bottom of an ungreased 13×9×2-inch baking pan. Spread cooled chocolate mixture over batter in pan. Spoon remaining peanut butter batter into small mounds over chocolate mixture. Sprinkle with chopped peanuts and sesame seeds.

4 Bake in a 350° oven for 30 to 35 minutes or until a wooden toothpick inserted in center comes out clean. Cool on a wire rack.

Nutrition Facts per bar: 115 cal., 7 g total fat (3 g sat. fat), 21 mg chol., 57 mg sodium, 12 g carbo., 1 g fiber, 2 g pro. **Daily Values:** 3% vit. A, 2% calcium, 4% iron.

What is tahini?

A butter made from ground sesame seeds, tahini is an ingredient often used in Middle Eastern recipes. One traditional favorite, hummus, is a combination of tahini and mashed chickpeas (garbanzo beans) served as an appetizer spread for pita bread. Tahini also can be used in recipes such as Peanut-Sesame Marbled Brownies (see recipe, above). Look for tahini in specialty food shops or Asian markets.

MELTING CHOCOLATE

Melting chocolate can be tricky if you're not melting it with butter as you do in the recipe, left. For recipes that don't include fat, use these guidelines.

- Chocolate can be melted on the range top or in the microwave. To speed things along, chop or break up the chocolate before you begin.
- **To melt chocolate on the range top,** use a heavy saucepan or double boiler. Make sure the utensils are dry and avoid splashing any water into the pan. Even a little water will cause the chocolate to seize up and get grainy and lumpy. Place the saucepan over low heat or the double boiler over hot, but not boiling, water. Stir the chocolate often to keep it from burning.
- **To melt chocolate in the microwave,** place 1 cup of chocolate pieces or 2 ounces of chocolate in a small microwave-safe bowl. Heat, uncovered, on 100% power (high) for 1½ to 2 minutes or until chocolate is soft enough to stir smooth.

199

ROLLING OUT PIE PASTRY

You'll never have pie or tart pastry stick to the counter again if you use this simple trick: Roll out the pastry dough between two sheets of waxed paper. Place a large piece of waxed paper on the counter, then place a well-chilled ball of dough on top. Flatten the ball slightly into a disk. Place another piece of waxed paper on top and begin rolling from the center to the edge, turning the dough occasionally.

If the waxed paper tears or wrinkles, you may need to remove it and start with a fresh sheet. When the dough is the desired dimensions, peel off the top layer of waxed paper. Slide the bottom sheet with the dough onto your hand and invert it over the pie plate or tart pan. Gently peel off the waxed paper and carefully ease the pastry into the pan. Trim the crust, and it's ready to be filled or baked.

tangy lemon tart

prep: 45 minutes   *bake:* 13 minutes   *chill:* 4 hours   *makes:* 10 to 12 servings

1½ cups all-purpose flour	⅛ teaspoon salt
2 teaspoons sugar	2 teaspoons finely shredded lemon peel
½ teaspoon salt	¾ cup lemon juice
⅓ cup shortening	⅓ cup butter, cubed
¼ cup cold butter	⅓ cup water
3 to 4 tablespoons ice water	5 egg yolks
1¼ cups sugar	Candied Lemon Slices
¼ cup cornstarch	3 tablespoons orange marmalade, melted

1 For crust, in a bowl combine flour, the 2 teaspoons sugar, and the ½ teaspoon salt. Use a pastry blender to cut shortening and the ¼ cup butter into flour mixture until mixture resembles coarse crumbs. Sprinkle 1 tablespoon of the water over part of the mixture; gently toss with a fork. Push moistened dough to side of bowl. Repeat, using 1 tablespoon water at a time, until all the dough is moistened. Shape dough into a ball.

2 Place dough between 2 sheets of waxed paper; roll from center to edge forming a 12-inch circle. Remove top sheet of waxed paper and transfer pastry into a 10-inch tart pan with a removable bottom. Peel remaining sheet of waxed paper off pastry. Ease pastry into pan; trim edges.

3 Line pastry with a double thickness of foil. Bake in a 450° oven for 8 minutes. Remove foil. Bake 5 to 6 minutes more or until crust is golden brown. Set aside.

4 For lemon curd, in a medium saucepan, stir together the 1¼ cups sugar, the cornstarch, and the ⅛ teaspoon salt. Stir in lemon peel, lemon juice, the ⅓ cup butter, and the ⅓ cup water. Cook and stir until thickened and bubbly. Gradually stir about 1 cup of the hot mixture into egg yolks. Return all of the egg yolk mixture to saucepan. Cook over medium heat until mixture just begins to bubble. Reduce heat; cook and stir for 2 minutes more.

5 Pour hot lemon curd into crust. Cool on a wire rack. Top cooled tart with candied lemon slices, forming a ring of overlapping slices in the center. Brush top of tart lightly with melted orange marmalade. Cover; chill in the refrigerator for at least 4 hours or up to 24 hours.

Nutrition Facts per serving: 366 cal., 21 g total fat (10 g sat. fat), 137 mg chol., 266 mg sodium, 43 g carbo., 1 g fiber, 3 g pro. **Daily Values:** 15% vit. A, 15% vit. C, 2% calcium, 6% iron.

Candied Lemon Slices: In a medium skillet combine ¼ cup water and ¼ cup sugar; bring to boiling. Add 8 very thin lemon slices. Simmer gently, uncovered, for 12 to 15 minutes or until softened and white portion becomes almost opaque. With a fork, transfer slices to a wire rack to cool.

picking berries

Blueberries are versatile. They can be eaten fresh, frozen, baked in quick breads, or used to flavor vinegars.

Marionberries are elongated berries that hold their shape and excellent mildly tart flavor, even after freezing.

Heart-shaped and mildly sweet, **strawberries** are delicious fresh or used in baking and cooking.

It is tart, so the **gooseberry** shows off well in baked goods, jams, or jellies. Try it solo or with other fruits.

Delicate **golden raspberries** are fragile to the touch. This golden berry is a sweet cousin to the red raspberry. It's best eaten fresh.

A cross between blackberries and raspberries, tart **loganberries** need plenty of sweetening. They're great in jams, jellies, and pies.

Smaller and a bit firmer than their red counterpart, **black raspberries** are a treat eaten fresh or baked in pies.

Red raspberries are sweet enough to enjoy plain or to use in baking and cooking. Refrigerate right away. Avoid mushy raspberries by washing them just before using.

easy berry sorbet

prep: 10 minutes   ***makes:*** 6 to 8 servings

2 cups fresh blueberries
2 cups fresh raspberries
½ cup cold water

¼ cup frozen pineapple-orange-banana
    juice concentrate or citrus
    beverage concentrate
Sugar cones (optional)

1 Freeze berries as directed in the tip at right. In a large bowl combine the frozen berries, cold water, and frozen concentrate. Place half of the mixture in a food processor bowl. Cover and process until almost smooth. Repeat with remaining mixture. Serve immediately. If desired, scoop frozen mixture into cones.

(Or, transfer mixture to a baking dish. Cover and freeze about 4 hours or until firm.) Use within 2 days.

Nutrition Facts per serving: 66 cal., 0 g total fat, 0 mg chol., 4 mg sodium, 16 g carbo., 3 g fiber, 1 g pro. **Daily Values:** 1% vit. A, 46% vit. C, 1% calcium, 5% iron.

Sorbet versus sherbet

In the world of frozen treats, sorbets and sherbets are often confused. Both are a frozen concoction of a liquid, a sweetener, fruit, and sometimes gelatin. The difference between the two is the liquid that's used. Sorbets are made with water; sherbets include milk or another dairy product. This distinction gives sorbets a softer, icier texture than sherbets. Sorbets often are less rich and seem more refreshing than sherbets, making them ideal between-course palate cleansers as well as desserts.

STORING FRESH BERRIES

Fresh berries are so perishable that you should store them properly as soon as possible.

For short-term storage, keep berries refrigerated. Store them in a single layer, loosely covered, and refrigerate for a day or two. Heaping fresh berries on top of each other in a bowl can crush the fruit.

For longer storage, freezing is best. Place the berries in a single layer on a baking pan (see photo, above) and place them in the freezer. Once they're frozen, put the berries in freezer containers or plastic freezer bags and seal. Stored this way, berries will keep in the freezer for up to a year.

raspberries
& lemon cream

prep: 20 minutes   *makes:* 4 servings

- 2 cups fresh red raspberries
- 4 teaspoons raspberry liqueur
- 1 8-ounce carton lemon-flavored yogurt
- ¼ of an 8-ounce container frozen whipped dessert topping, thawed
- 3 tablespoons sugar

1 Reserve ¼ cup raspberries. In a medium bowl gently toss remaining raspberries with liqueur.

2 In a small bowl stir together yogurt and whipped dessert topping. Spoon berry-liqueur mixture into 4 dessert dishes. Spoon yogurt mixture onto berries. If not serving immediately, cover dishes and chill for up to 4 hours.

3 Before serving, place sugar in a small heavy saucepan. Heat over medium-high heat until sugar begins to melt, shaking pan occasionally to heat sugar evenly. *Do not stir.* Once the sugar starts to melt, reduce heat to low and cook about 5 minutes more or until all of the sugar is melted and golden, stirring as needed with a wooden spoon. Remove pan from heat. Let stand for 1 minute.

4 Dip a fork into caramelized sugar and let syrup run off tines of fork for several seconds before shaking fork over dessert, allowing thin strands of caramelized sugar to drizzle over berries. If sugar starts to harden in the pan, return to heat, stirring until melted. Top with reserved berries. Serve immediately.

Nutrition Facts per serving: 148 cal., 1 g total fat (0 g sat. fat), 2 mg chol., 41 mg sodium, 32 g carbo., 3 g fiber, 3 g pro. **Daily Values:** 1% vit. A, 26% vit. C, 8% calcium, 2% iron.

COOKING WITH LIQUEURS

Liqueurs add a hint of elegance and sophistication to almost any dessert. They are sweet alcoholic beverages flavored with everything from fruits and nuts to herbs and spices to flowers and seeds. Also called cordials, liqueurs can be served in small glasses or on the rocks as after-dinner drinks or used in cooking to add a special flavor.

Some of the most common flavors include orange, cherry, raspberry, chocolate, mint, almond, and hazelnut. Crème liqueurs are sweeter and have a fuller body than regular liqueurs.

To substitute one liqueur for another, choose alternates in the same flavor family. For example, substitute one nut liqueur for another. If you don't have raspberry liqueur to make Raspberries and Lemon Cream (see recipe, left), consider using cherry liqueur, orange liqueur, or crème de cassis (black currant liqueur).

205

CITRUS ZEST OR PEEL

Zest is appropriately named, as it adds flavor and life to all sorts of recipes. When used in cooking, the term refers to the intensely perfumed outermost colored layer of citrus peel (not the white pith, which is bitter).

There are several ways to shred citrus peel. One is to finely grate the peel with a grater. Or, you can use a citrus zester, which has a stainless-steel edge with a series of cutting holes that strip off fine threadlike pieces of peel. Innovative cooks have put a woodworking tool called the microplane (see photo, above) to use. A microplane allows you to shred tiny, uniform pieces of peel faster and with less pressure than a regular grater or citrus zester. It also can be used to create fine shreds of chocolate or fresh ginger.

ricotta-filled pears
with chocolate

prep: 20 minutes   **makes:** 6 servings

1   cup ricotta cheese
⅓   cup sifted powdered sugar
1   tablespoon unsweetened cocoa powder
¼   teaspoon vanilla
2   tablespoons miniature semisweet
      chocolate pieces
1   teaspoon finely shredded orange peel

3   large ripe Bosc, Anjou, or Bartlett pears
2   tablespoons orange juice
2   tablespoons slivered or sliced
      almonds, toasted (see note, page 198)
    Fresh mint leaves (optional)
    Orange peel curls (optional)

1 In a medium bowl beat the ricotta cheese, powdered sugar, cocoa powder, and vanilla with an electric mixer on medium speed until combined. Stir in chocolate pieces and the 1 teaspoon orange peel. Set aside.

2 Peel the pears; cut in half lengthwise and remove the cores. Remove a thin slice from the rounded sides so the pear halves will lie flat. Brush the pears on all sides with orange juice. Place the pears on dessert plates. Spoon the ricotta mixture on top of the pears and sprinkle with almonds. If desired, garnish with mint leaves and orange curls.

Nutrition Facts per serving: 166 cal., 6 g total fat (2 g sat. fat), 13 mg chol., 52 mg sodium, 24 g carbo., 3 g fiber, 6 g pro. **Daily Values:** 5% vit. A, 10% vit. C, 11% calcium, 4% iron.

CRYSTALLIZED GINGER

Crystallized ginger (also called candied ginger) is fresh ginger that's been boiled in a sugar syrup, then dipped in sugar and dried. It imparts a fiery sweetness to foods when used as a garnish (see recipe, right) or when added to baked goods and sauces. For a sweet-hot treat, it can be dipped in melted bittersweet chocolate, allowed to dry, and served as part of a dessert tray.

Look for crystallized ginger in the baking aisle or near the herbs and spices in your local supermarket. Don't buy pieces that are hard, stuck together, or missing their sugar coating; these signs indicate the ginger is either old or of poor quality.

gingered shortcake
with spiced fruit

prep: 25 minutes   **bake:** 18 minutes   **cool:** 40 minutes   **cook:** 3 minutes   **makes:** 8 servings

2 cups all-purpose flour	2 tablespoons granulated sugar
¼ cup granulated sugar	½ teaspoon vanilla
2 teaspoons baking powder	3 tablespoons butter
½ cup butter	3 medium cooking apples, thinly sliced
1 beaten egg	3 tablespoons brown sugar
⅔ cup milk	¼ teaspoon ground nutmeg
1 tablespoon grated fresh ginger	1 cup blueberries
1 cup whipping cream	Crystallized ginger, minced (optional)

1 For cake, combine the flour, the ¼ cup granulated sugar, and the baking powder. Cut in the ½ cup butter until mixture resembles coarse crumbs. Combine egg, milk, and fresh ginger; add to dry mixture. Stir to moisten. Spread in a greased 8×1½-inch round baking pan.

2 Bake in a 450° oven for 18 to 20 minutes or until a wooden toothpick inserted near center comes out clean. Cool in pan for 10 minutes. Remove from pan; cool on a wire rack for 30 minutes. Split into 2 layers.

3 In a chilled bowl combine whipping cream, the 2 tablespoons granulated sugar, and the vanilla. Beat with chilled beaters of an electric mixer until soft peaks form (tips curl). Cover and refrigerate.

4 In a large skillet melt the 3 tablespoons butter over medium heat. Add apples; cook for 2 to 5 minutes or until almost tender. Stir in brown sugar and nutmeg. Cook for 1 to 3 minutes more or until fruit is tender. Stir in blueberries.

5 Place bottom shortcake layer on serving plate. Spoon about two-thirds of the fruit mixture and half of the whipped cream over cake. Top with second cake layer and remaining fruit mixture. Pass remaining whipped cream. If desired, garnish with minced crystallized ginger.

Nutrition Facts per serving: 457 cal., 28 g total fat (17 g sat. fat), 111 mg chol., 280 mg sodium, 47 g carbo., 2 g fiber, 5 g pro. **Daily Values:** 30% vit. A, 6% vit. C, 12% calcium, 11% iron.

There are many secrets to great cooking, but having the right equipment, storing foods properly, and keeping a well-stocked pantry are not secrets. They are the foundation of cooking. The following pages include all the information you'll need to set up a kitchen you'll love to cook in.

EQUIPMENT

Having enough quality cookware certainly makes life easier. Enough means you won't have to clean the same pan before you make every meal. Investing in good quality cookware is the way to go for long-lasting use, and easy care and cleanup.

Start with the basics listed here and buy the best you can afford. Gradually build on that base by adding the cooking gadgets you need and want and will use often enough to justify the cost.

Following is a list of equipment that's considered key to a well-equipped basic kitchen.

Pots & Pans

Pots and pans are made of a variety of materials: aluminum, cast iron, stainless steel, copper, ceramic, enameled metal, and glass. In general, metal pans perform better and last longer than ceramic or glass ones. Copper and aluminum are the best heat conductors. All-copper pans are expensive and tarnish easily, but you can get heavy stainless-steel pans with copper bottoms that work well. Plain aluminum pans can react with acidic foods and are

hard to find. What you will find are pans clad with layers of aluminum sandwiched between stainless steel. The stainless steel is durable and easy to clean, and the aluminum core conducts heat quickly and evenly.

Heavy pans are often called for in recipes. These pans are thick so they heat foods evenly and gently, which is useful for melting chocolate or caramelizing sugar; they also help prevent burning. Copper-bottomed pans, cast iron, enameled cast iron, and clad aluminum pans are all good choices for heavy-bottomed pans. Following are basic pots and pans to have on hand (items with an asterisk are not essential but are useful to have):

- Double boiler
- Dutch oven (*3-quart with lid*)
- Grill pan*
- Roasting pan

- Saucepans (*1-, 2-, and 3-quart pans with lids*)
- Skillets (*8- and 10-inch; preferably a nonstick 10-inch skillet*)
- Stockpot (*8-quart*)
- Vegetable steamer* (*collapsible or insert*)

Baking Equipment

- Baking pans (*two 10×15-inch with a 1½-inch rim*)
- Cake pans (*two 8- or 9-inch round, 9-inch springform, 13×9-inch rectangle, 8-inch square*)
- Casserole dishes (*2- and 3-quart*)
- Cookie sheets* (*two without rim*)
- Cooling racks, wire
- Loaf pans (*two 9×5-inch*)
- Muffin pans (*two 12-cup*)
- Pie plate (*9-inch*)
- Rolling pin
- Soufflé dish*

Nonstick pans

Forget about buying the best nonstick pans you can afford because their coatings eventually will become damaged. However, don't buy the cheapest either. Look for fairly heavy, moderately priced nonstick pans. With proper care, they will last from three to five years before needing to be replaced.

equipment & pantry

UTENSILS/GADGETS
- Bottle/can opener
- Cheese slicer*
- Citrus juicer/reamer*
- Citrus zester*
- Colander
- Corkscrew
- Custard cups*
- Cutting boards (1 wooden and 1 plastic)
- Sifter
- Funnel
- Grater, for cheese and vegetables
- Kitchen shears
- Ladles
- Measuring cups, dry
  (¼ cup, ⅓ cup, ½ cup, 1 cup)
- Measuring cups, liquid
  (1 cup, 2 cup, 4 cup)
- Measuring spoons (⅛ teaspoon, ¼ teaspoon,
  ½ teaspoon, 1 teaspoon, 1 tablespoon)
- Meat mallet*
- Mixing bowls (set of four)
- Mortar and pestle*
- Parchment paper*
- Pastry bag with tips*
- Pastry blender
- Pastry brushes
- Pepper grinder
- Pizza cutter*
- Pizza stone
- Potato masher or ricer
- Rubber scrapers
- Salad spinner*
- Sieves or strainers (wire mesh;
  1 large and 1 small)
- Skewers (short and long; preferably metal)
- Slotted spoon (long-handled)
- Spatulas, metal and nylon
- Thermometers (candy*, instant-read, oven)
- Timer
- Tongs
- Vegetable peeler
- Wire whisks (tiny and 8-inch)
- Wooden spoons (assorted sizes)

APPLIANCES
- Blender
- Electric hand mixer
- Food processor*
- Mini food processor*
- Standing mixer*

KNIVES
Choose knives made of high-carbon stainless steel with blades that run through the handles (full tang) and are held in the handles with rivets. High-carbon stainless steel resists corrosion similarly to regular stainless steel, but it isn't as hard, so it sharpens more easily. Keep your knives sharp and store them in a knife block. Never store them loose in a drawer or wash them in the dishwasher, both of which can damage the blades.
- Boning knife (5-inch)
- Bread knife, serrated (10-inch)
- Chef's knives (6-inch* and 8-inch)
- Fillet knife* (7-inch)
- Paring knives (two 3½-inch)
- Slicer/Carving knife (10-inch)
- Utility knife* (5-inch)

The cutting edge
Dull knives are bad news. A dull knife won't cut food very well, but if you cut yourself with a dull knife, it can cause more damage than if you cut yourself with a sharp knife. Sharpen your knives regularly and follow a few tips:
- Polish the sharpened edge of the knife with a chamois cloth. This removes any metal shavings that may cling to the edge. The clean edge will cut better.
- Skip electric knife sharpeners. They make it difficult to control the amount of metal that is removed.
- Some knives can't be sharpened. Stainless steel knives are too hard to grind. Serrated knives may need to be sharpened professionally. Inexpensive serrated knives should be thrown away when they become too dull.
- To test whether you've sharpened your knife enough, hold a piece of paper in one hand and carefully draw the blade of the knife down through the paper with the other hand. A sharp knife will cut the paper easily.

PANTRY

Your pantry is anywhere you can store food: cupboards, closets, refrigerator, and freezer. The foods you store will either be dry goods that keep for a long time (like flour or canned foods) or fresh perishables that you regularly use up before they spoil (like eggs and milk). Keeping your pantry stocked means you have a fairly large supply of foods ready to be used. It also means a little more planning so you stock up on the right items, but it will save you those trips to the grocery store for just one or two things.

Following is a list of items for a well-stocked pantry. Don't go out and buy everything on the list, though. Gradually build your pantry by trying recipes, then stocking up on the ingredients you like.

Herbs & Spices

- Almond extract
- Basil leaves
- Bay leaves
- Cardamom (*ground*)
- Chili powder
- Cilantro
- Cinnamon (*ground, stick*)
- Cloves (*ground, whole*)
- Cumin (*ground, seeds*)
- Curry powder
- Dill (*dried*)
- Fennel seeds
- Garlic powder
- Ginger (*ground and fresh*)
- Marjoram leaves
- Mustard (*dry, seed*)
- Nutmeg (*ground*)
- Onion powder
- Oregano leaves
- Paprika
- Pepper (*black, ground red, crushed red flakes, white, mixed*)

Keeping spices nice

It's a shame to ruin a great recipe by using spices that have been sitting in your pantry forever. The flavors in spices come from their volatile oils, which begin to fade as soon as the whole spice is ground. Spices that have lost their punch can give baked goods a bitter or medicinal taste. Follow these tips for spices:

- Keep all spices sealed in airtight containers.
- Store spices in a cool, dry place.
- Buy spices in small amounts and throw out any spices older than 6 months.
- Grind whole spices just before you use them to ensure the most intense flavor.

- Rosemary leaves
- Sage leaves
- Salt (*fine, regular, kosher, coarse*)
- Sesame seeds
- Tarragon leaves
- Thyme leaves
- Vanilla

Staples (*Dry Goods, Canned Goods, and Condiments*)

- Baking powder
- Baking soda
- Beans, canned and dry (*black, garbanzo, kidney, pinto, white*)
- Bread crumbs (*dry*)
- Broth or bouillon (*beef, chicken, vegetable*)
- Catsup
- Chocolate (*cocoa powder, semisweet pieces, unsweetened*)
- Coffee (*instant crystals*)
- Cornmeal
- Cornstarch
- Couscous
- Cream of tartar
- Dressings (*Italian, vinaigrettes*)
- Dried fruit (*apricots, cherries, currants, raisins, dates*)
- Flour (*all-purpose white, whole wheat*)
- Garlic (*bulb, bottled*)
- Green chiles (*canned*)
- Honey
- Hot pepper sauce
- Maple syrup
- Milk (*evaporated skim, sweetened condensed*)
- Molasses

211

equipment & pantry

- Mustard (Dijon-style, yellow)
- Nonstick spray coating
- Nuts (almonds, dry roasted peanuts, pecans, pine nuts, walnuts)
- Oats (quick-cooking, rolled)
- Oils (olive, peanut, vegetable)
- Olives (green, kalamata, ripe)
- Onions (red, white, yellow)
- Pasta, dried (fettuccine, macaroni, penne, ramen noodles, spaghetti)
- Peanut butter
- Port wine
- Potatoes (red, russet, yellow)
- Rice (converted brown and white, instant white, long-grain white, pilaf mixes, wild)
- Salsa
- Sherry wine (dry)

- Soy sauce
- Spaghetti sauce
- Sugar (brown, granulated, powdered)
- Tomatoes, canned (diced, tomato paste, stewed, tomato sauce, whole roma)
- Tuna, canned
- Vegetable shortening
- Vinegar (balsamic, cider, distilled white, red wine, rice, white wine)
- Wines (dry red, dry white)
- Worcestershire sauce
- Yeast (active dry)

Fresh, Refrigerated, and Frozen Items

- Butter
- Capers

- Carrots
- Celery
- Cheese (cheddar, Parmesan, Swiss, American)
- Chicken (breasts, legs, thighs, whole)
- Eggs
- Fruit, frozen (blueberries, raspberries, strawberries)
- Lemon juice
- Lime juice
- Margarine
- Mayonnaise
- Milk
- Orange juice
- Puff pastry (frozen)
- Salad greens
- Tortillas (corn, flour)
- Vegetables, frozen (broccoli, corn, green beans, mixed, spinach, tomatoes)

Dry Goods Storage Guide

Food	Storage Time (70° F)	Storage Hints
Baking powder	18 months or expiration date	Keep dry and covered.
Baking soda	2 years	Keep dry and covered.
Bouillon cubes or granules	2 years	Keep dry and covered.
Cornstarch	18 months	Store tightly closed.
Flour, all-purpose	6 to 8 months	Store in an airtight container in a cool, dry place.
Pasta, dry	2 years	Once opened, store in an airtight container.
Rice, white	2 years	Store in an airtight container.
Shortenings, solid	6 months (if opened)	No refrigeration needed.
Sugar, brown	4 months	Store in an airtight container.
Sugar, granulated	2 years	Cover tightly.
Spices and herbs (whole)*	1 to 2 years	Store in airtight containers in a
Spices, ground	6 months	dry place away from sunlight and heat.
Herbs, ground	6 months	Replace when aroma fades.
Vanilla	12 months (if opened)	Keep tightly closed.

*Note: Whole cloves, nutmeg, and cinnamon sticks will maintain their quality slightly beyond 2 years.   Source: University of Florida Cooperative Extension Service

simple secrets menus

What is the secret to making great meals? Compatible flavors (all Italian), eye appeal (a variety of color), and interesting textures (creamy soup and a crunchy salad) should all be kept in mind when coming up with a balanced meal. The following menus will help you create great meals. Feel free to substitute recipes in the lineup, if, for example, there is a salad you prefer over one given in a menu. Wine suggestions are also included.

WINTER WEEKEND LUNCH

- Potato and Leek Soup *(p. 35)*
- Mesclun Salad with Walnut Vinaigrette *(p. 12)*
- Gingered Shortcake with Spiced Fruit *(p. 208)*
- Wine Suggestion: French Mâcon Villages or Pinot Grigio

Mesclun Salad with Walnut Vinaigrette

WEEKNIGHT ITALIAN DINNER

- Minestrone *(p. 39)*
- Simple Focaccia *(p. 174)*
- Italian Salad with Garlic Polenta Croutons *(p. 22)*
- Apple-Cranberry Pie *(p. 188)*
- Wine Suggestion: Italian Chianti or Valpolicella

Simple Focaccia

simple secrets menus

Irish Coffee Meringues

Slicing Fennel

Thai Rice Noodles

WINTER BARBECUE

- Mustard Chicken Barbecue *(p. 143)*
- Sautéed Brussels Sprouts *(p. 54)*
- Oven-Roasted Potatoes
- Irish Coffee Meringues *(p. 192)*
- Wine Suggestion: French Grenache,
      Côtes du Rhône, or Châteauneuf-du-Pape

SPECIAL SUNDAY BRUNCH

- Poached Eggs on Polenta *(p. 90)*
- Fennel and Orange Salad *(p. 10)*
- Crusty Italian Bread or Rolls
- Fresh Strawberries with Whipped Cream
- Wine Suggestion: Italian Arneis or Chardonnay

LIGHT THAI-FLAVORED LUNCH

- Thai Lime Custard Soup *(p. 42)*
- Thai Rice Noodles *(p. 71)*
- Fresh Pineapple with Toasted Coconut
- Wine Suggestion: German Riesling

SUPER SUMMER SUPPER

- Grilled Burgers with Caramelized Onions *(p. 102)*
- Couscous-Artichoke Salad *(p. 15)*
- Fresh Red & Yellow Tomato Slices
- Blueberry-Buttermilk Chess Tart *(p. 185)*
- Wine Suggestion: Chilean Cabernet Sauvignon

Couscous-Artichoke Salad

HOLIDAY BRUNCH

- Holiday Frittata *(p. 86)*
- Praline-Apple Bread *(p. 182)*
- Dried Cherry Scones *(p. 179)*
- Citrus Fruit Salad with Pomegranate Seeds
- Wine Suggestion: Chenin Blanc, French Vouvray or Pinot Grigio

Dried Cherry Scones

CHASE-THE-CHILL DINNER

- Smoked Salmon with Apple Glaze *(p. 109)*
- Roasted Root Medley *(p. 63)*
- Wilted Greens Salad with Port Dressing *(p. 18)*
- Whole Wheat Rolls
- Brownie Pudding Cake *(p. 189)*
- Wine Suggestion: Carneros Chardonnay or Oregon Pinot Noir

Root Vegetables

simple secrets menus

Using Vanilla Beans

SOUTH-OF-THE-BORDER LUNCH

- Smoked Turkey Dagwood with Chile Mayonnaise *(p. 99)*
- Black and Red Beans Ranchero *(p. 77)*
- Mexican or Spanish Rice
- Vanilla Bean Ice Cream *(p. 184)*
- Wine Suggestion: Côtes du Rhône or California Syrah

Asparagus and Carrots with
Asian Vinaigrette

LIGHT AND SPECIAL WEEKEND LUNCH

- Ginger-Marinated Sea Bass *(p. 107)*
- Asparagus and Carrots with Asian Vinaigrette *(p. 20)*
- Basmati and Wild Rice Blend
- Easy Berry Sorbet *(p. 203)*
- Wine Suggestion: Alsatian Gewürtztraminer

Roasted Capon with
Wild Mushroom Stuffing

EASY BUT ELEGANT DINNER

- Roasted Capon with Wild Mushroom Stuffing *(p. 127)*
- Green Beans with Vermouth Butter *(p. 62)*
- Garlic Mashed Yellow Potatoes
- Coffee Cheesecake *(p. 197)*
- Wine Suggestion: Viognier or French White Burgundy

MEDITERRANEAN FLAVORS DINNER

Fruit- & Nut-Filled Phyllo Packets

- Citrus-Marinated Cornish Hen *(p. 134)*
- Basmati Rice Pilaf *(p. 81)*
- Mixed Salad with Lime-Pistachio Vinaigrette *(p. 23)*
- Soft Pita Bread Loaves
- Fruit- & Nut-Filled Phyllo Packets *(p. 194)*
- Wine Suggestion: French Chablis or Sauvignon Blanc

EASY ITALIAN DINNER

Chicken Stuffed with Smoked Mozarella

- Chicken Stuffed with Smoked Mozzarella *(p. 132)*
- Italian Salad with Garlic Polenta Croutons *(p. 22)*
- Breadsticks
- Ricotta-Filled Pears with Chocolate *(p. 206)*
- Wine Suggestion: Napa Chardonnay

AUTUMN LUNCH

Fresh Spinach

- Vegetable & Smoked Turkey Chowder *(p. 32)*
- Raspberry-Cranberry Spinach Salad *(p. 19)*
- Pumpkin-Pecan Muffins *(p. 176)*
- Peanut-Sesame Marbled Brownies *(p. 199)*
- Wine Suggestion: French Sancerre

simple secrets menus

Frozen Caramel Custard

Chile Pork Ribs with Chipotle Barbecue Sauce

Peeling Sweet Peppers

TROPICAL SUMMER DINNER

- Grilled Trout with Cilantro & Lime *(p. 106)*
- Caribbean Salsa *(p. 60)*
- Cuban-Style Black Beans and Rice *(p. 78)*
- Warm Flour Tortillas
- Frozen Caramel Custard *(p. 186)*
- Wine Suggestion: New Zealand Sauvignon Blanc

SPICY SUMMER BARBECUE

- Chile Pork Ribs with Chipotle Barbecue Sauce *(p. 155)*
- Southwest Hominy Skillet *(p. 83)*
- Broccoli Slaw
- Gingered Shortcake with Spiced Fruit *(p. 208)*
- Wine Suggestion: California Zinfandel or South Australian Shiraz

CELEBRATE SPRING DINNER

- Herbed Strip Steak with Balsamic Sauce *(p. 149)*
- Roasted Asparagus and Red Pepper *(p. 55)*
- New Red Potato Salad
- Raspberries & Lemon Cream *(p. 205)*
- Wine Suggestion: Sonoma Cabernet Sauvignon

HEARTY COMPANY DINNER

- Grilled Steaks with Gorgonzola Butter *(p. 158)*
- Risotto with Leeks & Roasted Asparagus *(p. 82)*
- Romaine and Fruit with Balsamic Vinaigrette *(p. 14)*
- Easy Berry Sorbet *(p. 203)*
- Wine Suggestion: Tuscan Red, Brunello di Montalcino, or California Cabernet Sauvignon

Grilled Steaks with Gorgonzola Butter

FRENCH FLAVORS DINNER

- Pork au Poivre with Mustard & Sage *(p. 162)*
- Roasted Vegetables over Salad Greens *(p. 66)*
- French Baguette
- Tangy Lemon Tart *(p. 200)*
- Wine Suggestion: California Merlot or French Bordeaux St. Emilion

Tangy Lemon Tart

ITALIAN WEEKEND DINNER

- Italian Beef Braciola *(p. 157)*
- Fresh Greens Salad with Herbed Croutons *(p. 17)*
- Crusty Italian Bread
- Fresh Fruit Napoeons *(p. 191)*
- Wine Suggestion: Chianti Classico or California Sangiovese

Fresh Fruit Napoleons

219

glossary

a

adobo sauce [ah-DOH-boh] A dark red Mexican sauce made from ground chiles, herbs, and vinegar. Chipotle peppers are packed in cans in adobo sauce.

al dente [al-DEN-tay] Italian for to the tooth. It describes pasta that is cooked until it offers a slight resistance when bitten into, rather than cooked until soft.

Anaheim pepper A light to medium green chile that is long and narrow. It has a sweet, slightly spicy flavor that makes it wonderful stuffed and cooked or raw in salsas and salads.

ancho pepper [AHN-choh] A dried poblano pepper. It is 3 to 4 inches long with a deep reddish color. Its flavor is sweet and fruity and ranges from mild to hot.

anchovy paste A mixture of ground anchovies, vinegar, and seasonings. Anchovy paste is available in tubes in the canned fish or gourmet section of the supermarket.

arugula [ah-ROO-guh-lah] A brightly-colored salad green with a slightly bitter, peppery mustard flavor. It is also called rocket and resembles radish leaves.

b

bake Generally refers to cooking food in an oven using radiant dry heat. Regular (thermal) ovens simply radiate heat from a heating element during baking; convection ovens circulate that heat with air for faster, more even cooking. See also roast.

balsamic vinegar Made from white Trebbiano grape juice. Balsamic vinegar gets its distinctive dark brown color, syrupy body, and slight sweetness from being aged in barrels. See also pages 14 and 66.

batter An uncooked, wet mixture that can be spooned or poured, as with cakes, pancakes, and muffins. Batters usually contain flour, eggs, and milk as their base. Thin batters are used to coat foods before deep-frying.

beat To stir rapidly in a circular motion. Beating is often intended to incorporate some air into food to increase volume, as with cake batter.

boil To heat liquid in an uncovered pan until bubbles break the surface. A full rolling boil cannot be stopped by stirring.

bouillon cube A compressed cube of dehydrated beef, chicken, fish, or vegetable stock. Bouillon granules are small particles of the same substance, but they dissolve faster. Both can be reconstituted in hot liquid to substitute for stock or broth.

bouquet garni [boo-KAY gahr-NEE] A bundle of fresh herbs usually thyme, parsley, and bay leaf used to add flavor to soups, stews, stocks, and poaching liquids. They are often tied inside two pieces of leek leaf or in a piece of cheesecloth. See also page 31.

braciola [brah-chee-OH-lah] Italian for roulade , meaning a thin slice of meat rolled around a filling. The roll is then browned before being baked or braised.

braise To brown food in fat, then cook it in a covered dish in a small amount of liquid. Food is braised at low heat for a long time and can be done either on the stove or in the oven.

Brie A soft, creamy cheese with an edible white rind. Brie from France is considered to be the best in the world.

brine A salt and water solution used for pickling or preserving food.

broil Cooking over or under direct high heat, either in an oven or on a grill. Choose foods that are quick-cooking, tender, fairly lean, and relatively thin for broiling.

broth The strained clear liquid in which meat, poultry, or fish has been simmered with vegetables and herbs. It is similar to stock and can be used interchangeably with stock. See also page 30.

brown To cook with high heat, either on the stove or under a broiler, until the surface of a food turns brown. Browning adds flavor, texture, and eye appeal to a food.

butterfly To split food, such as shrimp or meat, through its center, cutting almost completely through. One edge is left attached so the food can be opened like a book to resemble the wings of a butterfly. See also page 157.

c

caper The pickled bud of a shrub native to the Mediterranean and parts of Asia. Its flavor is tangy and salty, and it ranges in size from the smallest French nonpareil to the much larger Italian caper. See also page 28.

caramelize To brown sugar, whether it is granulated sugar or the naturally occurring sugars in vegetables. Granulated sugar is cooked in a saucepan or skillet over low heat until melted and golden (see page 186). Vegetables are cooked slowly over low heat in a small amount of fat until browned and sweet (see page 58).

cheesecloth A thin 100-percent cotton cloth with either a fine or coarse weave. Cheesecloth is used in cooking to bundle up herbs (bouquet garni), strain liquids, and wrap rolled meats.

chiffonade [shif-uh-NAHD] A French word meaning "made of rags." In cooking, it refers to thin strips of fresh herbs or lettuces. See also page 160.

chipotle pepper [chih-POHT-lay] A smoked, dried jalapeño pepper. Chipotle peppers have wrinkly brown skin and a rich, smoky flavor. They can be found dried or canned in adobo sauce.

couscous [KOOS-koos] From North Africa, this granular pasta is made from semolina. Quick-cooking varieties can be ready to eat in 5 minutes. Look for it in the rice and pasta section of large supermarkets. See also page 15.

cremini mushroom [kri-MEE-nee] Also called brown mushroom, this mushroom resembles the popular white mushroom but has a deeper, richer flavor.

cut in To mix a hard, cold fat (butter or shortening) with dry ingredients (flour mixture) until the mixture resembles coarse crumbs. This can be done with a pastry blender, two knives, a fork, fingers, or a food processor.

d

deep-fry To cook food by completely covering with hot fat. Deep-frying is usually done at 375°.

deglaze To remove browned bits of food (usually meat) from the bottom of a pan after the food has been sautéed or roasted. Liquid is added to the pan, and the bits are loosened by stirring. See also page 153.

demi glace [DEHM-ee glahs] A thick, intensely flavored sauce that is the base for other sauces. See also page 164.

double boiler A two-pan arrangement where one pan nests partway inside the other. The lower pot holds simmering water that gently cooks heat-sensitive food in the upper pot.

glossary

dressed Fish or game that has had the guts (viscera) removed. In the case of fish, gills are removed, the cavity is cleaned, and the head and fins remain intact. The scales may or may not be removed.

e

enoki mushroom [en-OH-kee] A crisp, delicate mushroom with long, thin stems and a small white cap. Cooking destroys its fruity flavor and crunchy texture, so it is usually added raw to salads, as a garnish in soups, or at the last minute to stir-fries.

epazote leaves [eh-pah-ZOH-teh] A pungent herb with a flavor similar to cilantro. It is used in Mexican cooking and is a popular ingredient in bean dishes because of its gas-reducing properties.

f

fava bean A tan, flat bean that looks like a large lima bean. It is available dried, canned, and, occasionally, fresh. See also page 28.

feta A tangy, crumbly Greek cheese made of sheep's or goat's milk.

fillet The boneless meaty portion from a fish's side.

fish sauce Used primarily in Southeast Asian cuisine, fish sauce is made by fermenting fish, usually anchovies, in a brine. The resulting pungent brown liquid is used as a condiment and flavoring.

french To cut meat away from the end of a rib or chop to expose the bone, as with rack of lamb.

g

gelatin Pure protein derived from beef and veal bones. It is an odorless, flavorless, clear thickening agent that forms a jelly when dissolved in hot liquid and cooled.

glaze A thin, shiny coating. Savory glazes are made with reduced sauces or gelatin; sweet glazes can be made with melted jelly or chocolate.

goat cheese Also called chèvre, which is French for goat. Goat cheese is a white, tangy cheese with a texture ranging from moist and creamy to dry and semifirm.

grill pan A heavy, stove-top, griddle-type pan with ribs for giving food grill marks without actually using a grill. See also page 100.

gumbo The word gumbo is from an African word meaning "okra." This creole stew contains okra, tomatoes, and onions as well as various meats or shellfish such as shrimp, chicken, or sausage. It is thickened with a roux. See also roux and page 43.

h

habañero pepper [ah-bah-NYEH-roh] Considered by many to be the hottest chile around, habañeros are small and look like little lanterns. They range in color from light green to red-orange.

half-and-half A mixture of equal parts cream and milk. It has about 12% milk fat and cannot be whipped.

haricot vert [ah-ree-koh VAIR] French for "green string bean", these beans are particularly thin and tender.

heavy cream Also called heavy whipping cream. Heavy cream contains at least 46% milk fat and is the richest cream available. It can be whipped to twice its volume.

hominy Dried white or yellow corn kernels that have been soaked in lime or lye to remove the hull and germ. It is available canned or dried. Ground hominy is used to make grits.

j

Japanese eggplant Small, slender eggplant that can be solid purple or striped. It is more tender and sweeter than regular eggplant.

jicama [HEE-kah-mah] A large, bulbous root vegetable with tan skin and white crunchy flesh. The skin is easily peeled, and the sweet flesh can be eaten raw or cooked.

k

kalamata olive [kahl-uh-MAH-tuh] A medium-size greenish-black olive from Greece. It is cured in a wine vinegar brine and has a pungent, fruity flavor. See also pages 74 and 150.

kosher salt A coarse-grained or flaky salt used in preserving foods according to Jewish laws. It is favored by chefs because it dissolves quickly and has a clean flavor.

l

light cream Also called coffee or table cream. It usually contains about 20% milk fat and cannot be whipped.

m

marinade A seasoned liquid in which meat, fish, or vegetables are soaked in order to flavor them and sometimes tenderize them. Most marinades contain an acid such as wine, lemon juice, or vinegar.

marinate To soak food in a marinade.

Marsala A fortified wine made in Sicily. Its flavor ranges from sweet to dry. Sweet Marsala is a dessert wine used both for drinking and in making desserts. Dry Marsala makes a nice predinner drink.

mesclun (MEHS-kluhn) A mix of assorted baby salad greens, including arugula, dandelion, oak leaf, sorrel, and radicchio, among others. See also page 96.

mince To chop food into very fine pieces, as with minced garlic.

o

oyster sauce A popular Asian condiment and seasoning made with oysters, brine, and soy sauce. This concentrated brown sauce has a rich flavor but is not overpowering.

p

pancetta [pan-CHEH-tuh] Italian type of bacon that is cured with salt and spices but is not smoked. It has a distinct, mildly salty flavor, and it usually is available in a roll.

parchment paper Parchment paper is a grease- and heat-resistant paper used to line baking pans, wrap foods in packets to be baked en papillote (see page 117), or to make disposable pastry bags.

parsnip A white root vegetable that resembles a carrot. Parsnips have a mild, sweet flavor and can be cooked like potatoes.

pastry blender A kitchen tool that has five or six parallel curved wires or blades attached at the ends to a handle. It is used to cut cold fat into flour when making pastry dough.

glossary

phyllo [FEE-loh] Also spelled filo, this dough consists of tissue-thin sheets of pastry used in Greek, Turkish, and Near Eastern dishes. It is available frozen in large supermarkets.

pine nut High-fat nut that comes from a variety of pine trees. Their flavor ranges from mild and sweet to pungent. They go rancid quickly and so must be stored in the refrigerator or freezer.

poach To cook food in gently simmering liquid. The liquid can be anything from water or broth to a sugar syrup (used to poach fruit).

poblano pepper [poh-BLAH-noh] A blackish green chile with a flavor that ranges from mild to quite spicy. About 3 inches wide and 4 to 5 inches long, its size makes it perfect for stuffing. Dried poblanos are called ancho peppers.

polenta [poh-LEHN-tah] Italian for "cornmeal mush." This mush can be eaten hot or spread out and cooled until firm. The cooled polenta is then cut and fried or broiled.

pork hock The lower portion of a hog's hind leg. Hocks are sold in 2- to 3-inch pieces. Fresh hocks are available, but usually they are sold cured and smoked as ham hocks.

port wine A sweet fortified wine from Portugal. Vintage port is made from the grapes from a single year and is considered the best. Tawny port is blended from the grapes of several years and can be aged up to 40 years. Ruby port is considered the lowest grade of port. It is made the same way as Tawny port but is not aged as long.

prosciutto [proh-SHOO-toh] Ham that has been seasoned, salt-cured, and air-dried (not smoked). Pressing the meat gives it a firm, dense texture. Parma ham from Italy is considered to be the best.

provolone [proh-voh-LOH-nee] A southern Italian cheese made from cow's milk. Provolone is firm and creamy white with a mild, smoky flavor. Because it melts so well, it is an excellent cooking cheese.

puff pastry A butter-rich, multilayered pastry. When baked, the butter makes steam between the layers causing the dough to puff up, creating many flaky layers. See also page 191.

puree To process or mash a food until it is as smooth as possible. The resulting puree can be used as a garnish, side dish (mashed potatoes), or as a thickener. See also page 35.

r

reduction A liquid (stock, wine, vinegar, or sauce) that has been boiled until its volume is decreased. The resulting liquid is thick and intensely flavored. See also page 149.

rice vinegar Vinegar made from rice wine. It has a mild flavor and is popular in Japanese and Chinese cooking. See also page 66.

roast A specific kind of baking. Roasted food is usually baked uncovered in a shallow pan, which permits browning and crisping.

roux [ROO] A thickener made by cooking equal measures of flour and fat over low heat. The color (white, blond, or brown) and flavor (mild to rich) is determined by how long the roux is cooked. See also page 43.

rub A mixture of spices and herbs pressed into meat to flavor it. See also page 133.

rutabaga A large yellowish root vegetable that looks like a big turnip. The flesh is pale and slightly sweet. Rutabagas can be prepared like turnips.

S

sauté [saw-TAY] From the French word *sauter*, meaning "to jump." Sautéed food is cooked and stirred in a small amount of fat over fairly high heat in an open, shallow pan. Food cut into a uniform size sautés the best.

score To make shallow, diamond-patterned cuts in the surface of foods, usually meats. This is done for looks and to allow additional flavor absorption from marinades and rubs.

Scotch bonnet pepper A small fiery chile that ranges from yellow to red in color. It is closely related to the habañero and is as hot.

sear To brown food, usually meat, in a skillet over high heat or under a broiler. Searing adds color and flavor to food.

shallot A member of the onion family that looks like a large purplish or tan garlic clove covered with a brown papery skin. It has a mild onion flavor and is used in place of onions to lend a delicate flavor to dishes.

shortening A solid white fat made by hydrogenating vegetable oil. It is flavorless and is used in baking and cooking.

sift To pass ingredients, such as flour or powdered sugar, through a fine mesh sieve to remove any large pieces and make the ingredients lighter.

simmer To cook food in lightly bubbling liquid. Bubbles should just break the surface of the liquid. Simmering gently cooks fragile foods, tenderizes tough ones, allows flavors to blend, and slightly thickens some liquids.

snip To cut up foods, such as herbs, with scissors. See also page 83.

sorbet [sor-BAY] French for "sherbet." Sorbets are made from water, sugar, and fruit juice or puree, then churned when freezing. They are different from sherbets in that they don't contain milk.

soufflé [soo-FLAY] A light, airy food made with an egg yolk base that is lightened with beaten egg whites. It may be savory or sweet. Hot soufflés are very delicate and should be eaten soon after baking, as they will deflate. See also page 87.

springform pan A round pan with high sides and a removable bottom. The bottom is removed by releasing a spring that holds the sides tight around it. This makes it easy to remove food from the pan.

stock The strained clear liquid in which meat, poultry, or fish has been simmered with vegetables and herbs. It is similar to broth but is richer and more concentrated. Both can be used interchangeably. See also page 30.

t

tahini [tuh-HEE-nee] Tahini is a sesame seed paste used in Middle Eastern cooking as a flavoring agent.

v

vermouth [ver-MOOTH] White wine that has been fortified and flavored with herbs and spices. Dry vermouth is white and is used as a predinner drink or in nonsweet drinks such as a martini. Sweet vermouth is reddish brown and can be drunk straight or used in sweet mixed drinks. Vermouth often is used as a cooking ingredient.

tip index

a-b

c

d-f

tip index

main index

C

main index

main index

main index

t-z

emergency substitutions

If you don't have:	Substitute:
baking powder	1 teaspoon = ½ teaspoon cream of tartar plus ¼ teaspoon baking soda
bread crumbs, fine dry	¼ cup = ¾ cup soft bread crumbs; ¼ cup cracker crumbs; or ¼ cup cornflake crumbs
broth, beef or chicken	1 cup = 1 teaspoon or 1 cube instant beef or chicken bouillon plus 1 cup hot water
buttermilk	1 cup = 1 tablespoon lemon juice or vinegar plus enough milk to make 1 cup (let stand 5 minutes before using); or 1 cup plain yogurt
chocolate, semisweet	1 ounce = 3 tablespoons semisweet chocolate pieces; or 1 ounce unsweetened chocolate plus 1 tablespoon granulated sugar
chocolate, sweet baking	4 ounces = ¼ cup unsweetened cocoa powder plus ⅓ cup granulated sugar and 3 tablespoons shortening
chocolate, unsweetened	1 ounce = 3 tablespoons unsweetened cocoa powder plus 1 tablespoon cooking oil or shortening, melted
cornstarch	1 tablespoon (for thickening) = 2 tablespoons all-purpose flour
cream, heavy whipping	1 cup = ¾ cup whole milk plus ⅓ cup melted butter
egg	1 whole = 2 egg whites; 2 egg yolks; or ¼ cup frozen egg product, thawed
flour, all-purpose	2 tablespoons (for thickening) = 1 tablespoon cornstarch; or 2 teaspoons arrowroot; or 2 tablespoons quick-cooking tapioca
flour, cake	1 cup = 1 cup minus 2 tablespoons all-purpose flour
flour, self-rising	1 cup = 1 cup all-purpose flour plus 1 teaspoon baking powder, ½ teaspoon salt, and ¼ teaspoon baking soda
garlic	1 clove = ½ teaspoon bottled minced garlic; or ⅛ teaspoon garlic powder

If you don't have:	Substitute:
gingerroot, grated	1 teaspoon = ¼ teaspoon ground ginger
half-and-half or light cream	1 cup = 1 tablespoon melted butter or margarine plus enough whole milk to make 1 cup
herb, dried	1 teaspoon = ½ teaspoon ground herb
herb, snipped fresh	1 tablespoon = ½ to 1 teaspoon dried herb, crushed
honey	1 cup = 1¼ cups granulated sugar plus ¼ cup water
lemon or lime juice	1 teaspoon = ½ teaspoon vinegar
margarine	1 cup = 1 cup butter; or 1 cup shortening plus ¼ teaspoon salt
milk, whole	1 cup = ½ cup evaporated milk plus ½ cup water; or 1 cup water plus ⅓ cup nonfat dry milk powder
molasses	1 cup = 1 cup honey
mustard, dry	1 teaspoon (in cooked mixtures) = 1 tablespoon prepared mustard
onion, chopped	⅓ cup = 1 teaspoon onion powder; or 1 tablespoon dried minced onion
sour cream, dairy	1 cup = 1 cup plain yogurt
sugar, granulated	1 cup = 1 cup packed brown sugar; or 2 cups sifted powdered sugar
vinegar	1 teaspoon = 2 teaspoons lemon juice
yeast, active dry	1 package = 1 cake compressed yeast; or 1 scant tablespoon active dry yeast
yogurt, plain	1 cup = 1 cup buttermilk; or 1 cup milk plus 1 tablespoon lemon juice

metric cooking hints

By making a few conversions, cooks in Australia, Canada, and the United Kingdom can use the recipes in this book with confidence. The charts on this page provide a guide for converting measurements from the U.S. customary system, which is used throughout this book, to the imperial and metric systems. There also is a conversion table for oven temperatures to accommodate the differences in oven calibrations.

Product Differences: Most of the ingredients called for in the recipes in this book are available in English-speaking countries. However, some are known by different names. Here are some common U.S. American ingredients and their possible counterparts:

• Sugar is granulated or castor sugar.
• Powdered sugar is icing sugar.
• All-purpose flour is plain household flour or white flour. When self-rising flour is used in place of all-purpose flour in a recipe that calls for leavening, omit the leavening agent (baking soda or baking powder) and salt.
• Light-colored corn syrup is golden syrup.
• Cornstarch is cornflour.
• Baking soda is bicarbonate of soda.
• Vanilla is vanilla essence.
• Green, red, or yellow sweet peppers are capsicums.
• Golden raisins are sultanas.

Volume and Weight: U.S. Americans traditionally use cup measures for liquid and solid ingredients. The chart, below, shows the approximate imperial and metric equivalents. If you are accustomed to weighing solid ingredients, the following approximate equivalents will help.

• 1 cup butter, castor sugar, or rice = 8 ounces = about 230 grams
• 1 cup flour = 4 ounces = about 115 grams
• 1 cup icing sugar = 5 ounces = about 140 grams

Spoon measures are used for smaller amounts of ingredients. Although the size of the tablespoon varies slightly in different countries, for practical purposes and for recipes in this book, a straight substitution is all that's necessary. Measurements made using cups or spoons always should be level unless stated otherwise.

Metric Information
Equivalents: U.S. = Australia/U.K.

$\frac{1}{5}$ teaspoon = 1 ml	$\frac{1}{4}$ cup = 60 ml
$\frac{1}{4}$ teaspoon = 1.25 ml	$\frac{1}{3}$ cup = 80 ml
$\frac{1}{2}$ teaspoon = 2.5 ml	$\frac{1}{2}$ cup = 120 ml
1 teaspoon = 5 ml	$\frac{2}{3}$ cup = 160 ml
1 tablespoon = 15 ml	$\frac{3}{4}$ cup = 180 ml
1 fluid ounce = 30 ml	

Baking Pan Sizes

American	Metric
8×1½-inch round baking pan	20×4-cm cake tin
9×1½-inch round baking pan	23×4-cm cake tin
11×7×1½-inch baking pan	28×18×4-cm baking tin
13×9×2-inch baking pan	32×23×5-cm baking tin
2-quart rectangular baking dish	28×18×4-cm baking tin
15×10×1-inch baking pan	38×25.5×2.5-cm baking tin (Swiss roll tin)
9-inch pie plate	22×4- or 23×4-cm pie plate
7- or 8-inch springform pan	18- or 20-cm springform or loose-bottom cake tin
9×5×3-inch loaf pan	23×13×8-cm or 2-pound narrow loaf tin or pâté tin
1½-quart casserole	1.5-liter casserole
2-quart casserole	2-liter casserole

Oven Temperature Equivalents

Fahrenheit Setting	Celsius Setting*	Gas Setting
300°F	150°C	Gas mark 2 (very low)
325°F	170°C	Gas mark 3 (low)
350°F	180°C	Gas mark 4 (moderate)
375°F	190°C	Gas mark 5 (moderately hot)
400°F	200°C	Gas mark 6 (hot)
425°F	220°C	Gas mark 7 (hot)
450°F	230°C	Gas mark 8 (very hot)
475°F	240°C	Gas mark 9 (very hot)
Broil		Grill

*Electric and gas ovens may be calibrated using Celsius. However, for an electric oven, increase the Celsius setting 10 to 20 degrees when cooking above 160°C. For convection or forced-air ovens (gas or electric), lower the temperature setting 10°C when cooking at all heat levels.